A Concise History of Mexico

KCl

A Concise
History of Mexico
from Hidalgo to Cárdenas
1805–1940

JAN BAZANT

Professor at the Center of Historical Studies
El Colegio de México

The right of the
University of Cambridge
to print and sell
all manner of books
was granted by
Henry VIII in 1534.
The University has printed
and published continuously
since 1584.

CAMBRIDGE UNIVERSITY PRESS

Cambridge

London   New York   New Rochelle

Melbourne   Sydney

Published by the Syndics of the Cambridge University Press
The Pitt Building, Trumpington Street, Cambridge CB2 1RP
Bentley House, 200 Euston Road, London NW1 2DB
32 East 57th Street, New York, NY 10022, USA
296 Beaconsfield Parade, Middle Park, Melbourne 3206, Australia

First published 1977
Reprinted 1978
Reprinted with corrections 1979, 1985

Printed in the United States of America
Typeset by Telecki Publishing Services, Yonkers, New York
Printed and bound by R. R. Donnelley & Sons Co., Crawfordsville, Indiana

Library of Congress Cataloging in Publication Data

Bazant, Jan

A concise history of Mexico
from Hidalgo to Cárdenas, 1805–1940

1. Mexico – History – 1810   I. Title

F1231.5.B38   972   76-50086
ISBN 0 521 21495 5   hard covers
ISBN 0 521 29173 9   paperback

Of all that extensive empire which once acknowledged the authority of Spain in the New World, no portion for interest and importance, can be compared with Mexico; – and this equally, whether we consider the variety of its soil and climate; the inexhaustible stores of its mineral wealth; its scenery, grand and picturesque beyond example . . . .

William H. Prescott, *History of the Conquest of Mexico*, Book I, Introduction

But it is the (Mexican) people, their origin and environment, their nature and development, their virtues and their shortcomings, their loves and hates, and the gross wrongs flung upon them by foreign foes, their long struggle for freedom, for physical and intellectual emancipation, – it is (in the description of these things) that the historian finds his most pleasing task.

Hubert Howe Bancroft, *A Popular History of the Mexican People*, Preface

Contents

Preface

Mexico, as indeed other Latin American countries and Latin America in general, has for a number of years been the object of considerable interest in the United States as well as in other parts of the world. Many monographs have been written on different aspects of Mexican modern history, most of them emphasizing, in accordance with the prevailing trend, social and economic developments. The time has arrived to attempt a synthesis. Given the limited amount of space at my disposal, I have chosen to focus attention on what I believe to be one of the dominant, central themes of Mexican history: the struggle for land on the part of those who do not possess it at all or do not possess it in sufficient quantity to satisfy their basic needs; yet not everyone is driven by the hunger of land or more land and wealth. Some men, motivated more by pride, strive for status, prestige, honor, power, and even glory. Other aspects of Mexican history such as foreign relations, military campaigns, art, and other cultural achievements are also important, but I think that they can be best understood in the light of the basic theme I have outlined.

Considering all this and taking into account recent literature, I have constructed a political narrative set against the dark background of socio-economic forces. One chapter has been devoted to each period of modern Mexican history, with a short introduction covering the conquest and the colonization.

I am deeply grateful to my wife and to Professor John H. Elliott for many valuable suggestions and comments on the language as well as on the balance and focus of the book. I also wish to thank Otakar Pacold for inviting me to his winter home in Florida where I was able, in peace and quiet, to finish this book.

J. B.

August 1976

Introduction

[The conquest] was neither a victory nor a defeat; it was the painful birth of the Mexican nation, the Mexico of today.

Inscription placed in 1964 on Tlatelolco Square, Mexico City

In 1519 the Spanish captain Hernán Cortés landed with five-hundred men on the Mexican coast, in front of the snow-capped cone of the Star Mountain, Citlaltépetl, on the very spot where the port of Veracruz now stands. Two years later, the Spaniards seized the capital of the Aztec empire, Tenoch-titlan, now Mexico City. Before the middle of the century, the Spaniards were masters of central and southeastern Mex-ico and were beginning to expand to the arid North. The vice-royalty of New Spain was set up in the conquered country in 1535.

With the exception of the coasts and the peninsulas of Yu-catán and lower California, Mexico then, as now, comprised a series of plateaus, some fertile, others which had been salt lakes, sterile—plateaus surrounded in most cases by moun-tains, or, as in the vicinity of Guadalajara, dropping off to the sea as if cut by sharp knives. They become gradually higher towards the south. About half of the country lies within the tropics, but the mountains produce a temperate climate. There is no lack of sunshine in the Mexican territory; water is the critical element. The prevailing winds come from the humid Gulf of Mexico, but the eastern escarpment which rises behind the coast and runs parallel to it forms an effec-tive rain barrier part of the year.

Thus, geographically Mexico consists of three distinct areas — the Southeast, the Center and the North. The first corresponds roughly to the ancient land of Olmecs, believed to be the first civilized nation in Mexico, and of Mayas; most of it is lowland with abundant rainfall for more than six months a year. The Center is separated from the Southeast by the eastern escarpment; its common feature is a rainy season lasting four to six months, from June to September or November, according to the year. Its valleys range from 1,500 to 2,600 meters above sea level and the climate is warm to cool, which explains why the Center has been the heart of the country since before the conquest. It is neither too hot nor too cold; neither too humid nor too dry. Central Mexico was first the home of the Teotihuacán culture and then of the Nahuatl-speaking, warlike Toltecs and Aztecs, and it was here that a high civilization was flourishing when the Spaniards arrived; the Mayan civilization in the Southeast had already declined The district of Oaxaca, an isolated pocket southeast of the Valley of Mexico, had been the seat of one of the most advanced civilizations, of which the ruins of Monte Albán give witness.

Maize, beans, and squash, often grown simultaneously on the same field, were staple crops in most of Mexico. Maize was ideally suited for the Mexican rainy season with its irregular showers, its weeds and pests. The Spaniards found out soon after the conquest that European cereals, especially wheat, could not be cultivated during the rains so they began to grow wheat during the dry season with the help of irrigation. Many varieties of maize flourished, from the lowland tropical maize which ripened in three months to the high-altitude variety that required more than half a year to mature. The large agave, source of the alcoholic beverage *pulque,* was grown between 1,800 and 3,000 meters above sea level in Central Mexico.

Maize cultivation was restricted to Southeastern, Western, and Central Mexico. Approximately north of the east-west line, Querétaro — the Lerma River — Guadalajara, rainfall begins to be too irregular or insufficient, or both, for maize. The characteristic plant of the country north of this line was cactus, many varieties of it. This northern desert was the home of the hunting and food-gathering Chichimecs. It fell to the Spaniards to extend sedentary civilization into the enormous arid North.

Everywhere they went, the Spaniards — soldiers, priests, miners and farmers — spread the Catholic faith and the Spanish language and culture. As few Spanish women chose to emigrate, the natural result were unions of Spaniards and Indian women, out of which Spanish-Indians or *mestizos* were born. Another consequence of the conquest was that most land fell to the Spaniards who began to transform it with Indian labor into farms and cattle ranches. Colonial society emerged slowly. It can be said that it took its shape about one hundred years after the seizure of Tenochtitlan.

Towards the end of the eighteenth century, the central, viceregal government as well as the high ecclesiastical positions and foreign trade were in the hands of European-born, so-called "peninsular Spaniards." Mexican-born Spaniards called creoles, many of whom had Indian blood in their veins but were registered as Spaniards, were miners, merchants and hacendados, owners of large farms or estates called "haciendas." "Mestizos" were mostly workers and artisans, and there were a comparatively small number of black slaves and mulattoes. Indians, exempted from taxes as well as tithes in exchange for a yearly head-tax called tribute, lived either in their villages under the protection and supervision of special authorities, or as peons, laborers, on haciendas or in towns.

Both peninsular and Mexican-born Spaniards considered themselves gentlemen. Many of them were wealthy. A few of the wealthiest acquired titles of nobility from the crown. Some creoles or Mexican-born Spaniards had been to schools of higher learning but nevertheless they had to be satisfied with minor government positions, although they were often more cultured than their Spanish-born cousins who ruled the country. They resented it and quite naturally began to abhor the conquest and extol the Indian resistance. Their feelings were waiting for an opportunity to express themselves.

I

Birth of Mexican Independence 1805–1821

Every colony that is well treated honours its parent state, but becomes estranged from it by injustice. For colonists are not sent forth on the understanding that they are to be slaves of those who remain behind, but that they are to be their equals.

Thucydides, "Causes of the War,"
The History of the Peloponnesian War

Revolutions are often promoted by segments of the upper class, who see their interests endangered by political or economic events and as a result become critical of the conditions. In this chapter I will show how this happened in New Spain, how this discontent reached and then passed the point of no return, and what its ultimate consequences were.

When war broke out between Great Britain and Spain on 12 December 1804, the Madrid government was subjected to a severe financial strain. Under these circumstances, it decreed two weeks later the compulsory redemption of mortgages belonging to chantries and pious works in Spanish America and the Philippines, as well as the sale of their real estate; the proceeds would go to the royal treasury in Madrid to redeem or "consolidate" the government paper money, circulating in Spain. It had been customary in New Spain for wealthy people to institute in their wills a chantry, by mortgaging their property for a certain amount at 5 percent. This interest would support a chaplain who had the duty in return to say a certain number of masses each year for the soul of the benefactor. Similarly pious works were sums willed by their donors to form a charitable foundation. Another common cause of indebtedness was the endowment of daughters and sisters entering a nunnery, which was usually effected by mortgaging the property in perpetuity for a specified amount of interest that would be paid to the nunnery.

In theory, the redemption, or *consolidación* as the measure came to be known, was a forced loan: the metropolitan government would borrow funds estimated at the enormous sum of over 40 million pesos from the endowments. But these did not have the money, which thus had to be collected from the debtors; as these did not have it either, and as the government would be satisfied only with cash, the debtors' property would have to be sold in public auction. In reality, the redemption, disguised as a harmless loan, threatened to become a wholesale expropriation of Mexican landowners. A storm of protest arose all over the hitherto peaceful country; farmers (hacendados), merchants, miners, and town councils sent petitions to the authorities asking them not to carry out the decree and warning them of the consequences.

The compulsory redemption began to be carried out in New Spain on 6 September 1805. The authorities accepted part payments of larger sums. But many people were simply unable to raise enough funds; in 1807 and 1808, the journals of the capital were full of notices concerning public auctions of houses, large and small farms, cattle, and businesses of all sorts. But in general, the largest debtors, who happened to be at the same time the richest landowners, did not suffer so much; a dozen case studies reveal that their estates did not have to be auctioned. If the richer landowners were unable or unwilling to pay, the authorities threatened to sell one of their haciendas, and after considerable haggling, a new agreement was reached ... and so it continued until the latter part of 1808. All in all, Spain succeeded in extracting from her colony around 12 million pesos, approximately one fourth of the total debt to chantries and pious works. It was sufficient to estrange the landowning elite from the mother country.[1]

Religious motives were also present. Spain was at the time a satellite of France and it was widely believed that the large sums were not used for war against Great Britain, but were transferred to Paris. Whatever the truth, this belief influenced public opinion in Mexico and strengthened local opposition to the extraction of money. In the mind of the Mexican landowner, France was the symbol, the incarnation, of hateful atheism. As a consequence of various reforms of the Spanish Bourbons, the power, influence, and wealth of the church in the colonies had been considerably reduced. Many Spaniards brought to their new home a more liberal spirit. But Mexican hacendados, especially those resident in provincial towns, retained their conservative turn of mind; some of them remembered the brutal expulsion by the Spanish government of the Jesuits.

The already docile church in New Spain hardly protested against the redemption although this affected the security of its investments; the funds would no longer be guaranteed by real estate but only by the insolvent Spanish government. The church hierarchy—the bishops and cathedral chapters—lived from tithes and therefore were not affected by the redemption. Curates of wealthy parishes lived mainly from parochial dues; while poorer parish priests and clerics with no fixed benefice, who represented the majority of Mexican secular clergy, depended partly or completely on the income from chantries. This applied also to many friars.[2] As Spain was soon unable to pay the interest, the lower clergy were drastically impoverished. Their interests converged with those of landowners, and when the time was ripe, the lower clergy readily supplied the hacendados with an ideology.

They did not have to wait long. In June 1808, news arrived in Mexico of revolutionary changes in Spain: the fall of the royal favorite, Godoy, and of Charles IV, the succession of Ferdinand VII, the popular uprising in Madrid against the French occupation army, and finally the arrest of Ferdinand VII by Napoleon, who forced his abdication. Spain was submerged in a civil war and, at the same time, was fighting a

war of national liberation against foreign invasion. Viceregal
authority in Mexico rested on that of the crown in Spain. But
now the king fell into captivity and nobody in the colony
thought of recognizing the usurper. Sovereignty had returned
to the people. *Juntas* were springing up in Spain in the name
of Ferdinand VII,[3] and in Mexico City the town council
moved toward independence under the direction of two
creole lawyers Primo de Verdad and Francisco Azcárate. The
friar Melchor de Talamantes provided the program, which demanded the end of the redemption, indemnity for damages
and restitution of conditions to their original state. He obviously spoke for the landholders and lower clergy.

It seemed logical to expect that the viceroy would uphold
the authority of Spain. By one of the curious inversions of
history the opposite occurred. The viceroy, Iturrigaray, des-
paired of the Spanish cause in the colony over which he presided, since Spain was unable to lend him military support.
Perhaps he was influenced by his contacts with the silver
miners of the country, for it was later revealed that his distribution of imported mercury for the amalgamation of silver
ore had not been a disinterested endeavor and that in the few
years of his government he had amassed an enormous fortune,
not in real estate to be sure, but in coin, precious metals, and
gems.

Now the Creole party representing Mexican-born Spaniards
offered to appoint him captain general of the colony. The
royal officials were to be confirmed in their posts, but all
civil and ecclesiastical vacancies were to be filled by creoles.
The creoles, who owned haciendas but were not interested in
managing them, who had acquired culture and education but
were deprived of the opportunity to exercise their knowledge
except on the small scale of town councils, would finally
achieve political power. The Bourbon reforms had helped to
create an affluent group that later turned to the professions
and finally to politics; if at first they benefited Spain, in the
long run they undermined the regime.

The creole lawyers of Mexico City envisaged a peaceful

revolution. But this was not to be. One of the viceroy's first decisions was to suspend the forced redemption, which he did on 9 August with the purpose of quieting the influential elements of the country. But it was too late. Larger issues were looming now on the horizon. Peninsular traders of the capital sensed danger to their monopolistic position. A cleavage of interests became apparent between the Spanish-born importers of goods from Spain or via Spain and creole landowners who, as consumers, wanted cheaper goods imported directly from England or other countries; this could have been achieved only by making Mexico independent. Thus the peninsular Spaniards were pushed into allegiance for their mother country, even though many were married to daughters of Mexican landowners. They decided to act and under the leadership of the Basque merchant Yermo organized a conspiracy to depose the viceroy. The coup was successful thanks to perfect planning and execution by a volunteer force composed of 300 employees of Spanish shops. These were usually poor immigrants working day and night as salesmen and servants for their employers, sometimes their relatives, with the hope of eventually becoming partners or sons-in-law or of saving enough money to establish businesses of their own. Their morals were strict but their more visible manners were brusque and coarse; their voices were loud and they were uneducated. These people, standing behind the counters in shops, were in daily contact with the Mexicans, and it is not surprising that they were a target of jokes and popular hatred. These men had everything to lose in case of Mexican independence, certainly more than their employers who already had their property and their creole connections. They proved reliable; on the misty night of 15 September 1808, these storm troops, led by Yermo, assaulted the viceregal palace and imprisoned the viceroy and the creoles known as leaders of the movement for independence. A new viceroy was promptly appointed.

This act pushed New Spain on the path of a violent revolution. For centuries, the principle of legitimate succession had been rigorously observed. Now the spell was broken. If the Spaniards broke the existing law and order, reflected the creoles, it was now their duty to restore it. If a handful of Europeans succeeded, why not the Americans, as the creoles began to call themselves with a pride behind which was barely hidden a resentment at being deprived access to the highest posts in their own country? After 1808 it was easier to organize conspiracies in the provinces because the capital city was under strict control of Spanish forces. Spanish power was also strong east of Mexico, in Puebla and Veracruz; since the conquest this had been the route along which European immigrants settled before spreading from the capital all over the country. The immigrants were numerous there and they were thus able to help to keep this life-line open. On the other hand, there were fewer European-born Spaniards in other provinces, especially in the Bajío.

The Bajío was a broad fertile valley stretching roughly from Querétaro in the east almost as far as Lake Chapala in the west and from the town of León and the village of Dolores in the north to Lake Cuitzeo in the south, near the important city of Valladolid, today Morelia. Until present times the climate of the Bajío has been rather arid and it had little sedentary population at the time of the conquest. The Spaniards introduced a new type of agriculture there: maize would be grown during the rainy season, occasionally with the help of irrigation, and wheat during the dry season, always with the waters of the Lerma River and its tributaries as irrigation. Indian laborers were brought in or migrated from the South.

At the beginning of the nineteenth century, the Bajío was the most prosperous part of the country. It contained the richest silver mining community, Guanajuato; woolen cloths were produced in Querétaro and San Miguel el Grande (later renamed San Miguel Allende), and leather goods were made in León. It had the highest population density of all New Spain. Compared to other regions, it had many towns, mainly commercial centers for the surrounding farms and with large populations of Indian peons, many small farms called ranchos owned or leased mostly by mestizos, and in contrast to the valleys of Toluca, Mexico, and Puebla, surprisingly few Indian villages. In the Bajío, at least in the Intendancy of Guanajuato, the Indians were culturally integrated, for most of them lived as peons on haciendas and ranchos and as laborers in towns. This is evident from the fact that most of them paid their tribute through a hacienda or directly themselves; a minority paid through the villages in which they lived. The acculturation of Indians, the growing proportion of mestizos and the rising national feeling of creoles showed itself in the cult of the dark Virgin of Guadalupe who became patroness of New Spain in 1746.

As everywhere else, most creoles of the Bajío were landowners and most landowners were creoles. One can surmise that they were less Spanish in their ways than, let us say, the creoles of Mexico and Puebla; or, putting it more positively, they were more Mexican. For certain national characteristics began to develop in the Bajío as a result of the blending of the races. If the Indians at one end of the spectrum were more culturally integrated than in the central part of the country, it can also be said that the Spaniards at the other end of the same spectrum had also become more assimilated by the interplay of the same forces. Many Bajío Indians and creoles were in reality mestizos.

Hence it should not be surprising that the revolt against colonial rule broke out among the creoles of the Bajío. The leader himself, Miguel Hidalgo y Costilla, came from an old creole family. His paternal forefathers were in the country by the early seventeenth century, and the ancestors on his mother's side had been on Mexican soil since before the middle of the sixteenth century. Miguel was born in 1753 on the large hacienda of Corralejo in the western part of the Bajío; his father was its manager. While large estate owners were in most cases creoles, they often had Spanish immigrants as managers. Following the traditional pattern, these immigrants worked hard, and as their basic necessities were satisfied in kind from the hacienda, they were able to save most of their earnings. In due time — after ten years, at least — they married and acquired property for themselves, large or small farms. Hidalgo's father, however, was not interested in becoming a hacendado; he viewed his position as permanent, recalled his youngest son from medical school to help him in his work, and the son eventually succeeded him as manager. His other three sons all completed their studies, two as priests and one as a lawyer. The main legacy the father could offer them was education. He was not poor, though. According to an inventory of 1764, he had 338 head of cattle, four horses, five Negro and mulatto slaves and, as an indication of his cultural propensities, a clavichord, an object certainly not very common in a faraway hacienda.[4]

In 1765 Hidalgo entered the Jesuit college at Valladolid. Two years later, the fourteen-year-old boy witnessed the arrest and expulsion of his teachers; he then enrolled in the diocesan college of San Nicolás in the same city. His career was brilliant and in 1790 he became rector of this institution. Situtated at the very southern edge of the Bajío, Valladolid was the ecclesiastical capital of this wealthy district; it was the seat of the bishopric of Michoacán and of large Augustinian and Franciscan provinces. These ecclesiastical jurisdictions covered most if not all the Bajío. As a result, Valladolid was the cultural center of the Bajío, together with Guanajuato, a prosperous silver mining city. A part of the Bajío's wealth flowed in tithes and other payments to Valladolid, where it was reflected in the high standard of living of the churchmen. From his salary, Hidalgo was soon able to buy three farms. Valladolid was also fortunate in having two enlightened bishops, both Spaniards from the Asturias: Antonio de San Miguel and his younger relative Manuel Abad y Queipo, later to become famous for his reform proposals and friendship with Hidalgo. Hidalgo seemed destined to play an important role. Then, in 1792, he resigned all his posts and accepted a curacy in a distant town near the Pacific coast. Whatever the cause of this demotion, it gave a different direction to his life, for parish priests are by the nature of their posts closely connected with the common people. In 1803, Hidalgo succeeded his brother in the parish of Dolores, a prosperous village fairly near Guanajuato. He soon became the friend of Juan Antonio Riaño, the enlightened governor of the Guanajuato intendancy and husband of a rich creole from Louisiana. Their home in Guanajuato was the center from which French culture spread; it was there that Hidalgo continued to meet his old friend Abad y Queipo, now bishop-elect of Michoacán. These two men had a common interest in introducing badly needed reforms. But destiny was to separate them soon.

Hidalgo's fellow conspirators were also creoles. Take for example, the three rebels of San Miguel el Grande: Ignacio Allende, Juan Aldama, and Mariano Abasolo. They all were sons of Spanish-Basque merchants. Their fortunes varied, Abasolo being the richest, for besides his own inheritance he managed considerable properties belonging to his wife. None showed any inclination to commerce; they all became captains in the small colonial army, the militia.[5] As landowners, some were affected by the forced redemption: the Allende family had to pay annual installments; Hidalgo himself was unable to redeem his debt and therefore his hacienda was embargoed.[6] The redemption did not increase their sympathy for Spain.

The conspiracy in which these men took part was organized in Querétaro, the important city at the entrance to the Bajío from Mexico, with the participation of the local governor himself, Miguel Domínguez, a native of Guanajuato, and especially of his wife, Doña María Josefa Ortiz. The social composition of the group was a familiar pattern, wealthy creoles, militia officers, and clerics forming its core. The program was simple enough: imprisonment of rich Spaniards, confiscation of their property to finance the revolution, and, of course, overthrow of any authority that might oppose them. The goal was national independence, disguised as the struggle to save New Spain from that atheistic monster Bonaparte, for the legitimate king, Ferdinand VII. These intentions appear clearly in a letter written by Allende to Hidalgo on 31 August 1810, informing him of the latest discussions of the Querétaro group. "It was decided to work with our intentions carefully concealed," wrote Allende, "since if the movement was openly revolutionary it would not be seconded by the general mass of the people; Second Lieutenant Don Pedro Septién" (a scion of an opulent family) "strengthened his stand saying that if the revolution was inevitable, as the Indians were indifferent to the word liberty, it was necessary to make them believe the insurrection was being accomplished only in order to help King Ferdinand."[7]

The uprising was staged for the beginning of October 1810. The government, however, managed to learn about it and on 13 September placed the members of the Querétaro group under arrest or surveillance. From then on, this cradle of Mexican independence was so closely watched by the Spanish authorities that it was never to play a role in the future independence movement. Unfortunately for Spain, the brave governor's wife secretly managed to send a messenger to her fellow conspirators in San Miguel el Grande. Warned in time, these hurried to the peaceful village of Dolores to consult with Hidalgo. As they did not wish to spend the rest of their lives in a royalist dungeon, they accepted Hidalgo's decision to revolt, in their firm belief that justice was on their side, for they wanted only to reestablish the law overthrown two years before by the Spaniards.

There was no time to lose. In the early hours of 16 September 1810, Hidalgo called his parishioners and proclaimed the revolution. Prison doors were opened, local Spaniards were arrested, their shops and homes sacked. Nobody was killed yet. With a crowd numbering several hundred men, Hidalgo and his companions proceeded the same day to San Miguel el Grande. On the way, Hidalgo took from the Atotonilco church the image of the dark Virgin of Guadalupe, to be used as a revolutionary banner. Haciendas belonging to Spaniards were sacked along the road, including the fields where the maize was almost ready to be harvested. Haciendas of "Americans" were at first respected, but in the course of the war, all were treated in the same way. As no clear social reforms were offered to the poor, starving as a result of crop failure in 1809, they were attracted to the rebellion mainly as an opportunity to plunder. Yet organization of the army was attempted; Hidalgo became captain general of America. Allende became Hidalgo's lieutenant; Hidalgo's brother was appointed treasurer but he could not introduce much order.

The revolt spread through the Bajío like a prairie fire. The revolutionary army, swollen now to 25,000 men approached Guanajuato. The intendant Riaño was watching it with apprehension. He had fortified the impressive municipal granary, recently erected by him at considerable cost, and retired there with the local Spaniards and a batallion of militia. They took with them the contents of the royal treasury as well as their personal hoards of precious metal. They were all well armed and expected reinforcements. On 28 September, Riaño confidently rejected Hidalgo's ultimatum to surrender. Hours later, on the same day, the almost unarmed mass of insurgents stormed the granary, butchered its defenders, and made off with silver bars and coins valued at 3 million pesos.[8] Some of this found its way to Hidalgo's revolutionary treasury. The granary still stands there, a silent witness to mob violence. If there was any prospect for a peaceful solution to the conflict, the bloodbath in Guanajuato ended it. It also became clear that the undisciplined crowds were sacking not only the property of peninsular Spaniards, but also that of Americans; after all, it was impossible to distinguish between a Spanish-owned and an American-owned shop, house, or hacienda. Wealthy creoles both in cities and the country wavered in their support of the revolution and finally lined up behind the government.[9]

After appointing new authorities in Guanajuato, Hidalgo turned south. The next objective was Valladolid, the city where he had spent his student days, where he had later been professor and rector of the college, and where he resigned his post to become a simple parish priest. Here was perhaps an opportunity to humble the proud canons of the cathedral chapter. He knew he would not find his old friend Abad y Queipo there any more. As early as 24 September, before the insurgents' entry to Guanajuato, the bishop-elect of Michoacán hurled excommunication against all four principal leaders of the rebellion and left his see for Mexico City. For years, he had urged the need for a profound reform in social and economic conditions of the country, including abolition of the tribute to which Indian adult males were subject and the distribution of land to landless peasants whose number was growing. Abad y Queipo sensed that unless a reform was carried out soon, the tensions accumulated over centuries would explode. He called himself an "American by voluntary adoption." It may thus seem surprising that he should have reacted so violently against the revolt.[10] As he himself admitted in the decree of excommunication, Hidalgo "had merited my confidence and friendship until now." In common with many other Spanish residents of the colony, he had warm feelings for the creoles, but like the rest, when the time came to choose, he chose the viceroy, the king, Spain, the church, in one word, authority. If Spain was momentarily in trouble, she would recover; from the outset it must have been clear to him that Hidalgo's talk about the nonexistent king of Spain was a justification for a revolt in which the victims would be the Spaniards. And finally, he predicted that the revolution would spell ruin and destruction; wars, especially civil wars, usually cause widespread ruin and destruction, and it was not difficult to prophecy correctly. Thus, when passions took hold of the nation and no one listened to reason anyway, Abad y Queipo threw himself vehemently behind the government and became the most virulent pamphleteer against insurgency.

Valladolid had been the center of a conspiracy in 1809 — from which the one in Querétaro possibly branched off — and the town, since then inclined to independence, surrendered to the rebel army without resistance on 16 October.

Hidalgo promptly asked the Count of Sierra Gorda, a canon in charge of the bishopric in place of Abad y Queipo, to lift the excommunication, which he did.[11] Such changes, dependent upon whether royalists or revolutionists were in control of a town, became frequent and, consequently, bans were not taken seriously.

Having captured most towns of the Bajío — although he was not always able to hold them long — Hidlago now was ready for the big leap to Mexico City. Marching at the head of 80,000 people, Hidalgo arrived in the mountains separating the Valley of Mexico from that of Toluca and there defeated a smaller peninsular army. But after a few days, Hidalgo inexplicably turned back, overruling Allende who wished to attack the capital. The reasons underlying Hidalgo's decision are unknown. It can be assumed, however, that he was disillusioned by the failure of the Mexico City populace to rise against the authorities and discouraged by the intelligence that a well organized army was approaching to relieve the capital.[12] So the insurgents marched westward to Guadalajara, together with Puebla one of the most important cities of the country after the capital. They entered Guadalajara on 26 November.

Guadalajara became the rebel headquarters for over a month and a half and was one of only four Mexican cities with a printing press; the other three cities, Mexico City, Puebla, and Veracruz, were in government hands, and their presses were used profusely in the war propaganda. Hidalgo now had an opportunity to clarify his ideas and make his program known to the country; so far, his speeches had not been recorded in print, and therefore it is not clear whether Hidalgo had proclaimed the abolition of the Indian tribute from the very beginning or later in the course of his campaign, for instance in Valladolid where on 19 October such a proclamation was issued in his name.[13] Judging from the mass of Indians — both village dwellers and those living in towns as well as on haciendas as peons and squatters — who had followed Hidalgo from the beginning, it would seem obvious enough that they flocked to him with the hope of having this hateful tax abolished. Now that one press was at his disposal, all doubts as to his program were dispelled for not only were manifestoes printed, but a newspaper, *El Despertador Americano*, also appeared. All of these publicized the abolition of tribute, of taxes on alcoholic beverages, which had made them too dear for the poor, of the government tobacco monopoly in order to offer cheap smoking to the poor, and also of course of slavery, though not many slaves were left in New Spain at that time.

Hidalgo finally approached the sensitive subject of agrarian reform. In the Guadalajara region Indian villages managed to own land not only to the end of the sixteenth century,[14] but up to the very beginning of the nineteenth, in contrast to Central Mexico where many villages had lost land by repeated sales of their portions. Villagers in the Guadalajara region, however, had the habit of leasing land to nearby haciendas for a very low rent. As the leases were automatically renewed, it seemed that the haciendas might eventually appropriate the lands. In order to safeguard them for the peasants, Hidalgo decreed on 5 December that all rents due should be paid and that in the future the lands should not be leased but should be enjoyed by the Indians.[15] The demographic recovery preceding 1810, with an increased pressure on land as its result, must have played a part in creating an agrarian problem.

In the meantime, the adversary had not remained idle. Several days after Hidalgo's revolt in Dolores, the army commandant of San Luis Potosí, Felix Calleja, a Spaniard married to a wealthy local creole, took matters in his hands without awaiting instructions from Mexico. With funds confiscated from the local government treasury, he organized an army which was to defeat Hidalgo. Some officers trained by him, like Armijo, Barragán, Bustamante, and Gómez Pedraza, became prominent much later in independent Mexico.[16] Some hacendados of San Luis lent him their employees, guards or servants, with whom he formed an efficient unit.[17]

With his small but well equipped army, Calleja recaptured

the towns held by the insurgents, where ferocious slaughters were now repeated on an increased scale, and on 17 January 1811, he routed Hidalgo's much more numerous but poorly equipped, undisciplined, and disorganized army on Calderón Bridge, near Guadalajara. The dream of independence had lasted only four months.

Hidalgo and his entourage took flight, but on their way to the United States they were captured on the dusty northern desert, in a place ironically named Our Lady Guadalupe of Baján, and taken to far-away Chihuahua. First the laymen were executed — Allende, Aldama, Hidalgo's brother Mariano, the treasurer of the revolutionary army, and Mariano Jiménez, a former mining engineer in Guanajuato. The parish priest of Dolores himself was executed on 30 July 1811, after a humiliating trial. His last days must have been sad enough; his companions were already dead. The cause of independence seemed irretrievably lost, and he had little reason to suspect that ten years later his dream would come true. Four iron cages were then placed on the corners of the quadrangular Guanajuato granary and in them were hung the heads of Hidalgo, Allende, Aldama, and Jiménez. They remained there until after independence was won.

Hidalgo was neither a systematic thinker nor a man of orderly habits; however, he was well suited to lead the first, chaotic, revolutionary stage of the war. It was his tragic destiny to bring destruction to a part of Mexico. Though his faults were many, he is justly remembered as the father of Mexican independence, for he was the first to have challenged the established rule. On his death, New Spain was not the same country as before the night of 16 September 1810.

After Hidalgo's death, the revolt reappeared in the South under the leadership of another priest. On 20 October 1810, José María Morelos had sought out the captain general of America, who had just left Valladolid to march on Mexico City. Morelos had studied at the Colegio de San Nicolás when Hidalgo was its rector. Abad y Queipo had recently ordered him to publish in his far-away tropical parish of Carácuaro the edict excommunicating his admired teacher, and the worried Morelos, already interested in the movement, decided to see Hidalgo personally. In their talk, the captain general justified the revolution from a religious point of view and, on the same day, commissioned Morelos to raise troops and wage war in southern Mexico. The interview proved to be of momentous consequence for the future course of the insurrection.

So far, the movement had been restricted to the Bajío or to the central plateaus in general. Now a new commander appeared who, apart from an inborn talent for leadership which Hidalgo must have instantly recognized, had an intimate knowledge of the "hot country," the land situated between the Pacific coast and the central plateaus, a land with few, sometimes inaccessible, roads, with rugged mountains and fertile plains, with an unhealthy climate in which few people raised in cooler regions would want to live, with a sun so scorching that fields could be worked only in early morning, in the evening, and on moonlit nights, and where life was not highly prized by local mulattoes, mestizos, and Indians.

In his background, Morelos was different from the creole commanders of the revolutionary army. He had been born in 1765 in Valladolid (later renamed Morelia), the son of a poor, honest family. His father was a carpenter and his mother the daughter of a schoolteacher who had once been connected with the church. The birth certificate described the parents as Spanish, but this was not necessarily so; it is generally held that Morelos was a mestizo. His mother taught him how to read and write, but at the death of his father the fourteen-year-old boy was sent to his uncle's hacienda near Apatzingán, a town in the hot country. There he spent ten years as a farmer and as muleteer.[18]

But he was not to remain there. Perhaps in part to please his widowed mother, he entered at the age of twenty-five the Colegio of San Nicolás and after several years of hard work was admitted to the priesthood. The happy mother accompanied him to his first assignment in a village of the hot country; the poor and no longer young new priest could not hope to obtain a parish in a more agreeable climate. The heat proved fatal to his mother's health and she died in less than a year, leaving José María in mourning and perhaps also in bitter reflection on the hard lot of curates and the pleasant lot of the bishop and the canons in Valladolid. His situation did not improve much when he obtained a chantry, but with his practical knowledge he was able to become a successful cattle raiser and thus to supplement his meagre income from parochial fees, few of which were paid either in cash or goods. It should surprise no one that at least 400 secular and regular clerics – over 5 percent of the total cleric population – have been counted as having participated in the insurgent movement.[19]

So Morelos departed southward. Even if Hidalgo's days were numbered and the Bajío was pacified by the royalist sword, the revolt spread like an oil stain to other parts of the country. It fell to Calleja to fight Morelos, who, after Hidalgo's death, became head of a revolutionary army until his capture in November 1815. Almost from the beginning, Morelos was fortunate to find excellent commanders in Galeana and the Bravo brothers, sons of hacendado families of the hot country, as well as in Vicente Guerrero, also born there but of humbler origins. In time, Morelos was able to organize an efficient army, to be sure a comparatively small one, but a disciplined army for which looting and indiscriminate killing were not permitted. His understanding of basic human psychology and his unique knowledge of local geography enabled Morelos to overcome his lack of military training; he managed to hold parts of the hot country for several years, and this gave him and his collaborators time to clarify their ideas and to think out a political strategy.

The rebels in their isolation gradually drifted away from Spain and eventually declared the independence of the country. Developments in Europe also influenced this process. The French forces were being defeated on all fronts and were retreating from both Russia and Spain. It was becoming obvious that Napoleon was doomed. The liberation of Spain from the foreign yoke would, of course, mean the restoration of the legitimate government and of the church in all its privileges. The argument that the Mexicans had to preserve their country for the true religion from the atheistic French would no longer be valid. Fortunately, the idea of national independence, which had been discreetly fed to the public, first by Hidalgo and then by Morelos, was taking root. It was then the right moment to proclaim it, before Ferdinand VII regained power. So might Morelos have reflected just before deciding to call a national congress of provincial representatives.

The Congress — the American, not Spanish constitutional terminology was used — assembled in September 1813 in Chilpancingo, a town on the road to Acapulco. Morelos had prepared for its consideration a program which he unassumingly named *Sentiments of the Nation:* America should be free and independent of Spain and any other nation, government, or monarchy. The Catholic religion should be the only religion, without the toleration of any other; its ministers should be supported by the tithes and the first fruits only and the dogma should be upheld by the hierarchy consisting of Pope, bishops, and curates, "for every plant which God did not plant should be torn out," probably a reference to the unpopular inquisition. Morelos made it clear that the form of government should be republican. Slavery, tribute, and all ethnic distinctions were to be abolished and all Mexicans — called "Americans" — would be equal. Their property should be respected and laws should regulate poverty and destitution and increase the wages of the poor. The property of Spaniards, "Europeans," once confiscated, should be carefully administered with the view of financing the war.

The Congress acted on the first recommendation of Morelos and on 6 November declared "that under the present circumstances in Europe, . . . the dependence on the Spanish throne should be dissolved." The Congress would celebrate treaties with the Holy See; it recognized the Catholic religion only and prohibited the use of any other in public or in secret, and it would protect with all its powers the purity of the faith and the preservation of the regular orders. In spite of the fact that the high church hierarchy had no use for the Mexican insurgents, these did not harbor any resentment against the church and all they yearned for was to be taken into account. It is an irony that the church turned its back on these poor, devout, village priests and gave full support to a Spain that was to become liberal. The Declaration of Independence was followed the same day by a decree reestablishing the Society of Jesus, apparently upon the initiative of Morelos himself.[20] There had been no Jesuits in Mexico to lead, or at least to inspire the rebels but their memory was cherished, and it can be said that they had belated revenge for their expulsion not so much in the decree but in the establishment of Mexican independence itself.

On 7 November Morelos and his forces left for Valladolid. The attempt to conquer that city was a mistake, for there the insurgents were decisively beaten by another native of Valladolid, Augustín Iturbide. From then on, the star of Morelos began to decline; his army lost ground under the systematic assaults of Calleja, general commander and virtual viceroy, although according to the 1812 Spanish Constitution he was only a *jefe político*.[21] The Congress fled from Chilpancingo and took refuge in Apatzingán in the heart of the hot country; here it worked on a constitution, unmolested but also in complete isolation while Morelos was away with the remnants of his forces. The constitution, proclaimed on 22 October 1814, embodied more or less the ideas expressed earlier in Chilpancingo; it was never to be carried out in practice, for under the ever-increasing royalist offensive the Congress was dispersed. Morelos himself was captured and executed on 22 December 1815.

In the Mexican struggle for independence, Morelos occupies a place second only to Hidalgo. Morelos no doubt possessed qualities Hidalgo lacked; he revealed himself as a soldier and organizer; above all, he was a man of character. Loyal and modest, Morelos refused to accept the pompous title offered to him by Congress and preferred to call himself a servant of the nation. If Hidalgo was a hurricane, Morelos was a steady rain that nourished the soil. Morelos developed the movement started by Hidalgo and gave it coherent form. In his conduct of war, he showed considerable humanity. Many inhabitants of New Spain who had been scared away by the violence of Hidalgo's crowds began to see independence in a more favorable light as a result of Morelos's efforts. Thus, when a propitious moment arose some years later, public opinion not only did not oppose, but welcomed independence.

The Spanish government considered that the end of Morelos meant the annihilation of the independence movement; a few groups of insurgents resisting here and there were not dangerous. So in 1816 it recalled Calleja, and the new viceroy, Apodaca, count of Venadito, attempted pacification by offering conditional surrender to the remaining rebels. Many accepted; others went into hiding. By 1820, the country was apparently tranquil, except for a small section of the hot country, where Vincente Guerrero refused to surrender. He would probably have died as guerrilla leader had an occurrence in Spain not given a different turn to events.

On 1 January 1820, a group of officers in Spain proclaimed the liberal constitution which had been approved by the Cortes in 1812, but annulled by Ferdinand VII upon his return to Spain in May 1814. The revolutionary wave overpowered the king so that he was forced to accept constitutional rule. The results soon became apparent. After the middle of the year, Spain began to witness a series of anticlerical measures including the suppression of the Society of Jesus and certain other religious orders. Surviving orders were not allowed to have more than one monastery in a district and no new monasteries or nunneries could be established. Other measures were decreed affecting the personal immunity of the clergy and the right of the church to acquire property. The church was facing a frontal attack on its privileges and possessions more serious than any liberalization attempted by previous governments.

In high ecclesiastical circles of New Spain the idea arose that the church might save itself by establishing an independent Mexico. The bishop of Puebla, Antonio Pérez, and the rector of the University of Mexico and canon of the metropolitan cathedral, Matías Monteagudo — the former a Mexican, the latter a Spaniard — promoted this idea.[22] Obviously they were not alone in this enterprise; they must have acted with the acquiescence of some of their colleagues and superiors. The high clerics naturally wished to avoid a repetition of Hidalgo's popular uprising; they were seeking a bloodless change of government. To accomplish it they needed the help of the secular arm, an alliance with the army or a part of it — with its highest levels, of course, not with the soldiers whose obedience was taken for granted. An opportunity soon presented itself with the appointment of Colonel Agustín Iturbide as military commander of southern Mexico.

Iturbide was born in Valladolid, son of a wealthy Basque merchant and a creole mother. His background was about the same as that of the rebels of San Miguel el Grande; unlike them, on receiving the news of Hidalgo's revolt, he offered his services to the crown. He was not the only creole in the royalist army; the civil war split the nation vertically, so that members of all social and ethnic strata fought on both sides. In the war, Iturbide became known as a ruthless and sanguinary army officer who executed insurgent priests without benefit of trial.[23] In 1815 he was accused of lack of scruples in financial matters and a year later retired from the army, probably harboring a grudge against the viceregal authorities who were persecuting him now that he was no longer needed. But for the 1820 revolution in Spain, he would have spent the rest of his life as an hacendado.

Hence it seems strange that in 1820, the viceroy should have offered him an appointment to an important army command and that he should have accepted; it was in fact

suggested that the clerical conspirators had persuaded Apodaca to do so as part of their scheme.[24] A simpler explanation is that Iturbide was chosen as the best royalist officer
available to deal with the guerrillas operating in the south
now that Colonel Armijo had resigned the post because of ill
health. Whatever the reason, this was an opportunity for Iturbide, and when he accepted, he perhaps had already decided
what to do. Soon after the beginning of his official mission
Iturbide attempted to gain the good will and confidence of
his former adversaries Vicente Guerrero and Nicolás Bravo,
the two most distinguished living independence fighters.
Bravo had been recently freed from a royalist prison and
Guerrero was resisting in the hot country.[25] Naturally, Guerrero was distrustful; Iturbide's written overtures sounded like
typical attempts to lure him into a trap. Guerrero's suspicions
were overcome, however, when Iturbide made public on 24
February 1821 his program for Mexican independence in
Iguala, deep in the hot country and not far from where Guerrero was operating.

In the document which Iturbide may have brought from
Mexico, at least in an outline or rough draft, he invited all
"Americans, under whose name are included not only those
born in America, but also the Europeans, the Africans, and
the Asiatics who live here," to join in a common effort toward the goal of independence.[26] All great countries had once
been ruled by other nations; they all eventually outgrew their
mother countries. Now this moment had come for Mexico.
"European Spaniards!", continued the manifesto in a more
emotional tone, "your country is America, for you live here;
here you have your beloved wives, your tender children, your
haciendas, your businesses and other possessions. Americans!
Who among you can say that you are not of Spanish descent?
Behold the sweet chain that unites us; consider the bonds of
friendship, interdependence of interest, education, language,
and harmony of feelings. . . . The time has arrived . . . that
our union should emancipate America without need of foreign help. At the head of a brave and determined army, I pro-

claim the Independence of Northern Ameri<
dependent Mexico all of whose inhabitant,
birthplace, would be equal. This proposition se<
able enough, for hostility between peninsulars an
must have worn out in the course of years; neither had
succeeded in unseating Spaniards nor these in subduing t.
creole cousins. Other problems now stood before the coun
try; hence it was time for a reconciliation. It was necessary to
defend the Catholic faith. With this issue, the author of the
manifesto — whoever he was[27] — found the common denom-
inator for Spaniards and Mexicans, for landowners and landless, for whites, mestizos, and Indians, for higher and lower
clergy. To the Spaniards who were worried about their properties and lives, he offered guarantees that they would live
unmolested in the new country, and he offered the long-
awaited independence to the Mexicans, especially to the insurgents who by now had lost hope that their dream would
ever come true. By uniting the nation, neutralizing the
Spanish forces and isolating the handful of royalist officials,
he proposed to carry out a bloodless transfer of power.

His appeal proved to be remarkably successful. Iturbide
was now committed to a cause deemed treasonable in royalist
eyes. All doubts about his intentions were dispelled. Two
weeks later, Guerrero sent Iturbide a message in which he
placed himself under his command.[28] The suspicion among
Guerrero's soldiers was, of course, not entirely overcome, but
the two armies met — one of the most bizarre sights possible
to imagine. Well dressed officers and well fed troops on one
side and typical mountain guerrilla fighters on the other eyed
each other distrustfully; they had met as enemies on battle-
fields in the course of the last decade. But it worked. The insurgents in other parts of Mexico followed Guerrero's example, giving Iturbide their support. Royalist officers who,
like Iturbide, had fought the insurrection, followed suit, including Anastasio Bustamante, a commander in the important Bajío. The viceregal power slowly disintegrated and the
count of Venadito himself was forced to resign on 5 July.

It was prudent, if not necessary, to persuade Spain to accept the independence of Mexico by formal treaty. A new viceroy, Juan O'Donojú, nominally only a *jefe político*, was on his way to Mexico and it was with him that Iturbide proposed to confer. They convened in Córdoba, the center of a fertile tobacco-growing district at the foot of the volcano Citlaltépetl, and on 24 August signed the Manifesto of Iguala as the basis of the future independent state, with several modifications, one of which did not seem important at the moment. According to the original document, Mexico was to be a constitutional monarchy under Ferdinand VII or, in the case of his refusal, under another prince of Spanish or any other reigning dynasty. The Córdoba Treaty did not specify that the future Mexican emperor — the term echoed the memory of both Napoleon and Montezuma — must be chosen from a European dynasty; in case the candidates named in the text did not deign to accept the crown, the ruler should be selected by the Mexican Congress.[29] O'Donojú overlooked the omission.[30]

Iturbide rode into Mexico City as liberator of the country on 27 September, his thirty-eighth birthday. After an effort which extended back fifteen years to the initial resistance to forced redemption of mortgages, Mexican landowners — spiritual, if not real, heirs of the conquerors — attained political power. In 1810, Mexicans alone were not strong enough to overcome the power of Spain and the church. Taking advantage of an unusually favorable constellation of circumstances, Iturbide succeeded where Hidalgo had failed, by enlisting the support of the royalist army as well as of the church. Thus he achieved independence by an almost, comparatively speaking, bloodless and short revolution.

However, ironically, Iturbide is the least admired of all those involved in the Mexican struggle for independence. First he fought against his fellow creoles; then he turned against Spain. Opportunists have never been loved by the people. This explains why Mexico has monuments to Hidalgo, Morelos, and Guerrero, but none to Iturbide. Each of the three heroes also has a province named after him; the state of Guerrero covers the same region in which its namesake spent ten years fighting for independence. And Valladolid was renamed after Morelos, not after Iturbide, also its native son. One would prefer Guerrero, who had sacrificed himself for a decade, to have been the liberator instead of Iturbide, who reaped the fruits of other's labors. Yet, ultimately, Iturbide's accomplishment cannot be denied.

2

The Troubled Years
1821–1855

> The cause of all these evils was the lust for power arising
> from greed and ambition; and from these passions pro-
> ceeded the violence of parties once engaged in contention.
> The leaders, . . . on the one side with the cry of political
> equality of the people, on the other of a moderate aristoc-
> racy, sought prizes for themselves in those public interests
> which they pretended to cherish.
>
> Thucydides, "Corcyraean Revolution,"
> *The History of the Peloponnesian War*

Iturbide, acclaimed as liberator, issued a proclamation: "Mexicans! . . . You know already how to be free; it is up to you
to show how to be happy." This was easier said than done, as
the following years showed. On the next morning, 28 September, a governing junta chosen by Iturbide from among the
conservative elements proclaimed the independence of Mexico.

The junta, with "the first chief of the imperial army" as its
president, included the canon Monteagudo and the bishop of
Puebla, well known promoters of independence; José María
Fagoaga, of the opulent silver mining family; and several
members of the creole nobility. Old fighters for independence like Guerrero were not members; on the other hand,
the junta included O'Donojú, the former viceroy, whose presence was supposed to lend legitimacy to the new régime and
to guarantee a smooth transition between the viceroyalty and
a future monarchy under a Spanish or European prince. It is
a curious fact that O'Donojú did not sign the declaration of
independence although he was at the session where it was ap-

proved. Perhaps he disagreed with its tone; perhaps he was not feeling well, for soon after he fell ill and died on 8 October.[1] O'Donojú had been the sole living link between Mexico and Spain; now this link was broken. Had he lived, the course of Mexican history might have been different, for with all the prestige of Spain behind him, he might have somewhat restrained Iturbide's ambition. Now Iturbide was left free to cut his way through the political jungle.

Another peculiar event occurred. The Córdoba convention specified that two commissioners appointed by O'Donojú should proceed to Madrid in order to negotiate a settlement. O'Donojú died before he could comply with this clause of the agreement, but the commissioners still could be sent by the junta or the regency — the executive body of five persons presided over by Iturbide. However, this was not done; moreover, the new government began to show hostility to Spaniards attempting to repatriate funds.[2] This was understandable given the disastrous financial situation prevailing in Mexico, but it could also be interpreted as a deliberate attempt to block a settlement with the mother country. In view of later developments, this possibility should not be excluded.

In a conflict between nations, it is usually difficult to decide who threw the first stone or fired the first shot. After O'Donojú's acceptance of Mexican independence, the Spanish army stationed in Mexico followed his example. A group of royalists refused to submit, however, and withdrew to San Juan Ulúa, a powerful fortress in front of Veracruz harbor, built on the same island on which Cortés had paused before disembarking and which was now a dungeon for political prisoners. From here the royalists continued to rule the sea, obviously waiting for reinforcements with which to recapture Veracruz and eventually reconquer the country. News traveled slowly in those days, about two months from Mexico to Europe or vice versa. Signs were multiplying that Madrid would react negatively to Mexican independence; the final decision was taken on 13 February 1822 by the decree of the Spanish Parliament, declaring the Córdoba agreement null

and void.[3] If it is true that the Spanish liberal government denied Mexico its right to independence, it is also true that the
Mexican government did very little, or nothing, to make its
independence palatable to Spain. Perhaps the whole outcome
of events was inevitable. Mexico's economy was ruined;
mines were flooded, haciendas burned down and many villages and even towns razed to the ground. Needless to say,
the state treasury was bankrupt. Expenses soared, for the insurgent forces had been incorporated in the army and the
Spanish troops had to be fed, pending their return to Spain.
The fiscal deficit was mounting day by day. Guided by the
best intentions, Iturbide's government contributed to the
economic disaster by lowering taxes; inspired by Alexander
von Humboldt's predictions, the new rulers had confidence in
the unlimited resources of the country. Humboldt, of course,
had assumed a peaceful future for Mexico. Unfortunately,
this assumption proved false. Consequently, the lowering of
certain tax rates worsened the deficit.

When an attempt to raise a loan failed, Iturbide resorted to
a forced loan. As the main holders of cash, the Spanish import houses of Mexico City were now expected to finance the
public treasury, even though their funds — as almost everyone else's — were exhausted. At the same time the Spaniards
were not inclined to lend a helping hand to Mexico, despite
the security offered to them by the Plan of Iguala and the
Córdoba Agreement. Many merchants refused to pay up and
instead preferred to emigrate with their savings; some of
them were imprisoned. Iturbide appeared to be violating
the solemn promises embodied in the two documents, although he did keep his word in other spheres: for instance,
many Spanish government officials, both high and low, remained at their posts.

In this difficult situation, the constitutional Congress
assembled on 24 February 1822, its members having been
chosed by electors selected by townships. In many of these
local elections, the influence of the United States and the
Spanish constitutions was apparent.[4] So it happened that to

Iturbide's unpleasant surprise, most deputies were either republicans or bourbonists (monarchist followers of a Spanish prince on the Mexican throne). Iturbide, who held different ideas about the future regime of the country, clashed with Congress from the first day when he insisted on occupying the most prominent seat. Although Congress admitted that he, as liberator, was the first citizen of the empire, it declared that it could not assign him the highest seat, for this belonged to its own president; Iturbide's personal escort was forbidden to enter the hall, and he himself was told not to unsheath his sword during the session.[5] Clearly this situation could not last long. An opportunity to do away with the troublesome legislature presented itself after the Spanish rejection of the Córdoba convention. On the night of 18 May 1822, army garrisons proclaimed Iturbide as Emperor Agustín I and on the next morning Congress approved this decision under military and popular pressure. Now that the Córdoba agreement had been nullified by Spain, reasoned deputy Valentín Gómez Farías, a physician later to become a liberal leader, Mexico was free to pursue its course.[6] Iturbide finally took the coveted seat under the canopy.

The emperor was promptly recognized by insurgents like Bravo and Guerrero. The latter had been rewarded by the liberator with the title of marshal and the command of southern Mexico; he did not seem envious of Iturbide's position. In his congratulation, Guerrero expressed the confidence that the liberator would not become a tyrant.[7] Iturbide did not heed the warning. With the legislature deprived of freedom, conspiracies mushroomed and by the end of August, nineteen deputies and several army officers were in prison. Two months later the emperor dissolved Congress altogether. It is a wonder that with all his long record of cruelty, Iturbide was satisfied with depriving his enemies of personal freedom; he did not deprive anyone of his life. Too much blood had already been shed. Iturbide obviously wished to remain a humane tyrant; nobody knows what would have happened had he resorted to the extreme measure that was applied to himself two years later. Mexico was still in the idyllic dawn of its independence.

As was to be expected, the new emperor was welcomed by the church, which also had good reason to view Congress with suspicion. Three weeks after installation, the legislative body suspended the forced loan; as bourbonists, many deputies were opposed to the arbitrary arrest of Spanish merchants. Most of them were mild liberals influenced by the then liberal Spain (against which Iturbide had revolted) and thus they voted that, if the government did not receive sufficient funds from a volunteer loan, it should proceed to the public auction of the already nationalized properties of certain religious orders, especially the Jesuits.[8] Jesuit property had been confiscated half a century ago and, of this, the amount which remained still unsold and under state administration was not considerable. Many people in Mexico had been yearning for the reinstatement of the Jesuit order; after all, this restoration had been part of the program of Morelos. Even if the Manifesto of Iguala had not specified restoration, restoration was implied by the unconditional guarantees given to the church. Hence it seemed strange that the reintroduction of this order was being postponed and that its former property was to be sold to the highest bidder instead of being kept for the Jesuits.

Moreover, the emperor was compelled by the increasing plight of the treasury to declare another forced loan which would also affect ecclesiastical corporations.[9] Congress or no Congress, the government was turning in its desperation to the church with the hope of obtaining funds. If the church had expected to receive security in independent Mexico, it was soon disappointed. Of the three basic points of the Iguala Plan — namely, establishment of independence, protection of Spanish lives and interests, and defense of the church — only the first was honored. The other two fell victim to fiscal need and deeply rooted, mutual distrust among Mexico, Rome, and Madrid.

It was in the troubled latter part of October 1822 when

Joel R. Poinsett, the special envoy of the United States government, landed at Veracruz. As early as the beginning of
January, Mexico had taken the initiative in regard to her
relations with Washington, London, and the Holy See.[10] Two
months later, President Monroe recognized independent
Mexico. When he finally sent his representative, Iturbide
was already emperor and Poinsett's mission was restricted
to an inquiry. He reached the city beneath the slumber-
ing volcano a few days before Iturbide dissolved the Congress. After returning to the United States, Poinsett described
his impressions in *Notes on Mexico made in the Autumn of
1822*,[11] in which he made no effort to conceal his dislike of
both the bourbonists and the followers of Iturbide and his
sympathy for republicans. Before he called on the emperor
on 3 November, Poinsett visited the political prisoners in the
Dominican monastery. This visit — it is interesting that it was
allowed — could hardly have been interpreted as a friendly
gesture to the government and it may account for the apolo-
getic attitude of the emperor during his meeting with Poinsett. Iturbide complimented the United States on their republican institutions and lamented that these were not suited to
the circumstances of his country. He then explained that he
had accepted the throne only to please the wishes of the
people and to prevent misrule and anarchy. However, Poinsett, commenting on the desperate plight of the treasury,
prophetically concluded his *Notes* by saying that "as long as
he possesses the means of paying and rewarding them — officers and soldiers — so long he will maintain himself on the
throne; when these fail he will be precipitated from it."[12]

The prediction proved correct. True, the government was
negotiating a loan in Britain, but since it needed money urgently, it laid hands on a convoy carrying 1.2 million pesos
from Mexico to Veracruz to be shipped to Spain. The most
pressing needs of the treasury were momentarily lifted, but
this arbitrary act showed that Iturbide was unable to rule the
country by orderly means. As the conservative leader Alamán
later pointed out, the empire combined all the defects of a re-

public with all the drawbacks of a monarchy. Before sailing from Tampico on 23 December — the departure had been delayed by furious northern winds — Poinsett received news of a military uprising in Veracruz against Iturbide's government.[13]

The intelligence was correct. The young military commander of Veracruz Antonio López de Santa Anna, a former royalist officer who had fought for the Manifesto of Iguala and then supported the empire, took matters in his own hands and during the first days of December, at the head of his soldiers, proclaimed a revolution. He then sent a letter to Iturbide, in which, after profuse accusations, he called for the reinstallation of Congress and the formation of a constitution based on "religion, independence and union," in other words on the Manifesto of Iguala, which had been infringed by the emperor. Generals Bravo and Guerrero promptly seconded the movement. In his own proclamation, the hero of the South modestly stated that Mexican independence had not been solely Iturbide's achievement.[14] The bulk of the army influenced by two former Mexican liberal deputies to the Spanish Parliament, Ramos Arizpe and Michelena, also adhered to the revolution,[15] and while his empire was crumbling to pieces, Iturbide abdicated on 19 March, one and a half years after the establishment of independence. His reign had lasted only ten months. Having got rid of the troublesome liberator, Congress and the new government were finally free to shape the destiny of the nation.

The Manifesto of Iguala was in fact no longer valid. A congressional committee recommended that it should officially be declared null and void and that Mexico should be at liberty to adopt whatever constitution it wished.[16] By implication, Mexico was free to become, for example, a federal republic. Congress followed the recommendation on 8 April; it also granted a pension to the former emperor providing he would reside in Italy. Iturbide was not happy in exile, however. Perhaps inspired by Napoleon's return from Elba, he landed in July 1824 near Tampico, unaware that in the meantime Congress had declared him a traitor. Mexico was not France, either, for nobody was there to acclaim him, and four days later Iturbide faced the firing squad.

After Iturbide's abdication, the reassembled Congress promptly appointed a provisional governing body. It was a triumvirate called the Supreme Executive Power, consisting of Generals Guadalupe Victoria, Nicolás Bravo, and Pedro Negrete. The first two were well known insurgent fighters; the third a Spaniard who had offered his services to the new country. The Executive Power — ·the name had a republican flavor — proceeded to appoint four cabinet members. From the very beginning, the most outstanding of them was Lucas Alamán, the minister of internal and foreign affairs, a young man of thirty who had just returned from a prolonged stay in Europe.

Alamán has already been mentioned as a conservative leader and historian. He was born into an opulent mining and banking family of Guanajuato in 1792, the son of a family which had crowned its fortune by acquiring a Spanish title of nobility, the marquisate of San Clemente. His childhood and adolescence appear to have been happy; it was the *douceur de vivre* for the provincial upper class. He was creole by birth, but — as he wrote much later — in the Guanajuato of those times no distinction was made between American and European born Spaniards, for they were all closely knit in the web of family, friendship, and business interests.[17]

During Iturbide's empire, Alamán was in Spain as a Mexican delegate to the Parliament; he did not have to face the emperor whom he considered to be an upstart. As marquis of San Clemente, Lucas Alamán would have been the perfect prime minister of a Bourbon Mexican monarch, for in his abilities and culture he towered above his contemporaries. As it was, he was not to use his title, for the government into whose service he had just entered was pronouncedly republican.

A new alignment of forces in Congress had given a majority to the republicans. If, before its dissolution by Iturbide,

the legislature maintained more or less a balance between republicans and bourbonists with Iturbide's followers in the
middle, those formerly in the middle now joined the republicans out of spite against the bourbonists who had so much
contributed to the empire's downfall. This majority effectively blocked the establishment of a European monarch on
the Mexican throne: if Iturbide was not to be emperor, they
reasoned, then no one else would be. In his defeat and his
death, Iturbide could claim this negative triumph.

The pro-Hispanic bourbonists were associated with freema-
sons of the Scottish rite; as such, they were called "Scottish
Rite Masons." They were the core out of which the conservatives would rise in the future. Now that a republic was becoming an established fact, monarchism began to be seen as
treasonable; hence, everyone now called himself a republican.
And as all were now republicans, new distinctions were
needed. So the bourbonists became "centralists," followers
of a strong central regime. The anti-Hispanic republicans became "federalists," favoring a federation on the United States
model. The capital city had been identified with the viceroyalty and the different revolutionary currents had been strong-
est in the provinces. This continued after independence, and
as the progressives' stronghold lay in the provinces, they
naturally argued for a high degree of provincial autonomy.
Later, this group would transform themselves into liberals
but, as political parties were as yet unknown, a suitable arche-
type was needed; it was found in freemasonry. Thus, in 1825
the federalists — with the help of Poinsett, now American
minister to Mexico — succeeded in organizing lodges of the
York rite; and so the federalists became known as "York Rite
Masons."

It did not surprise anyone that the constitution, finally
approved by Congress at the beginning of October 1824, one
year and a half after the collapse of the empire, was not only
republican — a republic was taken for granted — but also
federal and that the presidency should fall to a federalist,
namely Guadalupe Victoria, a man of obscure origin, perhaps

a mestizo. The propertied classes had their representative in the vice-president, Bravo, the well known leader of the Scottish Rite Masons (according to the constitution the vice-presidency went to the candidate coming in second) and in the most influential cabinet member, Lucas Alamán. Esteva, the minister of finance, a bookseller from Veracruz, was a federalist. Hence, in the government, upper-class and middle-class elements were balanced. It is easy to see why Congress and Victoria did not attempt to establish a purely middle-class regime. Together the upper and middle social strata formed only a small proportion of the total population. However, the middle class had no desire to share power with the lower sectors; they saw such an experiment as dangerous. The middle class was of course more numerous than the upper class, but the latter compensated for its small number by its wealth and connections. Thus a *modus vivendi* between them was set up.

After Iturbide's fall, the treasury had been in the greatest disorder. The situation improved when Mexico obtained two loans in London: 16 million pesos were borrowed at the beginning of 1824 with Goldschmitt and Company; the second loan, for the same amount, was obtained a few months later from Barclay and Company.[18] Thus Mexico assumed a burden of 32 million pesos in foreign debt. However, due to a low contract price and banker's deductions, Mexico received only about one third of this amount, approximately 10 million pesos. In November 1823, the finance minister expressed hope that the proceeds of the loan would be used for long-range improvement of the country; but when the cash arrived, it was all spent on current government expenses. At least, the bureaucrats were regularly paid, and this may well explain the relatively long duration of the truce between the centralists and the federalists, for "when salaries are paid, revolutions are extinguished."[19]

British investors also showed an interest in Mexican mining ventures. The total amount invested during 1823—1827 was over 12 million pesos, of which the Real del Monte, the property of the counts of Regla but now operated by a British company, received about 3 million[20] and the United Mexican Mining Association, one of whose directors was Alamán, received about 4 million pesos.[21] True, the British speculation in South American and Mexican bonds and mining shares soon collapsed, leaving behind many casualties, but the money was already sunk deeply in the Mexican earth. Even if the amount invested in Mexico was perhaps smaller than the damages caused both directly and indirectly by the War of Independence, it was sufficient to instill new life into the economy of the country.[22] Thanks to an instantaneous injection of funds, Mexico enjoyed a few years of civil peace.

During this period, there was complete and unrestricted freedom of the press and a surprisingly large number of newspapers.[23] However, political tensions were slowly rising and factions were piling abuse on each other. The pendulum was swinging toward the left; Alamán was forced out of the cabinet in 1825. The heat increased after the congressional victory of the federalists in 1826 and after the discovery, in January the following year, of what is known as the Father Arenas Plot to restore Spanish power in Mexico. At this juncture, Spain was the only important country that had not recognized Mexican independence. Considering also that many European-born Spaniards still held to their government posts, it was fairly easy to inflame public opinion against all things Spanish. In this situation a law was passed expelling certain groups of Spaniards from the country. The York Rite Masons were reaching out for the control of the government. The well intentioned President Victoria was unable to handle the situation. Fighting on the defensive, the Scottish Rite Masons first took revenge in a noisy campaign against the American minister Poinsett and finally resorted to arms. It was the vice-president himself, General Bravo, who lost patience and revolted against the government. He was promptly defeated by Guerrero and sent to exile. This proved to be just a preliminary skirmish.

The issue which had been looming on the horizon for some

time was the coming presidential election, scheduled for 1828. Bravo had spoiled his chances and now Guerrero's star began to rise. Guerrero, not only one of the liberators but also the man who had recently restored order in the republic, was the favorite. General Gómez Pedraza, the war minister and a former follower of Iturbide, ran against Guerrero as a moderate. The conservative elements rallied behind the moderate war minister; Guerrero was the champion of the middle and lower classes, and Lorenzo Zavala, the radical journalist from Yucatán, supported him. Gómez Pedraza was elected president by a slim margin but Guerrero refused to accept the result and, on his behalf, Zavala organized a revolution by which he took over the capital in December of 1828 — the only instance in Mexican history when a civilian seized power almost without army support. Zavala instead obtained help from the urban lower classes; in exchange, he had to tolerate the sacking and burning of shops, both Spanish and Mexican. Formalities followed: in January of the following year, Guerrero was elected president and on 1 April, received the office from Victoria. Thus constitutional government fatally collapsed after four years.

Guerrero and his finance minister Zavala now had an opportunity to carry out their program. Zavala had come from a prominent creole background in Mérida in the far-away peninsula of Yucatán. While the Indians in Central Mexico had revolted, the Mayas had remained in submission; unlike Alamán and later Mora, Zavala had not witnessed the social violence of the War of Independence.[24] The struggle in Yucatán was exclusively between creoles and viceregal authorities; there was no third party involved. This may well have influenced Zavala's outlook; for in contrast to the intellectuals of Central Mexico, he became a radical. Later, in independent Mexico, he was governor of the large state of Mexico with its capital in Toluca and, on a provincial scale, attempted a few social reforms.

Guerrero and Zavala complemented each other. Guerrero was a silent man, provincial in his outlook and devoid of ambition. Without Zavala, he would perhaps have remained military commander of the South. On the other hand, without Guerrero, Zavala would probably not have become a national figure. For despite his eloquence and his talent, Zavala had the handicap of being a Yucatecan, almost a foreigner, like a Guatemalan. Yucatecans even spoke differently, with the melodious inflection of the Mayas. Guerrero was in everybody's eyes the symbol of the resistance to Spanish rule. Clamor for a full expulsion of Spaniards increased, and this was decreed on 20 March 1829. Although thwarted in actual practice, the decree came as a shock. The Spaniards, who had been masters of the country for three centuries, were to be expelled, deprived of their posts and social position, and perhaps also of their property. Surely Spain would not let these actions pass unnoticed. To these measures Finance Minister Zavala added his own. He found the treasury empty, just as empty as his predecessor had found it six years ago, following the collapse of Iturbide's empire. Toward the end of 1827, when the domestic situation had become aggravated, Mexico was unable to pay interest on its two foreign loans and its debt had been piling up since then. In view of the rapidly mounting deficit which amounted at that moment to more than 3 million pesos a year, Zavala proposed to adopt a variety of emergency measures and thus to restore credit and public confidence.

In the first place, Zavala decided to sell the formerly nationalized church property, disposal of which had been considered in 1822 but then dropped in the following year, so as not to inflame the conflict between clerical and anticlerical groups. Guerrero himself was probably a good Catholic; as Morelos he would not have viewed with sympathy an auction of former Jesuit possessions. But now it was Zavala's chance to carry out his anti-Hispanic and anticlerical program. So he ordered the sale of church property on 1 May.[25] As a result, properties valued at somewhat less than 1 million pesos were sold, yielding about one fourth of their value to the national treasury.

Zavala combined these measures with what was to be the first Mexican attempt at a clear-cut progressive taxation. At his suggestion, Congress approved on 22 May a 5 percent tax on yearly rents and incomes between 1,000 and 10,000 pesos:[26] incomes lower than 1,000 would be tax-exempt; incomes over 10,000 pesos, however, would be taxed at 10 percent. Rents and incomes between 1,000 and 10,000 pesos corresponded roughly to the middle class, those over 10,000 to individuals of upper classes. Zavala proposed to strike at those in the highest income bracket; but all propertied groups would be affected. Other, similar measures followed. This was perhaps the only Mexican government of the nineteenth century which attempted to benefit the common people and to establish what would be called later a democracy; the only time in Mexican history up to the present century that the government favored the poor over the rich.

The landing of Spanish troops near Tampico at the end of July rallied the nation to a unified effort, and the intrepid General Santa Anna, always on the lookout in his Veracruz headquarters, hurried to the scene and promptly defeated the invaders, thereby becoming a national hero. This first Spanish attempt at reconquest was also the last; Spain eventually resigned itself to Mexican independence. For a moment, the victory bolstered Mexican national pride. But now the danger from abroad that had served to unite the country so far vanished and internal dissentions took on a new and ugly face. The Zavala tax proposals affected not only the upper but also the middle classes. These two groups now joined hands — for the first time since their common opposition to the empire — in an effort to oust the champion of the lower classes. The campaign against the regime did not dare touch President Guerrero, still a national hero for most people; it was restricted for the moment to attacking the finance minister and his friend, the United States minister Poinsett. The attacks became so fierce that the president was unable even to protect his minister; Zavala was forced out on 2 November and the Protestant Poinsett, a convenient scapegoat in a universally Catholic nation, soon followed. These were only preludes designed to prepare the country psychologically for the removal of Guerrero himself, a screen behind which an army revolt was brewing.

Vice-President Anastasio Bustamante, a former royalist officer, revolted in December with the support of Bravo, already back in Mexico. The revolt quickly succeeded and, on 1 January 1830, Vice-President Bustamante acting as president formed his cabinet. Alamán was again minister of foreign and internal affairs; however, in a reaction against Guerrero's attempts at social reform, Alamán had come to believe in a strong government. The new cabinet consisted of conservatives or centralists in contrast to the governments of 1823–1827, which combined elements of both federalist and centralist groups.

Guerrero retired to his hacienda in the South. In those days, a hacienda was not synonymous with wealth, for most estates guaranteed their owners only a middle-class standard of living. To retire to one's hacienda was a symbolic act: it meant that Guerrero did not wish to be in the way; in fact, he recognized Bustamante as acting president. But it also meant that Guerrero would be surrounded by his faithful peasants in case events took an unfavorable turn. A man of different tastes, Zavala chose not to accompany Guerrero but to remain in the capital. Alamán himself, his adversary now in power, warned him that he could not guarantee his life, and so Zavala left for the United States. Opposition was suppressed and it seemed that a period of economic and financial stability would lie ahead. First, Mexico agreed with the foreign bondholders to capitalize the arrears of debt amounting to more than 4 million pesos; confidence was restored at the price of increased principal of the debt. Secondly, Alamán resolved to revitalize the sagging national economy; mining was in a depressed state as a result of the overexpansion of previous years and of military and civil disturbances. So Alamán turned his attention to other spheres of economic life, in particular the textile industry. He set up a government bank which was to introduce cotton spinning and weaving machines.[27] This was coupled with strong protectionist measures, designed especially to prohibit the import of mechanically woven English cottons. Even though the bank eventually failed, it did while it lasted promote an industrial revolution; with the result that a dozen years later, the country could boast of about fifty textile factories which could reasonably supply the people with cheap cotton cloth. The factories were particularly prominent in the old textile city Puebla and in the cotton-growing state of Veracruz, where water power was abundant. The manufacturers were recruited from among merchants and financiers connected with the government, like Escandón, Barrón, and Martínez del Río.[28] Alamán was also interested in agricultural improvements, but here he accomplished little; he himself, a devout Catholic, had to confess that Mexican agriculture was burdened by tithes collected by the church. As in other previous and subsequent instances, it was fairly easy to modernize mining, industrial, and urban economy; but as a result of the rigid social structure of the countryside agricultural practices resisted change.

While the first foundations of an industrial revolution were being laid, Guerrero again revolted in the South, seconded by loyal Alvarez. This was the fourth time Guerrero had taken arms against the established government: first against Spain, then against Iturbide, later against Gómez Pedraza, and now against Bustamante. This was also the last time. General Bravo, his fellow-countryman and former comrade-in-arms from the times of Morelos, was sent to fight him. This war was viewed by contemporaries as a class war in which Bravo represented the propertied elements of society. Guerrero was captured in January 1831 and in what looks like a belated Spanish revenge against one of Mexico's liberators, was executed in the solitary Dominican monastery of Cuilapam near the city of Oaxaca.

During 1830–1831 Bustamante's government undertook many measures in favor of the church, to which neither the

Holy See nor clerical Spain would be indifferent. These measures also had an internal purpose: after Zavala's attempts at what seemed a subversion of the social order, the conservatives had come to the conclusion that the church must be strengthened, for the church with all its hierarchy was the surest guarantee of the property rights and privileges of the existing order. However, the most articulate cabinet member Alamán went further in this direction than advisable and thus aroused the hostility of hitherto uncommitted persons, among them a professor of theology and son of an impoverished merchant José María Luis Mora.[29]

In 1830–1831 the axis of the political struggle shifted: now that, after Guerrero's and Zavala's downfall, property was definitely safeguarded, other, new issues appeared. The clerical turn of Bustamante's central government and the opposition of Francisco García, the liberal governor of the silver mining state of Zacatecas — against whom Alamán did not dare send the army — opened the way to an anticlerical alignment which would also capitalize on the unpopularity of Guerrero's execution. New men came to the fore. One of García's friends was Valentín Gómez Farías, a physician and senator from Zacatecas. Formerly a follower of Iturbide and then a moderate republican, Gómez Farías now suggested that Mora write an essay on church and state in relation to property. The essay, submitted in December 1831, proposed the disentailment of ecclesiastical property and provided the point of departure for future anticlericalism in Mexico.[30] No doubt, Mora was not the first anticlerical in Mexico, but he gave Mexican liberalism a coherent form.

Mora was more a theoretician than a man of action, so it fell to Gómez Farías to organize the opposition against Bustamante. He needed an ally in the army, however. The army had proclaimed and achieved independence. It was the army that had made Iturbide emperor; the army, not the people or Congress, had brought about Iturbide's downfall and helped Bustamante to seize power. Now to oust Bustamante, the military arm was again needed. It so happened that the restless General Santa Anna had been in revolt since January 1832 and it was with him that Gómez Farías made a pact. By the month of May, the opposition had become so strong that in order to placate it, Bustamante dismissed Alamán and War Minister Facio — the two men who, in public opinion, were responsible for Guerrero's execution. The resignations not having produced the desired effect, Bustamante left the capital in August at the head of government troops to fight the rebels, while Zavala landed at Veracruz, ready to take part in the revolution. In December, Bustamante admitted his defeat and Gómez Farías took control of the government on behalf of Santa Anna. In January 1833, Gómez Farías — not Zavala — was appointed finance minister; Zavala was not offered a cabinet post and had to be satisfied with the governorship of the state of Mexico. Santa Anna, now called "Liberator," retired to his hacienda, Manga de Clavo, on the road between Veracruz and Jalapa, leaving all power in Gómez Farías's hands. In March, Congress elected Santa Anna president and Gómez Farías vice-president of Mexico; they were installed on 1 April. Both apparently obtained what they had wanted: Gómez Farías, power to carry out liberal reforms; Santa Anna, the presidency of the Republic of Mexico.

Santa Anna was born in 1794 in Jalapa, the commercial depot on the highway from Veracruz to Puebla and Mexico City, a son of a government official and mortgage broker.[31] Finding that his boy lacked interest in schooling, the father secured for him a position as salesman in a shop of Veracruz. In this city it was considered honorable for a creole to be a merchant; its natives had a mercantile mind and they were not ashamed of it, in contrast to the creoles of Central Mexico. Santa Anna was an exception to the rule, however. He would not stand behind the counter serving the customers or behind a desk making accounts. As early as 1810, he entered the army as a cadet.

The people of Veracruz and other towns of the region have always been known for their lively intelligence, tempera-

ment, and imagination. Santa Anna soon showed that he was
well endowed with these qualities. As a royalist officer in
1821, he played a prominent part in the establishment of
independence and then, like the rest of the army, supported
the empire. It seems that Iturbide did not trust him and it is
likely that the emperor's reluctance to grant him the command of his native province drove the impetuous officer to
an early rebellion.[32] As commander and governor of Yucatán, from 1824 to 1825, he conceived the idea of invading
Cuba, ostensibly with the view of liberating the island from
the Spanish yoke, in reality to relieve the pressure on Veracruz. As the Spaniards in the fortress of San Juan Ulúa soon
capitulated, the soundness of Santa Anna's project was not
questioned. In 1829, as commander in Veracruz, he halted
the Spanish invasion; in December, he refused to join the revolt against Guerrero and in January 1830 resigned his governorship, recognized Bustamante, and retired to his hacienda.
Two years later, he again embarked on a revolt which this
time took him to the presidency.

He had always, or almost always stood on the side of liberty — the natives of Veracruz were noted for their liberal
views, at least in religious matters — and that is no doubt why
Gómez Farías could strike a bargain with him. But one thing
in his conduct was peculiar. After serving a limited time in a
government post, he would resign and retire to his hacienda
Manga de Clavo, attributing his decision to his "ill health." In
time the retreat would produce its effect and, with regained
health, Santa Anna would launch a new rebellion. He obviously did not need government posts, for he was rich: Manga
de Clavo was one of the best estates in the province and
Santa Anna eventually acquired other haciendas, so that almost all the land along the road from Veracruz to Jalapa
came to be his.[33] But he was not the only rich general or
politician. It was his attitude, his unwillingness to serve the
country in the posts assigned to him, which seemed strange.
It looked as if he considered these posts beneath his dignity,

as if he thought himself superior to haggling with people. When he finally obtained the highest post in the republic, he left the work to his vice-president and again went to Veracruz. Was the presidential chair not sufficient for him? Another characteristic was peculiar: his pompous oratory. He was always ready to sacrifice himself on the altar of the fatherland; he was always guided by the voice of liberty and justice. Verbose rhetoric had been practiced before him by Iturbide, and, it must be said, with success up to a certain point. And now Santa Anna had taken it up. Of course pompous verbosity is especially suited to conceal true intentions.

While Santa Anna was resting at Veracruz and perhaps also brooding sullenly over imaginary or real injuries, Gómez Farías began to carry out his anticlerical program: the end of October witnessed the removal of civil obligation to pay tithes — that is, removal of a tax on agricultural production. From now on, payment of tithes would be entirely voluntary. This measure was meant to benefit hacendados. Civil enforcement of monastic vows was removed at the beginning of November; friars and nuns were free to leave the convent whenever they wished. Two weeks later, all transfers of property belonging to the regular orders since independence were declared illegal.[34] While the first law affected the bishops and the canons, whose main income consisted of tithes, the last decree was a step towards a disentailment of monastic real estate which was already under discussion in Congress. The sale of church real estate had to be declared null and void, in order to prevent the church from selling its property to trusted persons and, thus, evading the disentailment. But there was conflict in Congress over the way in which disentailment should proceed. Zavala, who had so far restricted his activities to the state of Mexico, decided to stage a come-back; he proposed that Congress immediately assume possession of ecclesiastical real estate and then sell it at a public auction.[35] Mora suggested instead that properties should pass to the present tenants. Eventually, the law that was passed in 1856 combined both features. However, for the present Zavala's proposal was rejected and, his fortune on the decline, he had to accept appointment as Mexican minister to France. Although Mora won temporarily, he was not to see his idea transformed into law.

The church was not willing to submit to the proposal without struggle. It so happened that the liberals, true to their conviction that complete equality of all citizens before the law should be established in accordance with their principles, had also attempted to reduce the size and privileges of the army.[36] The army and the church whose privileges were known as *fueros* joined hands in a common effort to convince Santa Anna that he should act. In May 1834 several army officers and their troops revolted. The revolt spread and in the following month, Santa Anna took over as president. The consequences soon became apparent. Most anticlerical decrees were repealed. Payment of tithes remained voluntary, however; thus, conservative hacendados reaped the fruits of liberal reforms.

In foreign policy, Mexico finally achieved recognition by Spain and Rome. The first attempts to reach a settlement took place around the middle of 1831, and a peace treaty between Spain and the Republic of Mexico was signed at the end of 1836. The Holy See made its overture in August 1831 and it recognized Mexican independence at the beginning of December 1836, fifteen years after its establishment.[37] By that time Santa Anna was no longer head of the government.

Santa Anna obviously carried out Alamán's conservative program, both in domestic and foreign policy. The man who had for years supported the republican and then the liberal cause, became a conservative and turned against the very men who had elected him president. He himself supplied an explanation some time later when he was a prisoner in Texas. Upon Santa Anna's imprisonment, the former United States minister to Mexico Poinsett sent him the following message: "Tell General Santa Anna that when I remember how ardent an advocate he was of liberty ten years ago, I have no sympathy for him now; he has what he deserves." To which Santa Anna replied: "Tell Mr. Poinsett that it is very true that I threw up my hat for liberty with great ardor and perfect sincerity, but very soon found the folly of it. A hundred years from now my people will not be fit for freedom. They do not know what it is, unenlightened as they are, and under the influence of the Catholic Clergy; despotism is the proper government for them, but there is no reason why it should not be a wise and virtuous one."[38] The message, which of course was not intended for the Mexican public, is surprisingly matter-of-fact; it reminds us of the apology Iturbide had given Poinsett years before. Many years later Santa Anna admitted that his monarchist upbringing made him reject republican ideas as too radical in 1822 and that the dictates of his conscience drove him to defend the church in 1834. If this is true, then the liberalism of his youth must be seen as sheer opportunism.[39]

The suppression of liberals by Santa Anna put the damper on reformist endeavors for a generation. It exposed the whole weakness of the movement, which consisted mainly of the urban middle class. Its leaders and ideologists now went into exile. Mora left for Paris, never to return; he spent his life there in poverty, feeding on his bitterness and writing impressive volumes, some of which were published and others lost.[40] He died there in 1850, little knowing that his ideas would come to fruition a few years later. His former adversary Zavala was Mexican minister to France during 1834 and there he had time to record his impressions of the journey he had taken to the United States in 1830. His disillusionment caused him to modify his concepts: as he now explained in the preface to his book, it was not sufficient for Mexico to copy the American constitution; it would be more useful to copy the customs and habits of the American people.[41] To be sure, Zavala had in mind the northern, more Puritan sector of the United States rather than the South with its distasteful slavery. Central Mexico was too clerical; the future belonged, according to Zavala, to the northern Mexican states or provinces, especially Texas. Zavala predicted that eventually a civil war between the liberal and progressive North and army-dominated Central Mexico would ensue in which "the American system will gain a complete though bloody victory." Zavala did not suspect that his prophecy would come true — of course with somewhat different results — so soon. He himself did not live to see it. However, he did come back to Texas as private citizen and signed the Declaration of Independence on 2 March 1836. Zavala became vice-president of the Texan Republic, but died half a year later.[42]

Alamán fared somewhat better. True, at the beginning of 1833, he had been accused by Alvarez as being responsible for Guerrero's execution and soon after had gone into hiding for fear of assassination or of receiving the death penalty in a political trial. He emerged after the take-over by Santa Anna and was acquitted by the court. Nevertheless, he remained forever after a man branded by public opinion as guilty of the tragedy. While Bustamante's reputation was soon whitewashed, so that he was able to become president again, Alamán would not or could not accept cabinet posts any more, even though he now belonged to the victorious party.

Thus, three leading Mexican intellectuals failed as politicians or statesmen. The military caste which had been in power since independence was not willing to share its power with civilians. So Alamán, Zavala, and Mora turned to writing and produced, each in his turn, a history of contemporary Mexico.[43] It was their way of taking revenge on a treacherous reality. Their political defeat, with its bitterness and resentment, influenced their later views; hence their writings should be read with caution. Mora and Zavala became prophets of future developments and Alamán's writings became the source of conservative thinking up to the present day. Mora and Zavala managed to put a time-bomb under the political structure, which would explode after they were gone. Alamán failed in his effort to persuade others that Mexico was not ready to govern itself and needed a foreign monarch.[44]

Having stripped the liberal federalist Gómez Farías of the vice-presidency in January 1835, Santa Anna veered towards centralism and so, at the end of March 1835, Congress approved a motion to amend the 1824 Constitution.[45] Soon after, the "protector," as the president was now called, invaded the state of Zacatecas and deposed its liberal governor. A similar action was expected to take place against the province of Texas, where apprehension against Santa Anna's authoritarian policy was growing. In 1821, the viceregal government had given Moses Austin the right to colonize a part of that country; in one of his last acts as emperor, Iturbide confirmed the concession one week before his abdication to Stephen Austin, Moses' son,[46] and the privilege was later ratified by Congress. By 1835, Texas already contained a large population that was not willing to obey dictates coming from a far-away capital. Four months after the Mexican Congress decreed on 3 October that all state governors should hold office only with the approval of the central government[47] and that all state legislatures should cease to function, Texas declared its independence.

Santa Anna expected to crush Texas as he had crushed Zacatecas and, at the same time, punish Zavala who was thought to be behind the move to independence. However, Santa Anna knew little about the forces which were to oppose him. Before leaving for Texas at the head of the army, he told the French and British ministers that if he found that the United States government was aiding the rebels, "he would continue the march of his army to Washington and place upon its Capitol the Mexican Flag."[48] A few months later, he was defeated and became a prisoner of the Texans who wanted to shoot him as a war criminal — in fact, his definition of the rebels as pirates had led him to commit many atrocities against them — but he extricated himself by his charm and ability to talk and convince people.

Today it is perfectly clear that the final result, that is Texan independence, was inevitable, with or without war and with or without Santa Anna. "The colonists chose to separate from Mexico and to declare their independence, counting on the powerful support of the United States," the Mexican historian Justo Sierra wrote many years later.[49] "This was sad but also inevitable. Whatever ties the people of Texas had were with their brothers; none were with the Mexicans . . . If our politicians had been perceptive enough to see things as they were and if they had recognized the legitimacy of the secession of Texas, both the war with Texas, and its shameful and ruinous consequences, and the struggle with the United States, which was its inevitable aftermath, would have been avoided. . . . "

Justo Sierra was born in Yucatán; his grandfather, as governor, had fought for Yucatán's autonomy against the central Mexican government during the same years Texas was fighting for its independence. Yucatán at that time had little in common with Central Mexico; it communicated with New Orleans and New York easier than with Mexico City; its creole oligarchy had a culture of its own.[50] Hence for Justo Sierra it was not difficult to understand Texas. Perhaps this could also explain the comparative ease with which the Yucatecan Zavala had become a Texan patriot. Of the two evils, dismemberment of Mexico and continuation of Santa Anna's regime, he had chosen the first.

While Santa Anna was away, a centralist constitution was adopted toward the end of 1836. The conservative regime set up earlier by Santa Anna, continued to rule the country without him. Other generals, including Anastasio Bustamante, were presidents. Santa Anna returned to his hacienda, Manga de Clavo, unmolested, but also unnoticed. An event was soon to help him regain prominence. A French pastry cook whose shop in Mexico City had been ransacked some years before by a group of soldiers, demanded compensation; the unwillingness or the inability of Mexico to pay it gave France a welcome pretext to invade Veracruz in 1838. This episode became known as the Pastry War. Here was the opportunity Santa Anna had been waiting for. Popular clamor in his favor rose and he promptly marched to Veracruz. His conduct was brave; he lost a leg but restored his military reputation and once again became a national hero. Having captured the public eye once again, he pushed his way up to power, first aiding Bustamante against some federalist rebels, then by serving as interim president in the absence of Bustamante and, finally, in the autumn of 1841, by joining in revolt against Bustamante and becoming president himself.[51] This time he was granted dictatorial powers; statues of him were erected. He built theaters; a lover of ceremony, he allowed his leg be buried with great solemnity. However, pageantry is costly and so people slowly tired of high taxes and of the corrupt clique of favorites. A military revolt unseated Santa Anna at the end of 1844, after three years of power. This time the Mexicans exiled him for life.

But again a turn of events came to his aid. In the spring of 1845, the United States annexed the Republic of Texas. It was obvious to everybody that this aggressive step would sooner or later trigger a war between the United States and Mexico. The Mexican government under the presidency of General Herrera, a moderate, was preparing for it. But it could not do much, as Valentín Gómez Farías, the great liberal of 1833, now in exile in New Orleans, well knew. Mexico seemed hopelessly backward. While the United States had their steamboat traffic on the vast Mississippi-Ohio River system and now were extending their railroad network toward the West, Mexico still had to rely almost exclusively on mules and horses. Unlike Zavala, Gómez Farías was no friend of the United States; he wished to modernize his country in order to better its chances in the event of war. This could be achieved only by means of a violent revolution that would deprive the church of its privileges and its wealth. As before in 1832, Gómez Farías needed an ally in the army. Time was pressing.

Santa Anna arrived in Cuba, his place of exile, in June. He resented the moderates in power in Mexico and he must have felt a burning desire for revenge against the United States. Assuming that the end justifies the means, Santa Anna began to consider a new pact with his adversary Gómez Farías.

On 25 April 1846, the very day that fighting broke out between United States and Mexican troops, Santa Anna wrote Gómez Farías a long and friendly letter.[52] As if nothing had happened between them, he suggested that they should work closely together "so that in our future conduct your name will always be linked with mine, and so that we can bring about a real fusion of the people and the army. . . . " Finally, Santa Anna made an extraordinary proposal: "I will give you the affection of the army, in which I have many good friends and you will give me the affection of the masses over whom you have so much influence . . . In order to establish on a solid footing the rule of a prudent democracy, and acclimatize on our soil political liberty . . . we need that intimate union I recommend." Strangely enough, Gómez Farías accepted the proposal and closed the deal. On 4 August, General Mariano Salas revolted in Mexico City with the support of Gómez Farías who had been back for some time. The new government readopted the 1824 Constitution. Gómez Farías took charge of the ministry of finance, with the obvious purpose of feeding the army with ecclesiastical funds. Santa Anna landed in Veracruz, having been permitted by the United States navy to pass the blockade and in a manifesto apologized for his past conduct; he had leaned, he said, on men of wealth and high position "wishing to moderate in this way the vehemence of the popular masses by the inertia of conservative instincts," but now he favored "the political dogma of the sovereignty of the nation." The people of his own Veracruz received him cooly, but Gómez Farías apparently trusted him. On 16 September, the two of them rode through the capital in an open carriage, Gómez Farías in the front seat facing his would-be new friend and the general, in the back seat, dressed in a civilian suit without his military decorations.[53]

The situation of the Mexican army was desperate and Santa Anna promptly departed north, leaving his partner in charge of the government in Mexico City. Their relationship was formalized in December 1846 when Congress appointed Santa Anna president and his associate vice-president. While

Santa Anna was away, Gómez Farías was free to embark on anticlerical measures. The needs of the army were so pressing that a few weeks later he decreed the nationalization and public auction of clerical assets up to the value of 15 million pesos. As there was no time for a detailed valuation of properties, the government ordered the immediate confiscation of church property estimated to be worth 10 million pesos.[54] So far the partnership of the two men had worked in the same fashion as in 1833. It was also to have a similar end; the church protested and an army revolt spread in the capital toward the end of February. Santa Anna returned to the capital, took over the presidential office and repealed both confiscatory decrees on 29 March not without first receiving, however, a promise from the church that it would guarantee a loan of 1.5 million pesos. It is likely that Santa Anna had deliberately used Gómez Farías to blackmail the church, which was no more anxious than anyone else to lend money to the government.

Church funds could not save Mexico from disaster, however, for Santa Anna was defeated decisively and the capital itself was occupied by United States troops. Santa Anna resigned in September 1847 and went into exile. The peace treaty was signed on 2 February 1848: Mexico lost Texas, New Mexico, and California. As these vast provinces which amounted to almost half of Mexico's territory were almost entirely uninhabited and had few known natural resources, their loss as such did not have a disruptive effect on the Mexican economy. Nevertheless, the defeat was a shock to Mexico: conveniently it was explained as a result of Santa Anna's treason, incompetence, and ignorance.

It is ironical that this disaster was inflicted on Mexico by the nation originally admired by Mexican liberals. When Poinsett wrote in July 1846, "let us not by an unnecessary act of hostility convert into deadly animosity that kind of friendly feeling which was once entertained toward us by the federal republican party in that country,"[55] it was already too late. In his letters to Mora in Paris in 1844, Gómez Farías gave vent to a bitter enmity against the powerful neighbor. When as a result of the defeat, Santa Anna's conservative regime collapsed and a new liberal government had to face the hard reality of defeat, Gómez Farías had no part in it. Two generations later, Justo Sierra described the peace treaty as "a painful but not an ignominious agreement . . . (The Mexicans who signed it) did as much as they could; they accomplished as much as they should have."[56]

The war brought in its wake the danger of social dissolution and political disjunction. In the North, Indian tribes, pushed southward by the expansion of the United States, had invaded Mexican territory, burning haciendas and villages and killing their inhabitants. Then, in 1847, the Mayas of Yucatán revolted. When the American traveler John L. Stephens visited the peninsula in 1840–1842, he found the Indians singularly submissive. They had not forgotten the cruel suppression of their ancestors' 1761 uprising. As a personal friend of affluent local hacendados who were equally at home in Mérida, the state capital, as in New York City, Stephens witnessed the humility and even gratitude with which Mayan peons bore corporal punishment on haciendas. A few years later, Yucatán was in the throes of a race war which is known to history as the War of the Castes.

Yucatán was a unique mixture of modern and archaic features; a small group of landowning families ruled over a numerous Mayan-speaking population of peasants and peons subjected to what amounted to legalized serfdom.[57] The peninsula had weak economic and political ties with Central Mexico; the enterprising hacendados of Yucatán were successfully growing sisal and other crops for export. Hence it is not surprising that the landowners in Yucatán conceived the idea of becoming independent of Mexico with its perpetual political disorders. Against Mexico's armies they began to use Mayan soldiers. In return for service as soldiers, the whites — actually most of these were Spanish- and Mayan-speaking mestizos — offered to satisfy the grievances of the Indian peasants: abolition or at least reduction of parish fees, abolition of a personal tax which was exacted from the Indians as the tribute had once been in colonial times, and distribution or free use of public and communal land. As such promises were not fulfilled, three Indian village chiefs took advantage of favorable circumstances and revolted with the purpose of exterminating or at least expelling all the whites. In the war which ensued they almost succeeded in pushing their enemies, whom they anachronistically called Spaniards, into the sea. The landowners eventually enlisted the support of many of their peons by granting them the title of "hidalgo," an obsolete term meaning "gentleman." Thus Mayans fought Mayans. In this life and death struggle, the whites sacrificed the wealth of the church; consequently, when a decade later a civil war raged in Central Mexico over the issue of ecclesiastical property, the exhausted Yucatán remained practically neutral.[58]

Also Central Mexico became after the war with the United States a theater of agrarian unrest in which laborers, squatters, and peasants united to attack and destroy haciendas;[59] these spontaneous uprisings were probably the first clearly agrarian movements, of a kind which were to become important in later stages of Mexican history. The country seemed on the verge of collapse when its government received $3 million, part of the war indemnity of $15 million given to Mexico by the United States. With the help of these funds it was possible to reestablish social order; aid was dispatched to Yucatán and the Mayan insurrection was suppressed to the mixed joy of local creoles who thus saved their skins but forever lost their hope of becoming independent of Mexico. Rebel die-hards escaped to the jungles of eastern Yucatán where their descendants were subdued by the Díaz army at the beginning of the twentieth century.

Mexico was also able to put her public finances in order. Under the presidency of General Herrera and his successor General Arista, several liberals of the new generation, Melchor Ocampo, Guillermo Prieto and Manuel Payno, were finance ministers. After protracted negotiations in Mexico and

in London with the committee of bondholders, Payno succeeded in 1850 in having the rate of interest on the Mexican
foreign debt reduced from 5 to 3 percent per annum, while
its principal — which had been raised in previous conversions
to $50 million by a capitalization of unpaid interest — re-
mained the same. Mexico was to satisfy the fairly reasonable
biennial payments until 1854.

As long as revolution threatened the established social order in 1848, both liberals and conservatives joined efforts to
suppress it. When asked what should be done with rebellious
Indians, Mora, the liberal ideologist, replied from Europe that
they should be suppressed.[60] Once the danger was swept
away, the conservatives intensified their opposition to the
government. Lucas Alamán was afraid of the young liberals,
especially of the governor of Michoacán, Melchor Ocampo.
Again, army units began to revolt in various parts of the
country; still, the conservatives did not feel strong enough to
govern by themselves. So they turned to Santa Anna in his
South American exile. Alamán, the brains of the Conservative
party, explained his program to Santa Anna in March 1853:
full support for the Roman Catholic church, a strong army,
the abolition of federalism, and a strong executive led by
Santa Anna. As liberals and conservatives were of approximately equal strength, Santa Anna was in the privileged position of being able to decide which way the balance would
turn. This time he joined the conservatives.

Santa Anna assumed his fifth presidency on 20 April 1853.
After more than twenty years, Alamán again became a cabinet member; he probably felt that this was not only his last
chance but also the last chance of conservatism and that he
had no right to avoid responsibility. He died one and a half
months later. Providence had been kind to him, for after his
death, the government rapidly degenerated. The president
soon became an absolute monarch except in name. He would
not assume the title of emperor for Iturbide's lesson would
never be forgotten; instead Santa Anna acquired more real
power than the unfortunate emperor. In December 1853, he

was even given the right to name his successor and ridiculous titles were showered on him.[61] The young liberals were permitted to go into exile; it must be said to Santa Anna's credit that his political adversaries were not jailed for long periods, let alone assassinated. He needed money to finance the pageantry he so loved and so he sold what is now part of southern Arizona to the United States for the sum of 10 million pesos, thus enabling Mexico's northern neighbor to round off its territorial acquisition of 1848. (This transaction is known as the Gadsden purchase.) This was too much; in February 1854 Juan Alvarez, the old guerrilla fighter of the "hot country," rose in arms and on 1 March, a program of the new revolution was drafted in Ayutla. It was impossible for Santa Anna to suppress the revolt in the South. It spread slowly but irresistibly and in August 1855 the general relinquished the presidency and sailed into exile. Mexico then began a new chapter of its history.[62]

In all fairness it must be said that the governor of New Mexico had threatened to invade the district mentioned above and that the United States used all possible pressure to force Mexico to sell it. There can be no doubt that the United States took advantage of the weaker neighbor.

In the first twelve years of independence, Mexico had experimented with monarchy, moderate constitutional republic, radical populist regime, conservative government, and liberal government; each in turn failed to produce stability. This led many people to believe that only the charismatic Santa Anna might provide a solution by means of a personal rule free of ties with political groups. Sincere or not, he proved incompetent to govern the country. Now that he had left again for another, and hopefully permanent exile, would the new men be able to give Mexico a durable regime?

3

The Liberal Revolution
1855–1876

> Revolution thus ran its course from city to city, and the
> places where it arrived at last, from having heard what had
> been done before, carried to a still greater excess the refine-
> ment of their inventions. . . .
>
> Thucydides, "Corcyraean Revolution,"
> *The History of the Peloponnesian War*

After Santa Anna's downfall and departure from Mexico, the
leaders of the revolt elected Juan Alvarez, the dominant figure of the South, as president. Like Guerrero, under whom
he had fought, Alvarez had no clear political program for national reform — beyond the old federalist conception of
states' rights — which justified his personal control as a general and a hacendado of the region. His election was considered symbolic, for he had waged war against the Spaniards
with Morelos and Guerrero and after the latter's execution
had been in an almost permanent rebellion against the central
government; after Bravo's death he was the only surviving
hero of the War of Independence. His acceptance of the post
lent legitimacy and hence stability to the new revolutionary
regime.

Alvarez formed his cabinet during the first days of October: he offered the ministry of war to Ignacio Comonfort, his
comrade-in-arms in the recent revolt; as a moderate, Comonfort was expected to hold the army together. The other four
ministries, however, were entrusted to *"puros,"* exalted liberals: foreign relations to Melchor Ocampo, the ministry of jus-

tice to Benito Juárez, the treasury to Guillermo Prieto, and the ministry of development to Miguel Lerdo de Tejada. The appointments proved to be of far-reaching consequences for the future of the country.

Santa Anna had gone too far in his right-wing relations with the church: among other things, in 1854 he had repealed the law of 1833 which had removed civil enforcement of monastic vows. The Mexican landowners now wondered if he would now repeal the law of 1833 which had abolished civil obligation to pay tithes? Having swung to the far right, the pendulum now swung to the extreme left. The liberal cabinet members belonged to a new generation, untainted by the failures of previous liberal governments. With one exception, they were all born during the War of Independence; hence their personal experience was limited to independent Mexico and its disorders. They naturally dreamt of a Mexico with an orderly and progressive government; in their effort to find an explanation for the ever worsening conditions, they put the blame squarely on the church and the army. In this, of course, they were disciples of Mora and Gómez Farías. True, the latter had failed in his attempts to disentail ecclesiastical wealth, but his educational reform as well as the schools of higher learning established by several state governments were beginning to bear fruit; the church had lost its monopoly of education and it was now possible to become a lawyer and to practice a profession without having gone through ecclesiastical schools. The new generation was well equipped for the coming showdown with the church.

The war with the United States, with all the sufferings and humiliations it had inflicted on proud Mexico, acted as a catalyst; the defeat stimulated self-criticism.[1] The military defeat obviously demonstrated the decay of the army. As for the church, the upper clergy provoked the 1847 revolt against the requisition of clerical property, considered essential to finance the war. The lower clergy no longer led the nation against the invader or oppressor, as in the days of Hidalgo and Morelos; priests apparently contributed little to the war effort. Consequently, the two institutions which enjoyed legal privileges and which had ruled the country since independence, had proven incompetent and thus were held responsible for the outcome of the war. This was the rationale which shaped the younger generation's ideology and pointed the way to action.

The best known of the ministers, the temperamental Melchor Ocampo, was born an illegitimate child probably in 1814 and raised by an elderly unmarried lady on her hacienda in Michoacán. The boy inherited from his foster mother the hacienda then valued at the considerable amount of 120,000 pesos.[2] Melchor studied law but preferred to return to his hacienda; as manager, he showed an early interest in science and agriculture. But Ocampo was not a businessman; his personal wealth tended to decrease. His education was completed by a European journey during which he called, in Paris, on Mora who impressed him as authoritarian. Ocampo began to reveal himself as an extreme individualist; as he later observed, the liberal party was "essentially anarchical."[3]

A frequent cause of illegitimacy among the lower class at that time was the high fee charged by parish priests for performing weddings. Fees for baptisms, marriages, and funerals provided the basic livelihood of curates, in contrast to the upper clergy — bishops and canons — who drew their maintenance principally from tithes, and also in contrast to the regular orders which supported themselves mainly by their real estate. Even though parish priests had to pay their own assistants, the fees were singularly high. The fee was so exorbitant for a wedding that many poor peasant couples never got married. However, resident peons — that is, laborers living on a hacienda could normally get a loan from their employer to cover the marriage fee. But the fee for a wedding amounted to at least 10 pesos — Ocampo mentioned that 17 pesos were charged in his parish — and the peons earned about 1 peso per week. From this approximately one half had to be used to pay for food; peons did not pay rent for they were provided with either a ready-made cottage or a plot of land on which no rent was charged. A certain proportion of the rest was not paid to the laborers but was credited as part payment of loans for marriage fees or other expenses. Some were able to extinguish their debt after a certain time, but most laborers remained in debt, especially if they had many children who obviously had to be baptized, some of whom died in infancy and also obviously had to be buried in consecrated ground. The result was a constant drain on the finances of most workers which perpetuated the peonage or debt-servitude, a system considered by enlightened farmers like Ocampo not only as immoral but as not conducive to progress. Ocampo himself canceled the full debt of all his laborers four times,[4] but he could not expect other landowners to follow his example. Considering the illegitimacy of his own birth, it is not surprising that this matter was close to Ocampo's heart.

Ocampo published a short article on the debt-servitude system as early as 1844, when he was only thirty. It must have been one of the few essays on the subject, if not the only one, for the hacienda with its peons and their debts was taken for granted. One of the most unpleasant features of the system was that a laborer in debt was not permitted to leave until he paid it or unless somebody else paid it for him — somebody else was usually another landowner. In practice this meant that peons were bought and sold for the price of their debt which was always written in inventories. If a peon in debt fled, he could be hunted down and brought back. This was of course against the principles of freedom and equality. This may be another reason why so little was written on the embarrassing subject. Ocampo was perhaps the only hacendado who admitted publicly in writing that some of his laborers cost him whatever he had loaned them, others whatever he had paid for them, and finally those who owed nothing, cost him nothing. He added, however, that he treated them humanely and that if one of his peons in debt escaped from the hacienda — perhaps to find work with another employer — he reclaimed him only if he was guilty of a serious offense.[5] In 1844, Ocampo considered it sufficient to exhort laborers not to contract debts and employers not to advance the laborers any money except in a case of emergency.

The war with the United States distracted Ocampo's attention for the moment from high parish fees and laborers' debts. The new liberal government in Mexico appointed him provisional governor of Michoacán, a post he assumed early in September 1846. When the Mexican army was defeated in 1847, he proposed a guerrilla war against the invader.[6] The suggestion was ill-timed for the country was soon after beset with Indian and peasant revolts against landowners who consequently came to prefer national defeat to loss of property and perhaps life. The normally anti-American Alamán went as far as to deplore the withdrawal of the occupation army.[7] Ocampo resigned in March of the following year as a protest against what he considered an ignominious peace treaty.[8]

The liberal regime made it possible for Ocampo to return to his favorite theme. The opportunity presented itself at the beginning of 1851 when one of his laborers asked the curate of Maravatío to bury his son; as he was too poor to pay, he begged the priest to do it free of charge, which the latter refused to do.[9] Ocampo could obviously have paid for the funeral without any effort, as he must have done many times before; but this time he refrained from doing it and thus embarked on an acrimonious polemic with the parish priest.[10] He addressed the Congress of the state of Michoacán as a private citizen saying that the abusive practise of some curates must be terminated. This could be achieved by a new, clear and lower tariff of parish fees. Moderate as his demands were, they caused a storm which echoed through the republic and which eventually caused him his life.

This was the first time that somebody dared to attack the system on which the livelihood of the lower clergy was based. The prestige of this most important segment of the church was at stake. Although bishops and canons had been discredited many years ago by their hostility to Mexican independence and friars no longer held a monopoly on education, hospitals, and charity, parish priests had so far been spared. By 1850, however, parochial fees extracted from the poor began to offend the sensibility of the young, liberal intellectuals; they were to supplant the priests as leaders of the nation. In his attack on the church Ocampo received the approval of the public and he became governor of Michoacán again in June 1852. As before, he devoted much energy to educational reforms, but his goal to lower parish fees was to remain a dream.[11] Reactionary army units revolted in Michoacán and Jalisco; Ocampo himself resigned in January 1853 and five months later Santa Anna sent him into exile.

The exiles who grouped themselves around the brilliant Melchor Ocampo in New Orleans included the little known, modest former governor of the gold-bearing Oaxaca state, Benito Juárez. Juárez was born in 1806 of Indian parents in the village of Guelatao, not far from Oaxaca City. The village was in a wilderness area of forested mountains and streams impassable during part of the year. When the village was not cut off from the outer world, the journey to Oaxaca took one to two days. An orphan since early childhood, Juárez decided at the age of twelve to join his sister in the state capital where she was a domestic for the family of a kind Italian merchant; years later Juárez would marry the merchant's foster daughter. He found shelter there and soon learned to speak, read, and write Spanish; Zapotec had been the only language spoken in his small village. He graduated from the local Institute of Sciences and Arts in 1834 as a lawyer, at the age of twenty eight. He conquered the handicap of a difficult childhood spent in an isolated Indian village. He began to participate in politics and in 1847 became a state governor. Then in 1853, Santa Anna banished him from the country for having opposed him in the Mexican-American war.

Until then, Juárez had not distinguished himself as a liberal. In the first place, he had not had much opportunity to read liberal writings; secondly, his nature was pragmatic; his practical mind guided him to advance only as far as it was possible. In New Orleans a friendship sprang up between him and Ocampo. These two dissimilar men complemented each other. Ocampo influenced the ideas of his friend so that when both men returned to Mexico after Santa Anna's downfall, Juárez was an exalted liberal. In 1855 it seemed that Ocampo would forever preserve the leadership of the liberals he had assumed in exile. But it was shown soon that talent alone is not sufficient to bring one's ideas to a triumph; the other element which is difficult to measure but which is essential, is character. Juárez was richly endowed with the latter. Thus it happened that Ocampo resigned, disgusted, in the very same month of October 1855 after serving only two weeks as cabinet member, while Juárez stayed. Had Ocampo expected to be elected president instead of Alvarez? He certainly showed impatience whenever he did not have his way.

In contrast to the country squire Melchor Ocampo and the provincial lawyer Benito Juárez, the Finance Minister Guillermo Prieto was a product of Mexico City where he was born, the son of the manager of a large flour mill, in 1818.[12] Another cabinet member Miguel Lerdo de Tejada had a different background. He was born in 1812 in the port of Veracruz, a son of a Spanish merchant and a creole mother and grandson of a colonial governor.[13] Around 1821, the Lerdos moved to Jalapa; they were wealthy but, following the local tradition, Miguel was not allowed to devote himself exclusively to study but had to undergo mercantile training also. Meanwhile, a friendship developed between the Lerdo family and General Santa Anna.[14] It proved stronger than political differences. It is a typical feature of Mexican society that two men born or raised in the same town or region can hold conflicting political opinions but retain their friendship, especially if they become related by mutually christening their children; compaternity has been a common way of enlarging the family circle and is considered almost as strong a bond as kinship.

In 1848, Lerdo published his first brief essay, in which he accused the upper clergy of having betrayed the national cause first by their support of the monarchist General Paredes and then of the army revolt against a government that expected to finance the national defense with ecclesiastical funds.[15] An exalted, or "pure," liberal, Lerdo was sent in the spring of 1853 to Colombia to invite Santa Anna back from exile.[16] Obviously some liberals considered Santa Anna as still uncommitted and chose Lerdo as the most suitable envoy. Upon his arrival in Veracruz, Santa Anna asked Lerdo to write down for him in detail his views on the current situation in Mexico and explain his reform program. Lerdo complied in April with a long letter in which he quite openly criticized the army and the church and made a series of useful proposals for technical improvements.[17] Needless to say, Santa Anna did not heed Lerdo's liberal suggestions, but he did appoint him undersecretary of the new ministry of development. On the liberal victory, Alvarez appointed Lerdo head of the same department. In his post, Lerdo worked to promote the building of telegraph lines, important means of communication in the vast, mountainous country.

All four cabinet members under Alvarez were exalted liberals, but none of them was a systematic thinker or theoretician. This perhaps was not necessary, for Mora had worked out the liberal ideology in detail almost a quarter of a century earlier; what was needed now was action. Socially, the members of cabinet belonged to the middle class either by birth or marriage, in contrast to the conservatives who tended to be upper class members either by birth, as in the case of Alamán, or size of their possessions, in the case of Santa Anna. One of the new liberal ministers was a pure Indian; a fact which, by itself, shows how much Mexico had changed since independence.

Juárez proved to be the most hardworking cabinet member; he was the only one to have produced a significant legal reform — the law known as "Ley Juárez" abolished clerical immunities by restricting the jurisdiction of ecclesiastical courts to ecclesiastical cases. The law also proposed to divest the army of some of its privileges. Mild though it was, the law created such a storm that Alvarez resigned and General Comonfort became president at the beginning of December 1855 and promptly appointed a cabinet of moderate liberals. Alvarez returned to his property on the Pacific coast. Short as his presidency had been, it was decisive for the future of Mexico. From then on, the wheel of history could not be turned back. Clerical response to the Juárez Law was so instantaneous and violent that when Comonfort became president, the die had already been cast: revolt was brewing in the state of Puebla and it came into the open at the end of the year. In January 1856 the rebels occupied the city of Puebla and forced the local merchants and the bishop, Labastida, to contribute to their government. President Comonfort in person led the army against the rebel city and compelled it to surrender at the end of March 1856, at a cost to the goverment of around 1 million pesos. Although Labastida had refused to be identified with the rebels,[18] Comonfort put the blame squarely on the church and decreed the attachment of clerical property in the bishopric of Puebla with a view to collecting the corresponding indemnity. From then on, the people of Puebla unwaveringly supported the clerical cause and the city became the bastion of antiliberalism.

Feeling that the church should not be blamed for the insurrection of catholic laymen and of some clergymen, the bishop of Puebla protested against the decree establishing the indemnity. For Comonfort, who had so far tried to follow a moderate policy, the temptation to cover the high cost of the campaign from the possessions of the rich diocese of Puebla, which included the states of Puebla and Veracruz, was too strong. In the city of Puebla alone ecclesiastical real estate was valued at 5 million pesos, about one-half of the total real estate. When attempted negotiations failed and Labastida refused to pay the indemnity, he was expelled in May and the government embargoed all church property in the bishopric, in order to confiscate all revenues coming from it until at least 1 million pesos were acquired.[19]

By this time, even moderate liberals like President Comon-

fort must have come to the conclusion that the final showdown between the church and the state was inevitable. The
attachment of church goods in the Puebla bishopric was
planned as merely a temporary measure on a regional scale. It
now seemed convenient and even necessary to complement it
by some other measures which would affect church possessions permanently and on a national scale. Considering, however, the violent reaction unleashed by the Puebla confiscatory decree, it seemed advisable to attack ecclesiastical property indirectly, in a way that would not appear as anticlerical
at all. Perhaps with this intention, President Comonfort appointed Miguel Lerdo, former minister of development, as
minister of finance in the latter part of May.

One month later, on 25 June 1856, Lerdo presented his
new law, the main feature of which was that the ownership
of all urban and rural real estate belonging to ecclesiastical
and civil corporations would be assigned to the respective
tenants and lessees, for an amount resulting from the capitalization of the actual rent at 6 percent; that is, conversion of
the annual rent into the value of the property (the higher the
rate of interest, the lower the value). Clerical corporations included not only monasteries and nunneries but also confra-
ternities or brotherhoods, schools, or colleges – in a word, all
institutions associated with the church. The law also affected
the property of civil corporations in that, henceforth, no corporation could own real estate. The future owners would owe
the capital value of the property, secured by its mortgage, to
the church corporation and they could redeem at their convenience all or part of the debt whenever they wished. The
new proprietors would have to keep on paying to the corporation the same amount they had been paying up to then as
rent; the rent would instead become the interest on the capital. Lerdo thus envisaged the transformation of the church
into a giant mortgage bank and of the mass of tenants and
lessees into landowners, both urban and rural. The liberals believed that the disentailment by itself would bring economic
progress; the former lessees would improve the land and

make investments in their newly acquired property. Another purpose of the law was political and social: the liberals wished to create a middle class that would afford them a social base they needed so badly, especially in the countryside, for up to then they were a minority movement. It was expected that the future landowners would support them, since they would purchase the property with a 16.67 percent discount: this was the reason for adopting a 6 percent capitalization instead of the customary 5 percent, which Mora had recommended in his proposals.

The Lerdo Law anticipated the possibility that tenants hostile to the government might refuse to acquire the property it was offering them. If the tenant or lessee did not claim the property within three months, any other person could claim and purchase it; if there were no claimants it would be auctioned. A tenant or lessee was under obvious pressure to acquire the house in which he lived and perhaps had a workshop or a business, or the land which he farmed, for otherwise he might be deprived of the tenancy or leasehold by a complete stranger. Having once become a landowner under the Lerdo Law, he would probably be regarded by the clergy with hostility and thus be forced to embrace the liberal cause. To buy or not to buy would therefore be a difficult decision for a great many people: it involved material advantage on the one hand and scruples of conscience or threats of excommunication, on the other.

The law looked harmless enough; it certainly did not appear to be confiscatory. The church, however, saw it as a plot to deprive her of her property and, therefore, denied approval.

However, the law was implemented, and by the end of 1856, property valued at 23 million pesos was sold to more than 9,000 individuals.[20] Most buyers were tenants of the house they purchased; though poor, they now became small property owners and, as such, even if they had reservations about the law, they acquired an interest in the continuation of the liberal regime. But the disentailment had its darker side. A significant minority of tenants refrained from claiming the property; this was then auctioned and purchased by wealthy speculators some of whom were well known financiers specializing in loans to the government, as a result of which they had come to hold a considerable portion of government bonds. The financiers had been previously connected with conservative regimes, but by reason of their new investment, they would be tied to the destiny of the liberal party. The tenants of course resented the new landlords and waited for the day when the property would be returned to the ecclesiastical corporation. In the countryside, haciendas had been leased in one piece to a single person who then became a hacendado. With some exceptions, little in the way of forming a rural middle class was accomplished as a result of the disentailment of ecclesiastical estates. Besides, the existing hacendados saw in the disentailment an opportunity to round off their holdings; most of them were, of course, conservative and it is a curious fact that as far as is known none of them protested against the liberal Lerdo Law. On the other hand, many prominent hacendados, both liberal and conservative, protested in July 1856 against a few mild agrarian reform projects then before the Constitutional Congress.

In January 1857, Lerdo resigned. The country had had enough of disentailment for the moment; it needed time to adjust to the enormous transfer of property. The liberal efforts culminated at the beginning of February in promulgation of a new constitution which embodied ideas not included in the 1824 Constitution: for instance, it included the Juárez Law, that is the abolition of clerical and military immunities, and it incorporated the Lerdo Law. This was natural, for most congressmen were middle-class lawyers opposed to the privileges of the upper class. From then on, the government assumed a more conciliatory attitude and, on 1 May, it sent its representative to Rome.[21] It seemed that the Holy See was willing to accept the transactions under the Lerdo

Law, but that it demanded that the church should have the legal capacity to acquire and own property; this was not unreasonable, for under the Lerdo Law if any of the new owners and future buyers did not pay interest, the church could no longer put pressure on them with the threat of eviction. The conservative Mexican press suggested in August that in spite of having been "the origin of ruin for countless families," the disentailment should be legalized through an agreement with Rome.

Of course, the Lerdo Law also applied to properties of civil corporations such as city councils, townships, municipalities, and villages or communities of Indian peasants. Village lands traditionally consisted of dwellings with adjoining gardens and orchards, a plaza with a church and a town hall, agricultural land farmed by individual residents, and, finally, the so-called *"ejidos,"* or communal pasture land, and, whenever possible, communal forests. *Ejidos* were of paramount importance and as such were protected by Spanish colonial legislation. Their size was never made clear, however. Some privileged villages had been granted 632 square kilometers each, an enormous extension indeed; this was not uncommon in the North where land was abundant and dry and suited to raising cattle rather than farming.[22] The viceregal government, interested since the beginning in colonization, had settled Indians in these relatively inhospitable areas by offering them favorable conditions, such as freedom from tribute. In general an *ejido* of one village was equal to 17.5 square kilometers.[23] Naturally, when a village had the misfortune of lying near a land-hungry or prosperous hacienda or near a growing city, trouble was bound to arise. Then inroads into the *ejido* land would be made, either to bring it under cultivation or to convert it to urban uses. Thus, villages began to lose parts of their *ejidos.* The Lerdo Law did not wish to harm Indian communities; this is why it exempted *ejidos* from disentailment. It only wished to break down clerical control in villages by sales of village land destined to religious uses. Conflict over the disentailment was bound to arise, and many

Indian communities revolted in the latter part of 1856, led naturally by their priests.[24]

Events were further complicated a few months later when the new constitution proclaimed that ecclesiastical and civil corporations could not own land at all; *ejidos* were no longer exempt. This meant not only a breakdown of clerical control in Indian communities, but also a breakdown of the communities as well. The idea had spread that in order to integrate the Indians into modern society and economy, it was necessary to dissolve their communal life; their community should cease to exist; all its property should be divided among its members. How little the Mexican liberals understood their own countryside! Theirs was a city movement; its leaders were lawyers. It is curious that not even Juárez showed interest in Indian peasants as such. Liberals were engaged in a life and death struggle with the Catholic church and, so far, their following was restricted to towns. If they were to win, they had to gain a social base in the rural areas where, after all, most of the population lived. The countryside was basically conservative – not only Indian peasants but also most individual landowners, both poor and wealthy, were deeply religious. The Conservative party with hacendados on top was rooted there. The liberals, if they were to prevail, had to gain a foothold in the country at any price. City lawyers clashed with village priests; not only ecclesiastical land but also some village land was sold under the Lerdo Law, thus winning at least some adepts among the conservative country people. Disentailment of communal lands finally stopped because of Indian opposition.

Liberals had an antirural bias; most of them did not show any interest in protecting Indians against hacendados. This does not mean that they lacked an agrarian program. Their ideal was to promote middle-size farms, not latifundia or small peasant plots. The splitting up of haciendas had been hampered up to then by mortgage contracts; now the Lerdo Law opened the way by stipulating that buyers of corporate real estate were authorized to divide the land in as many lots as they deemed fit, despite opposition from the mortgagee. As a result, some clerical estates of Guanajuato were split in 1856 and 1857, thereby strengthening the rural middle class.[25] But the liberals never lost sight of their main objective, the destruction of ecclesiastical power. They certainly had no love for the hacendado with his peons bound by debts; but they had to concentrate on their most powerful adversary, the church. Furthermore, hacendados were often the financiers on whom the government depended for financial help. Thus, many valuable projects of agrarian reform were sacrificed. In sum, the liberal strategy against the church consisted of gaining the support of people of all classes by offering them a share of clerical property. This program succeeded in cities and urban areas. In the priest-dominated countryside, it was impossible to isolate the church. Here the liberals clashed with religious villagers; they could not afford to antagonize them and so they had to abandon the hope of transforming the Indian peasant into a middle-class farmer. Instead, they found support in landowners wishing to increase their holdings. As a result, some hitherto conservative hacendados embraced the liberal cause in order to protect their investments. Thus, the countryside was no longer solidly conservative.

By 1857, Mexico was divided into conservative and liberal forces of approximately equal strength. To prevent a new outburst of civil strife, a compromise was necessary. Both President Comonfort and the Holy See were working toward it when reactionary army elements struck in the capital; after a month of chaos, General Zuloaga assumed the presidency in January 1858. Just before relinquishing office, Comonfort released Benito Juárez, the head of the Supreme Court, from the prison where he had been taken by the army, thereby taking personal revenge against the conservatives whom he had helped and rendering the liberal cause an immense service. Comonfort, disillusioned, left the country and went to the United States; neither conservatives nor liberals wished him to stay in Mexico; a good-intentioned man who failed in his attempt to govern the country in a most difficult moment. Liberals do not cherish his memory, yet his momentous decision, seemingly unimportant at the time, to free Juárez saved the liberal cause.[26] Juárez proceeded immediatelly to Guanajuato where he established a liberal government; as head of the Supreme Court, he had the constitutional right to presidential succession; so he declared himself president of the republic. Civil war began. From the outset, the country split into factions: the conservative core — the states of Puebla, México, and Querétaro — against the peripheral areas where liberals were traditionally strong.

As the first act of his government, General Zuloaga declared null and void the Lerdo Law; all disentailment transactions were annulled and ecclesiastical corporations automatically regained full ownership of their properties sold under the Lerdo Law. The church was not to receive them as a free gift, however; in exchange, the metropolitan chapter of the church promised Zuloaga a loan of 1.5 million pesos.[27] Former landowners under the Lerdo law, became tenants again. Speculators who had bought property in an auction lost it. If in the meantime they had evicted former tenants, these should be restored to tenancy. This order proved difficult to enforce, however, for some speculators were persons of influence. Church corporations, soaked by the government as we shall presently see, did not care who the tenant was, providing he paid the rent. Thus, many of the pious poor were sacrificed on the altar of expediency.

The church was able to pay only one tenth of the promised total loan in cash; it paid the rest in notes or bills guaranteed by its property. The conservative government sold them with discount to financiers who eventually acquired ecclesiastical property with the acquiescence of the church. The risk was high, for Melchor Ocampo, the finance minister in the Guanajato liberal government, had from the very outset declared as illegal all acts and transactions of the Zuluoga government; in the event of liberal victory — which, of course, as seen from the capital, did not seem very probable — all prop-

;entailed and now returned to the church, would be
tically restored to buyers under the Lerdo Law.
conservative financiers would lose most properties
they were purchasing from the church. In time, the conservative government was able to extract more cash from moneylenders at the expense of the church. There was probably no other way to finance the war.

While the church was parting with some of its possessions voluntarily under the conservatives, it was losing them against its will in areas under liberal control. True, Juárez accompanied by Ocampo, Prieto, and others, soon had to leave Guanajuato and then Guadalajara, which had surrendered to the conservatives; finally he sailed from Manzanillo and arrived at the beginning of May 1858 in Veracruz where he settled down with his government under the protection of the liberal state governor. In the West, the liberal state of Michoacán held out and decreed a forced loan from the church. Liberal commanders in the North followed suit. For all practical purposes, church possessions were being confiscated. The war was becoming increasingly more cruel and destructive. Juárez had so far refrained from waging an open war against the church, for fear of offending popular religious feelings and thus prolonging the war.[28] But events forced his hand. The time had arrived to put the liberal aims squarely before the nation.

This was the meaning of the manifesto issued by the constitutional government in Veracruz on 7 July 1859. The document, signed by President Juárez and the two most prominent cabinet members Ocampo and Lerdo, put all the responsibility for the fratricidal war on the shoulders of the church and proclaimed a complete separation of church and state, suppression of monasteries, secularization of friars, abolition of novitiates in nunneries, confiscation of all the wealth owned or administered by the church, and elimination of the civil obligation to pay parish fees. These measures were considered urgent. Besides, the manifesto recognized the need for a division of landed property; for the first time, the liberal government admitted the necessity of an agrarian reform, which had been recognized a generation earlier by the governor of Zacatecas, Franciso García; but it added at once that such redistribution would take place in the long run as a natural consequence of economic and social progress as well as of population growth. For the moment, it promised only a law that would remove legal obstacles to the voluntary parceling of rural estates.

The laws affecting church possessions were decreed several days later, those carrying out the separation of church and state, toward the end of the month. These came to be known as the "reform laws." The liberal government felt that the outright confiscation of all ecclesiastical property was justified by the clerical loans to the conservative regime in Mexico City, which amounted to several million pesos. But we have already seen that the church had no choice; these loans were forced loans. Pressed on one side by the reactionaries and on the other by the liberals, the church helplessly watched as its wealth was taken from it. And now came the final, inevitable blow. The nationalized possessions, both real estate and capital, were to be sold to buyers of clerical real estate under the Lerdo Law. Meanwhile the buyers had returned the real estate to the church in the regions occupied by the conservatives; now they were to redeem its value to the government under favorable conditions of payment. True, most of this property was located in Central Mexico, which was under conservative control. Here the new law could clearly not be enforced, but it had a political objective: the former purchasers of church property in, for example, Mexico City and Puebla, would henceforth support the liberal cause because the law offered them the same properties for what amounted to a much lower sales price. Theoretically, the price which was about two thirds of the value was to remain the same, but it was to be redeemed partly in bonds of internal debt and partly in easy monthly payments; since the government bonds circulated at 5 or 10 percent of face value, it meant in practice that people would be able to buy a property at about one third of its price. Those able to pay cash would get an even better bargain, about one fourth of the price or less. No doubt, these terms were expected to attract many uncommitted or timorous persons to the liberal side at a time when the conservative armies still occupied the core of the country. Financiers, who held a considerable amount of bonds and who resided in the capital, would especially find it to their advantage to acquire former church property.[29]

A few financiers were based in Veracruz, engaged in imports and lending money to the constitutional government. A curious practice developed here: it was made possible for these financiers to pay the local liberal authorities in advance for the properties situated in regions under conservative control, especially the valuable houses in Mexico City. This transaction, which primarily involved a small group of French businessmen, was of course highly speculative: in case of a conservative triumph, these people would lose all their investment. Naturally the price was in inverse relation to the risk. Although public opinion disapproved of these sales, they clearly helped to keep the Juárez government afloat by a constant supply of cash, which, in turn, meant armaments.

Not all clerical real estate had been disentailed under the Lerdo Law. There were also ecclesiastical mortgages on private property — especially on large estates of conservative hacendados — monastic buildings, and some churches. All these possessions were now offered for sale on the same terms as the property sold in 1856 and 1857, that is for about one fourth or one third of its already depressed price. Again, many of these properties were located in conservative-controlled territory, but it was hoped that many people would swing to the liberals with the expectation of getting a bargain; this consideration must have weighed heavily in the minds of some hacendados. The July 1859 law offered them the right to redeem their mortgages, but if they did not do it within thirty days, anyone else could do it; in the last instance, the mortgage or property would be auctioned. The enormous discount was naturally the result of the government's need for cash. Again, people had to choose between conservative or liberal: those who sided with the conservatives were to be the losers.

Nunneries were to continue to exist, but the nuns would receive in private property the dowry they had given the convent in perpetuity. The nunneries were a customary refuge for unmarried daughters and sisters; their function was different from that of monasteries and hence they were treated differently, although their wealth was greater.

The last reform decrees dealing with the separation of church and state finally materialized Ocampo's dream of voluntary parish fees. All the reform laws drove political passions to highest pitch; the conservative armies made a last unsuccessful attempt to win the war, and then began to retreat. Merchants in the capital were no longer able, or willing to lend money to the government in exchange for clerical property, as such transactions would be annulled by victorious liberals. Desperate, President Miramón confiscated in November 1860 over 600,000 pesos kept at the British legation on behalf of the English bondholders, an action which was to influence British diplomatic attitude in the following year. One month later, Miramón was defeated in the battle for possession of the capital and on Christmas Day the liberal army entered. The war was over. Although conservative guerrillas continued to fight in some isolated regions, the constitutional government was for all practical purposes the master of the country at the beginning of 1861.

A scramble for nationalized property began in Mexico City and other urban areas. The houses were being restored to their buyers under the Lerdo Law. This was not always possible, however. Just as the Zuloaga regime in 1858 had to accept to a certain extent the *faits accomplis* created by the disentailment, so now the liberal government had to face certain powerful interests created by the previous regime. Loans had been made in Mexico City to the conservative government, with church property as security. Some financiers were foreigners; in particular, Nathaniel Davidson, the representative of the house of Rothschild, and Eustaquio Barron, descendant of an Irishman married in Spain, had together given the conservative authorities about 1 million pesos, in exchange for ecclesiastical real estate of approximately the same value. Juárez obviously did not wish to antagonize the two British firms and preferred to propose an arrangement whereby they would keep the houses in exchange for an additional payment. The persons who had acquired the property under the disentailment law and who, we may assume, were liberals were sacrificed in 1861 to political and financial expediency. The Swiss banker Jecker had invested 1.5 million pesos in bonds issued by the conservative government. Since the government did not make a deal with Jecker and his bonds were acquired by influential politicians in France, the issue later served as a pretext for the French invasion. One of the Frenchmen who had financed the constitutional government in Veracruz — the Breton ship captain José Yves Limantour — received a package of houses in Mexico City priced at 0.5 million pesos. Yet, in most cases, the mass of former tenants regained their property and this new middle class of small and medium landholders continued to be the backbone of the liberal cause and continued to support it during the coming difficult years. Thus, church possessions finally passed into private hands and, out of this medley of interests, a new Mexico was born.[30]

In the countryside, church lands and mortgages were being redeemed by private individuals, lessees, mortgagors, or merchants and money-lenders. In contrast to towns where foreigners were able to acquire a considerable amount of land, the nationalized rural real estate was purchased almost exclusively by Mexicans, foreigners traditionally shunning this type of investment. The liberal government did not forget its promise expressed in the 1859 manifesto regarding a law on the subdivision of landed property; the new law of February 1861 specified that owners of both nationalized and private real estate might divide it, even against the wishes of the mortgagee. Many hacendados found it attractive to parcel their estates into smaller units and offer them for sale; thus many people of the middle and even lower classes now found it possible to become landowners. With the middle strata of society strengthened, especially in the states of Guanajuato, Michoacán, Jalisco, Zacatecas, and San Luis Potosí, in other words the Bajío and its surroundings, the liberal regime gained new adherents in the hitherto hostile countryside.[31] If the confiscation of Jesuit property in 1767 and the forced loans of the first part of the nineteenth century alienated parts of the church wealth, the liberal revolution liquidated it almost completely.

Meanwhile Mexico City was in political agitation. As early as November 1860, the Veracruz regime had called for elections in 1861. The presidential campaign started practically from the first day Juárez and his cabinet set foot in the city. Conservative leaders having all fled, only liberal candidates remained. Nevertheless, the election of Juárez by no means appeared certain or even probable; as acting president of a victorious government, he was now a national figure, but in the public eye he still occupied a second row seat behind Ocampo and Lerdo. It was not easy for the nation to get used to this silent, reserved man; for most people, Ocampo was still the hero and Lerdo was the author of the disentailment and confiscation of church property. But Ocampo was so disgusted with politics that he was anxious to go and live in his peaceful Michoacán estate. In Veracruz a quite natural rivalry had developed between him and Lerdo; each one considered himself as the leader. Now the inconstant Ocampo had lost all his ambition, but in the face of Lerdo's candidacy he decided to give Juárez a helping hand. In a bitter polemic, Ocampo attacked his former companion in the cabinet; Prieto joined him.[32] In those days, Lerdo was the rising star on the liberal horizon and the other leading liberals possibly imagined they were just using Juárez as a counterweight to check Lerdo's ambition. Lerdo died of typhus in March while the presidential elections were in process. His rival Ocampo was to survive him only by slightly more than two months: although warned that conservative guerrillas were active in the area, the fearless Ocampo refused to leave his hacienda; he was captured there and executed two days later. There was another candidate, General Jesús González Ortega, a former journalist. As the man who had defeated the conservative army, he was a national hero. It was feared that following an old tradition, González Ortega would rally the military and attempt to overthrow the government, especially since the president was a civilian. González Ortega resisted the temptation and assured the nation that he would never lead a revolution. He kept his word in spite of the result of the elections. Juárez obtained 5,289 votes, Lerdo 1,989, and González Ortega 1,846. Lerdo had, of course, already been dead for some time.

Juárez stepped from the background into the limelight. He had weathered the political storm. But an even worse storm was coming in the shape of financial problems which were eventually to bring in their wake international complications. True, in 1861 nationalized properties worth 16 million pesos were sold in Mexico City and its surroundings alone, but only 1 million pesos were actually received in payment; the rest was compensated in credits, promissory notes, and bonds. The government tried desperately to raise funds by other means, but failed. The English bondholders expected some money from the sale of nationalized goods.[33] Similarly, France was pressing her claims for the Jecker bonds, but Juárez refused to be held responsible for the acts of the former conservative government. Although it seemed impossible, the liberal regime had barely enough money to survive. European creditors waited in vain and felt cheated when the Juárez government suspended all payments in July. Great Britain, France, and Spain agreed on military intervention in Mexico three months later and, before the end of 1861, the allied troops landed in Veracruz. Just emerging from a savage civil strife, Mexico was in for another war.

The conservative armies having been beaten decisively, the

enemy was no longer within; this time, Juárez was facing a foreign invasion. Britain and Spain soon disengaged themselves from the operation when it became clear that Napoleon III had special designs on Mexico. A few Mexican monarchists then residing in Europe conceived the idea that the time had finally arrived to establish a Mexican empire under European — namely, French — protection. They were joined by Mexican conservative refugees who saw in the French invasion a welcome opportunity to reconquer power for themselves and the church. It appeared that a civil war would be inflamed anew from abroad. The conservatives were clinging to the last straw; their participation in the attempt of a foreign country to conquer Mexico by force, whatever the pretexts and avowed reasons or motives, wrecked forever the chances of the conservative cause in Mexico.

The French invasion aroused genuine patriotic feelings in Mexico. Unexpectedly, Mexican armies under General Zaragoza repulsed the enemy at the battle of Puebla on 5 May 1862. For the first time in many, many years, Mexico felt the exhilaration of victory. The wounds caused by the war with the United States were suddenly healed. Juárez and the liberal cause became identified with the nation and its independence. The importance of the battle was mainly psychological. French forces were reorganized and Marshall Forey arrived in September to lead a new, more powerful campaign. General Zaragoza having died, Juárez had no other recourse than to appoint González Ortega, whom he had kept without military assignment, to the general command of eastern armies. González Ortega established his headquarters in Puebla and there financed the costly defense preparations by the sale of the remaining ecclesiastical properties, in particular nunneries and monastic buildings.[34] In the heat of the war, nunneries that had been allowed by the reform laws of 1859 to continue their normal life, were now all suppressed. In the belief that the invaders represented the clerical reaction, the government decided to strike where it would hurt; institutions exempted by earlier laws were closed down and their funds confiscated. However, nuns' dowries, as a private property, were respected.

Despite the extremely low prices at which nationalized goods were now being sold, the army in Puebla was able to store a large amount of munitions and supplies with which to defend the city. Puebla surrendered after two months' siege, in May 1863, one year after the victorious battle. Henceforth, the invading armies were free to extend the occupation to other parts of the country. But the defense of the city did show the world that Mexico was opposing the foreign invasion and that the spirit of resistance was alive. It was this that in the end was more important than all the French military victories.[35] González Ortega himself was taken prisoner, escaped while being taken to Veracruz, and found his way to the North. Juárez, his cabinet ministers, a few deputies, and a small group of advisers abandoned the capital in the evening of 31 May. Their carriages headed north.

Now that the French were in possession of Mexico City, Labastida, now archbishop of Mexico, expected from them a firm declaration of conservative principles, in the first place the annullment of the reform laws. However, in his manifesto of 12 June Forey recognized the validity of the nationalization and sale of church property. This policy was strengthened several months later by Marshall Bazaine, the new head of the French expeditionary army and for all practical purposes the master of Mexico.[36] France obviously felt no desire to restore to the church its wealth and power; Napoleon wished to have a stable regime in Mexico, along the lines of the one existing in his country; confiscation of clerical goods was expected to give rise to a large middle class and thus a stable society. By accepting the nationalization, the French wished to take the wind out of the sails of the liberal, republican government; once isolated, Juárez who was retreating further north and ever nearer to the United States boundary, was expected to pass into oblivion. The French adopted the program of the liberal party in Mexico and thus, no doubt, gained many adherents among both liberals and buyers of church properties. The disillusioned conservatives then turned to archduke Maximilian Habsburg but when he arrived as the emperor of Mexico in June 1864, he chose his ministers from among the liberals, or former liberals and sent well known conservatives such as Miramón abroad. For the moment, a liberal republic was seen as a thing of the past. True, the monarchy was under the protection of French arms, but Mexican liberals of the time had a predilection for everything French; France was for them a synonym of progress, as once the United States had been for the generation of Zavala. It was of course ironical that France had invaded the country, but the liberal supporters of the empire were not bothered by this, at least at this time.

The liberals welcomed the modernization which began under the French occupation. France poured a considerable amount of money into Mexico.[37] Actually, only a small proportion of it was used productively, but it was enough to make noticeable improvements, especially in Mexico City.[38] Under French protection, Mexico became again an attractive place for British investments. The abolition of usury laws by the Juárez government in 1861 had created a propitious climate for the foundation of a bank. The London Bank of Mexico and South America considered the local conditions sufficiently stabilized to justify opening a branch in Mexico City in 1864. The bank introduced the circulation of bank-notes for the first time in Mexico. Just as important for the economic development of the country, construction began on a railroad from Veracruz to Mexico City via the industrial town of Orizaba and with a branch line to Puebla. Antonio Escandón, a Mexican entrepreneur who had introduced modern stagecoaches on the Veracruz-Puebla-Mexico City highway was granted the concession for the railroad by the Juárez regime in 1861; due to constant disturbances, however, only insignificant stretches were completed. But Escandón managed to get a British firm interested in the project; a company was formed in London in 1862, to which Escandón's concession was transferred two years later and in which he retained a minority of shares. Work proceeded so fast that by 1867, when the empire collapsed, almost one half of the 424 kilometer line was completed, by no means an insignificant achievement. The liberal government had laid the groundwork on which the French and Maximilian later built.

The French did not consider the confiscation and sale of church property as sufficient to create a predominantly middle-class Mexico. Other measures were needed. In a manifesto to the Mexican nation of June 1863, Marshall Forey announced that thenceforth taxes were to be born mainly by the rich. He also hinted that Indians were to be accorded full equality in legal matters.[39] If Forey's approval of the nationalization displeased the conservatives, the proposed policy was bound to antagonize the wealthy landowners, both liberal and conservative. The French were unimpressed by the creole oligarchy, whom they saw as pretentious and conceited, and they were shocked by the abyss between the rich and the poor as well as by the treatment of the Indians. Such disparities had not existed in Western and Central Europe since the turn of the century, but in Mexico they were taken for granted. Indians — most poor were Indians and most Indians were poor — were considered children and treated as such by the rich landowners. Even a kindhearted hacendado like Ocampo declared, not without a touch of pride, that he brought back only the peons guilty of a transgression, presumably in order to punish them himself. The liberals did not implement Article 5 of the constitution, which stipulated full freedom of work and by implication prohibited debt-serfdom. A law expressly prohibiting debt-servitude was never considered by the liberal government.

It fell to the Mexican emperor to formulate such a law. In his decree of 1 November 1865, Maximilian granted to laborers the right to leave their employment at will. Hours of work and child labor were restricted and all debts over 10 pesos were annulled. Corporal punishment was forbidden and peddlers were permitted to enter the hacienda ground and offer their wares to peons, thereby breaking the monopoly of hacienda stores. The law specified fines for violators.⁴⁰ Unfortunately it came too late; the government tried to enforce it but the landowners boycotted it and the French were too preoccupied with the unfavorable trend of events. Had it been promulgated two years earlier, when the French were winning on all sides, it might perhaps have been enforced with reasonable successs and thus survived the empire into the republican era.

Meanwhile in another similar move Maximilian in 1865 restored to Indian villages the right to own property and one year later granted *ejidos* to those communities that did not have them.⁴¹ Again, these reforms came too late.

It is obvious that these measures did not make the empire popular among the landholders; even if most of them had welcomed it at the outset as giving more safeguards to life and property, in 1866 when the military situation turned against the empire as a result of Napoleon III's decision to withdraw his troops, the hacendados must have recalled that the Juárez government never meddled with their peons and their land.

Thus, Maximilian was abandoned by the conservatives and then by the propertied classes; with the worsening military conditions the monarchist liberals swung again to Juárez, who began to gain ground and three years after his withdrawal from Mexico City started to march southward from the United States border. The French army departed from the country, and the empire became restricted to Central Mexico; Maximilian found his last support and solace among conservative die-hards like General Miramón, whom he now welcomed back to Mexico.

Republican armies were slowly but surely closing the circle around Central Mexico. While an army under the young General Porfirio Díaz was moving against Puebla, the Northern army was moving on Querétaro. This is where Maximilian decided to make what was to be his last stand. He was defeated and captured together with General Miramón and General Mejía, a conservative of Indian origin. They became prisoners of war. Executions of war prisoners including civilians were quite common during the civil war of 1858–1860. During the French occupation, many republican guerrilla fighters were courtmartialed and shot by Mexican or French firing squads. Hence the execution of the three commanders was virtually a foregone conclusion. They were tried by a military tribunal, convicted of war crimes, and executed on the morning of 19 June 1867 on a hill overlooking the peaceful valley of Querétaro.

The execution stirred considerable criticism in Europe. It was expected that at least Maximilian's life would be spared. But the execution was meant as a warning to other countries not to invade or attempt to conquer Mexico again; as such it was effective. Maximilian's attempt at a social reform was forgotten and the agrarian reformers of the present century never suspected that the well meaning foreigner, and not Juárez, had been their precursor.

By the end of June 1867, order was reestablished in Mexico. In contrast to 1856 and 1861, in 1867 the liberal victory was complete; no monarchist or conservative guerrillas were disturbing the peace of the countryside with the hope of inflaming the civil war again. Both the Conservative party and the European attempts at conquest were irrevocably defeated. Mexico now had a republican government. The country had proven to the world that it could defend its independence; the liberal party had liquidated its old enemy, conservatism, even if it appeared under the guise of monarchy. In almost a decade of presidency, the civilian Juárez had revealed himself as a formidable war leader. But now that the peace had finally settled over the land, would the liberal regime be able to give it a stable government? Would Mexico be able to project the image of an orderly nation to the world? Now that Juárez was no longer harassed by hostile forces, would he rise to the occasion? These questions must have occurred to many people both in Mexico and abroad.

The temptation to punish all those who had collaborated with the empire was strong. Laws to this effect had been enacted by the republican government during the war. But what was needed was national conciliation. Half a dozen monarchist generals were executed and less than one hundred persons from those arrested in the capital were condemned to prison, to be freed three years later as a result of a general amnesty.[42] This was by no means simple magnanimity; given the fact that so many Mexicans had accepted the empire, it seemed wise to close this embarrassing chapter of Mexican history and open a new one.

A deep resentment against Western Europe was felt by Mexican republicans who had so admired the democracy and freedom of Great Britain and France. National pride bade Juárez to break off diplomatic relations with these two countries. On the other hand, there was appreciation for the attitude of the United States, which had continued to recognize Juárez and had sent military supplies to republican Mexico, especially after the end of the United States' Civil War.[43] A sign of better relations between Mexico and the United States was an agreement signed in 1868 regarding claims of American citizens for damages suffered in Mexican wars since 1848; the United States reduced these claims to an amount considered reasonable by Mexico.[44] On the other hand, the Juárez government not only repudiated all loans contracted in Europe by the empire, but also declared that it would not renew payments on the old "English" debt and that the bondholders who apparently had approved the military intervention in Mexico, at least in its initial phase, would have to wait. British investments in Mexico were left unmolested, however. The government considered that the London Bank of Mexico had remained neutral in the struggle; it had dealt of course mainly with the empire, but at least on one occasion it had advanced some money in London to the treasurer of the republican government. Besides, Mexico's economy was utterly exhausted so the bank was allowed to continue its operations. Juárez also pardoned the Mexican Railroad Company for its past collaboration with the empire, so construction could be continued.

Within this framework of pacification and economic development, Juárez sought reelection. His four-year term had expired in 1865, during the war when he was established in the northern state of Chihuahua; but, based on the extraordinary powers granted to him previously by the Congress, he had extended his presidency by decree until such time as new elections became possible again.[45] González Ortega also aspired to the highest office, but he did not have the nerve to attempt an army takeover; he was arrested by republican authorities and was still in prison in 1867. A new, younger, and more formidable military candidate for the presidency arose in the person of General Porfirio Díaz, the hero of the last war. However, Juárez's popularity was so overwhelming that he received 7,422 votes as against 2,709 votes for Díaz in the 1867 elections.[46] With the national mandate so clearly in his favor, Juárez applied himself to the task of pacifying the country. The now harmless González Ortega was freed in the following year. Porfirio Díaz retired to his native Oaxaca. There seemed to be some prospect that the government would endure. Amnesty was declared in 1870 for the enemies of the republic and the archbishop of Mexico, Labastida, returned in the following year and was treated by government representatives with respect.[47] After all, Juárez had inherited a predominantly Catholic country; he understood that a measure of tolerance was indispensable for the government's survival. He knew that sentiments and beliefs can be changed only by education and hence gave preference to a reorganization of public schools; for example, between 1857 and 1875 the number of primary schools more than tripled, from 2,400 to 8,100. Juárez's principal adviser was Gabino Barreda, a physician, who had received his degree in 1851 in France and who brought from there positivist philosophy with its accent on science.[48] It is sometimes thought that educational reform was one of Juárez's main contributions to modern Mexico.

The beginning of 1871 witnessed maneuvering for the coming presidential election. Sebastian Lerdo, a younger brother of Miguel, for years minister of foreign relations and the closest collaborator of the president, resigned and became a candidate himself in opposition to Juárez.[49] Díaz campaigned again. The elections gave Juárez 5,837 votes, Díaz 3,555 and Lerdo 2,874. Juárez's popularity had declined; he did not obtain an absolute majority. The impatient Porfirio Díaz charged that the repeated and indefinite reelection of Juárez was endangering national institutions, for it lead to personal control of the executive over Congress and the Supreme Court and, thus, to a dictatorship. Juárez retorted that the rebel wanted to return to the militarism and army rule of the past age. The reelected president died half a year later, in July 1872. The performance of Juárez had indeed not been so good since the death of his wife at the beginning of 1871. Perhaps he should have stepped down; but like so many statesmen, he considered himself indispensable and never thought of making provisions for a successor. He had had almost fifteen uninterrupted years in office, a duration so far unheard of in Mexico. Even conservative historians concede that he introduced a form of government which did away with civil wars.[50] Certainly, Juárez must have been an accomplished politician.

When Juárez died, the presidential chair fell to Sebastian Lerdo de Tejada, who had been the head of the Supreme Court and, as such, had the right to succession. Not much happened during his presidency. On 1 January 1873, Lerdo opened the Mexico-Veracruz railroad; this masterpiece of civil engineering had been for all practical purposes finished under Juárez but Lerdo was the first president to ride in it. He did not show much interest in economic development. He was distrustful of the United States and the dictum attributed to him, "between strength and weakness, the desert," signified that he did not wish to have any railways built between Mexico and the northern neighbor. In Mexican history, Lerdo is known for his extreme anticlerical policy. Under Juárez, religious processions were tolerated, for the reform laws had left the decision to local officials who in many cases respected popular feelings and beliefs. In 1873 Lerdo took the step of including the reform laws into the constitution and thus expressly prohibited popular religious ceremonies in the whole country.[51] He also carried his anticlerical policy to other spheres; he ordered the expulsion of the venerable Sisters of Mercy, who had been respected by Juárez. Lerdo's anticlerical policy makes no sense unless we bear in mind that as an old bachelor and scholar Lerdo had been nicknamed "the curate" or "the Jesuit." Perhaps he now wanted to show that he was a better, purer, liberal than Juárez.

If Juárez had barely won his reelection in 1871, it was not logical to expect that the much less popular Lerdo would be returned to office. And so, when Díaz made his third bid for the highest office at the beginning of 1876, Lerdo's support disintegrated and the military revolt succeeded before the end of the year. Lerdo left for the United States, leaving the battlefield to his rival.[52] The attempt to establish a permanent civilian government had failed.

4

The Era of Porfirio Díaz
1876–1910

> [With his guard] Pisistratus broke into revolt and seized the citadel. Thus he acquired the sovereignty of Athens, which he continued to hold without disturbing the previously existing offices or altering any of the laws. . . . [In his third government] Pisistratus set himself to root his power more firmly, by the aid of a numerous body of mercenaries and by keeping up a full treasury. . . Thus was the tyranny of Pisistratus established at Athens.
>
> Herodotus, *Persian Wars,* Book I

Porfirio Díaz was born in 1830 in Oaxaca City. His godfather, who held the infant in his arms for christening, was his uncle, a parish priest who later became bishop of Oaxaca. Porfirio's mother was the daughter of a peasant family that owned some cattle and land; his father, of an enterprising temperament, had been a muleteer and then a sugar-cane cultivator on a small scale; he finally settled down in Oaxaca and established an inn which in those days catered especially to muleteers and provided care for their animals.[1] In view of the family connections, it is not surprising that the boy was sent to a seminary; his mother dreamt of seeing her son in priest's robes. After the Mexican-American War, the whole country was seething with liberal ideas; even remote Oaxaca had its crop of anticlerical students. Influenced by his friends, Porfirio rebelled against his uncle, abandoned the seminary, and entered the Institute of Sciences and Arts. Benito Juárez, a lawyer and state governor, was on several occasions professor and director of the institute; many students fell under his influence, among them the twenty-year-old Porfirio Díaz and Matías Romero, a child prodigy seven years Porfirio's junior. Díaz was on the point of becoming a lawyer when Santa Anna engineered a general plebiscite at the end of 1854; everybody in the Oaxaca institute was ordered to vote. As anticipated, everybody voted for the dictator; only Díaz dared to dissent by publicly depositing a vote for Alvarez, the head of the insurrection against Santa Anna. After this, Díaz vanished and joined rebel troops in the mountains. He was to remain an army man for the rest of his long life. During 1858–1860 he fought the conservatives during the Civil War and was promoted to general in 1861. He became a national figure during the resistance against the French invasion and occupation; he captured Puebla in the spring of 1867 and soon afterward liberated the capital of the republic. Porfirio Díaz was a national hero.

In a photograph taken at that time Díaz, dressed in a civilian suit, still looks like a shy provincial lawyer with rebellious hair and beard; except for a domineering expression in his eyes, there is nothing that would point to his great future.[2] Díaz looks entirely different in a picture painted of him in the very same year of 1867.[3] He is dressed in a magnificent uniform. The epaulettes give the impression of broad shoulders and his hair and beard are carefully trimmed; the pose is imperial, napoleonic, typical of an army man of the time. Perhaps this portrait was painted toward the end of 1867, when Díaz ran for president. Had his character changed in this short lapse of time? Could he perhaps have been both a small town lawyer and a haughty general simultaneously? Or did the painter read in his face what did not exist there, in order to invent an image of a military hero?

Perhaps the general hoped that the aging President Juárez would offer him a cabinet post or the general command of the army. (It is not known if these were his expectations but they might explain later events.) Nothing of the sort happened of course. Juárez was not a friend of the army, even of a liberal army, the spectre of an army revolt haunted him throughout his presidency. But in 1867 he himself increased such a danger when he ordered, as one of his first acts after the military victory, a demobilization of the army, depriving 70,000 men of their livelihood.[4] Personal resentment against Juárez and discontent in the army thus pushed Díaz into the path of opposition.

The provincial lawyer, already a national hero, was becoming a military-political leader, a *"caudillo."* He learned to use the technique of his predecessors: he proudly retired to his hacienda La Noria — donated to him by his native state — surrounded by a retinue of loyal supporters. Then in 1871, when he launched an army revolt against the reelected President Juárez, Díaz proclaimed that "if triumph crowns our efforts, I shall return to the peace of my home, preferring in any event the frugal and tranquil life of the obscure laborer to the ostentation of power."[5] These words certainly sound familiar; apparently, Díaz had learned something from Iturbide and Santa Anna. Five years later, in 1876, triumph finally crowned his efforts, but he did not return to the peace of his home. Juárez was no longer alive, so Díaz did not have to excuse himself for disrupting the constitutional order and for opposing the president; now his adversary was only Lerdo.

The cabinet appointed by Porfirio Díaz toward the end of 1876 was composed of well known liberals:[6] the ministry of war went to General Pedro Ogazón, the former governor of Jalisco during the Three Years War against the conservatives; like Díaz, Ogazón was a lawyer and an army man at the same time. The ministry of foreign relations was given to Ogazón's son-in-law Ignacio Vallarta, already a prominent jurist, and the ministry of justice and public instruction to the atheist and socialist writer Ignacio Ramírez. Vicente Riva Palacio, the anti-Lerdo journalist who was grandson of Vicente Guerrero and son of an important liberal lawyer who was governor of the state of Mexico was appointed minister of economic development. Riva Palacio was to coordinate later the writing of a five-volume chronicle of the country, *México a través de los siglos,* in which he himself supplied the section on the colonial period. Díaz gave the ministry of finance to Matías Romero, the youngest of the generation raised by the Oaxaca Institute of Sciences and Arts and Juárez's godchild.[7]

The split of the liberals — first between the followers of Juárez and Díaz and four years later between the followers of Lerdo and Díaz — had left the new military president with a rather slender civilian base. Hence Porfirio Díaz made it clear from the beginning that he would welcome support from other quarters. He of course counted on the army and he was careful not to demobilize its superfluous elements; instead he guaranteed them permanent posts. His promise of 15 January 1877, that in contrast to Lerdo's presidency the Catholic religion would not be persecuted and that his administration would not discriminate against anyone, must have evoked a favorable response not only from the clericals, but also from the former supporters of Maximilian.

When Díaz had attained power toward the end of 1876, he was still considered and certainly considered himself a liberal. But what was his program for the government? Here Díaz singularly lacked ideas. He carried to the extreme the pragmatism practiced by Juárez, of whom it has been said that he was "not a leader who conceived and gave impulse to programs, reforms, or ideas. That task reverted to the men who surrounded him, and he acquiesced in or rejected their leadership."[8] Yet the situation under Lerdo's presidency provided a general framework. The Mexican economy lagged hopelessly behind the United States and Western Europe. Plans for railroad construction already existed, but remained on paper. Now that peace had been established after so many decades of war, it seemed necessary to promote economic development by attracting foreign investments. As early as 1867, immediately after the war, Juárez had accepted British capital. Now much more was needed, especially American capital; U.S. investors had already shown interest in Mexico. Lerdo had been too slow to act, hence it fell to his successor to lay the groundwork for the over-due introduction of modern transport, mining and industry. This could be facilitated by the es-

tablishment of order; but only the army, not a civilian regime, could enforce it. Thus, Díaz became the president of
order and progress.

In the mind of Porfirio Díaz as well as of his collaborators,
order and economic progress came to justify army rule. This
of course brought in its wake a gradual restriction of the
press which had been entirely free under Juárez and Lerdo.
In fact, the press had been so free that it helped to under-
mine the regime of these two civilian presidents. Díaz had
used this freedom in order to attain power but, knowing its
corrosive effect, he justified its suppression on the ground
that Mexico was not ready for it. In 1908, in the last years of
his long rule, he declared "democracy to be the one true, just
principle of government, although in practice it is possible
only among highly developed peoples."[9] These words, spoken
in an interview with an American correspondent which was
apparently intended for foreign consumption, remind us of
similar words spoken by Iturbide and Santa Anna. "Here in
Mexico we have had different conditions," Díaz continued;
"I received this government from the hands of a victorious
army at a time when the people were divided and unprepared
for the exercise of the extreme principles of democratic government. To have thrown upon the masses the whole responsibility of government at once would have produced conditions that might have discredited the cause of democracy."
And, "we preserved the republican and democratic form of
government. We defended the theory and kept it intact. Yet
we adopted a patriarchal policy in the actual administration
of national affairs, guiding and restraining popular tendencies, with full faith that an enforced peace would allow education, industry, and commerce to develop elements of stability and unity." The general concluded that "the principles of
democracy have not been planted very deep in our people;
the individual Mexican as a rule thinks much about his own
rights . . . but not about his duties." He referred to the educated middle class. On the other hand, "the Indians, who are
more than half of our population, care little for politics.

They are accustomed to look to those in authority for leadership instead of thinking for themselves."

If Porfirio Díaz used the methods of Iturbide and Santa Anna to reach power, he certainly did not imitate these *caudillos* once he was president. They had utterly failed as rulers; they must have taught Díaz precisely how not to govern the country. Instead, Díaz must have learned from Juárez, who in his unobtrusive, almost invisible way, managed to rule Mexico for almost fifteen years. Of course, the continuous war from 1858 to 1867 had helped Juárez to perpetuate himself in the office; once the war was over, he had begun to lose his control of politics and he was not far from losing his reelection in 1871. At that time, liberalism was being weakened by complete freedom of the press, and it was still basically restricted to cities; the countryside — villages, settlements of rancheros and haciendas with their population of laborers — soon reasserted its traditional nature. It was from here that the army and the church had always drawn their strength. In sum, the situation was fundamentally the same as had occurred in 1834. Consequently, the result was similar, that is, the establishment of an army regime, with the difference that the long duration of the Juárez presidency had prepared the country for the even longer presidency of Díaz.

There can be little doubt that the victorious general was determined to follow the example established by Juárez, of a life-long presidency. However, Díaz had campaigned against Juárez and then Lerdo with the slogan of "no reelection," and now he had to fulfill his electoral promise. This he did by a constitutional amendment which prohibited the reelection of the president and of state governors for the following term; a president could be reelected, but not immediately. This subtle difference passed unnoticed by most people. Díaz obviously had it in mind to install for the four years of 1880–1884 a place-holder who would return the office to him at the expiration of his term. It is also quite likely that by 1878 he already knew who the man would be on whom he could rely for such an important service. He passed over his cabinet members, who were all men of recognized ability but did not fit into his scheme, for they were his superiors intellectually and they might thus attempt to revert to a permanent civilian regime. Nor did he choose his man from among the liberal army commanders; here the risk was that such a person might perhaps sway the army in his favor and so replace Díaz as the ruler of Mexico. It had to be a man who would not only be an intimate friend but who would also depend on Díaz; friendship certainly was not enough, for even the best friends can forget their friendship once they become presidents. By a process of elimination, Porfirio Díaz began to consider General Manuel González. Díaz and González were of course "compadres" but, in addition, González had a peculiar military career: other commanders had to their credit many years of service in the liberal cause, going in many cases back to a participation in the 1854 revolt — not González, however. As a professional officer, he had fought during the civil war of 1858–1860 on the conservative side and he and Díaz had met as adversaries. At the outset of the French invasion he volunteered to enter the republican army in which he then fought always under the orders of his compadre; perhaps no other commander would have been willing to accept him. Recently, in 1876, he had proved his loyalty to Díaz by playing an important role in the revolt against Lerdo. González was naturally a man of ability, but his record would make it impossible, or at least very difficult, for him to become a dominant figure in the army and overshadow Díaz in the esteem of the liberal public. The man on whom Díaz could rely was found.

In due time González was elected and installed president. He included Díaz in his cabinet as minister of development but could not hold him very long: the former president preferred to "retire" as state governor to his native Oaxaca; to be governor — a president on a small scale — was more to his taste than to be in the cabinet where other ministers would be equals and difficulties between him and the president might arise. He could count on González not to interfere with his governorship; from Oaxaca he would also be able to watch developments and return in time to claim the presidential chair for himself. Everything happened as foreseen, with the additional advantage that González discredited himself by the corruption of his government and by his licentious personal life. The last year of his term, 1884, was full of discontent and riots in the capital; the free press had its share in rousing the people to opposition and it is not unlikely that, had not Díaz resumed office, a violent upheaval would have taken place and Mexico would have returned to the disorders of the Santa Anna era. It can be easily imagined that Mexico felt relieved when Porfirio Díaz finally took over the government on 1 December 1884. After the experience with González, the nation would perhaps accept future reelections of Díaz; after all, he was known to be financially honest and to possess domestic virtues. The prospect of an indefinite reelection and a life-long presidency, however, was bound to evoke memories of Santa Anna; Díaz knew he would have to face a determined opposition from liberal public opinion. His first task then consisted in curbing the press, the same press which had been his ally in 1876, which had treated him well during his first term and which, by attacking President González, had helped to raise his image in public eyes. The four years of his second term witnessed the imprisonment of several dozens of newspapermen and the assassination of a few more recalcitrant ones.[10] Santa Anna had been satisfied with sending his critics abroad, but experience showed that the liberals could successfully plot an overturn of the dictatorship from their exile. This then had to be prevented and Díaz prevented it, for one generation at least.

With the press now at his disposal, Díaz was ready to prepare his second reelection. The constitution had to be amended again so as to permit immediate reelection and this was done in 1887. Díaz cautiously asked Congress to approve a single reelection for the following term only. Once reelected in 1888, Díaz felt secure enough to throw off the mask: in 1890, Congress reestablished the original text of the 1857

Constitution, which contained no restrictions on reelection and which had made it possible for Juárez to remain in office so long. From now on, Díaz could stop worrying about his continuous reelections, which came to be taken for granted. Díaz used to his advantage the discredit to which González had fallen. He left nothing to chance, however. Just in case his "compadre" dreamt of becoming president again, he kept him in check by permitting an accusation against him for corrupt practices to be presented in courts. Such precautions exemplify Díaz's political cunning and ability.

Thus, Díaz became president for life after fourteen years of effort and waiting. In 1890, he was sixty. His slow rise to permanent power contrasts with that of Iturbide and Santa Anna, who had let themselves be elected emperor and perpetual dictator, respectively, after half a year in power. Díaz had learned to be patient; he was a young man at fifty, and he probably felt he would live until his eighties or nineties. Hence he could wait. The nation had to forget, as far as possible, his original program of no reelection, and this of course took time. Juárez having become the national idol, it was advisable to stress the similarities between them; dictatorship had to be disguised under the cloak of a normal, democratic reelection. The early opposition of young Díaz against Juárez was played down and, in the official literature, the general was pictured as carrying on the task begun by his great predecessor in office. Díaz knew from the outset that a considerable measure of religious toleration would help him to rule the country; certainly, the church must have welcomed his defeat of the anticlerical Lerdo who had thwarted the conciliatory policy of Juárez. If the civilian Juárez had in mind a peaceful coexistence with the church, this was even more true of Porfirio Díaz, for the natural complement of military authority is the authority of the church.

Besides, Díaz had already taken one step toward this goal. In 1880, in the last months of his first term, Díaz had met the brilliant, wealthy, and ambitious young priest Eulogio Gillow.[11] Gillow was a friend of two cabinet members and of the lawyer Manuel Romero Rubio, minister of foreign relations under Lerdo; Romero Rubio was of course a liberal but his wife was connected with the church hierarchy and high society. It so happened that in April of the same year Díaz had become a widower; he began to visit the Romero Rubio family, especially the attractive daughter Carmen, more than thirty years his junior. While González ruled, Porfirio Díaz had been laying the groundwork for his future and, at the age of fifty three, he married the Romero daughter with the approval of the high church hierarchy. The symbolic reconciliation with the church brought in its wake a rapprochement between the mestizo, middle-class president and the upper class.

The upper class which, in the absence of a titled nobility, consisted of a group of the largest landholders and financiers had been associated with the conservative governments of Bustamante and Santa Anna. It had suffered a setback during the liberal revolution when the middle class came to the fore but it regained its place under Maximilian's short-lived empire. Some of its members — for example, the Martínez del Rio and Sánchez Navarro families — were punished as collaborationists by Juárez and some of their land was confiscated. In the years following the definitive collapse of the conservative cause, the upper class stood aloof from the government. Yet its wealth, even if momentarily diminished as a result of fines and confiscations, was still there. The liberal regime did nothing to harm hacendados; on the contrary, they seem to have reaped the fruits of the nationalization of church property. After the end of the empire, the liberal government centered its efforts on the division of communal lands among peasants, in accordance with the 1857 Constitution. The liberals had been prudent enough to postpone implementation of the constitution until their final victory. Then, in August 1867, the government began to implement this part of its program. This was accomplished to a considerable degree under the presidency of Juárez;[12] the program was completed under Díaz, with the last decree ordering division signed in

1890. The results disappointed those who had expected to transform Indian peasants into independent farmers. In many cases, peasants sold their lots for a small amount of money to neighboring hacendados; as a result, villages lost their communal lands to haciendas and even to ranchos, for small and middle-sized farms also benefited from the repartition.[13] After the church and village lands came the national lands, mostly unoccupied desert with no value at the time. Their quantity was unknown but it certainly amounted to a considerable portion of the national territory. With the purpose of promoting colonization and economic progress as well as of obtaining funds for the continuation of the war, Juárez issued a law in 1863 offering 2,500 hectares to each interested party for a modest sum. This was considered a small amount of property in the North, where most of the national lands were to be found. The law was modified in 1883: henceforth the government could grant contracts for surveying national lands;[14] as payment, the surveyors would receive one third of the surveyed land. The government was entitled to sell the remaining two thirds in blocks of 2,500 hectares or less; purchasers and surveying companies were required by law to bring in immigrants but they found it difficult to comply with this condition. They were relieved of this duty by the law of 1894, which also eliminated the maximum amount of land that could be acquired by one person. By that time, those national lands which appeared to be of any use were already in private hands; all that remained were enormous desert stretches and tropical primeval forests.

It is clear that in regard to land, too, Díaz continued the policy initiated by his illustrious predecessor. The result, by 1890, of the transfer of church, village, and national lands was an important increase in the number of small and middle-size farms, ranchos and haciendas.[15] No doubt, the ownership of land in many parts of the country was dispersed, thus creating or strengthening the middle class. Also, already existing haciendas had an opportunity to extend their boundaries and thus to become latifundia. The old liberal politician Luis

Terrazas, for example, acquired in his enormous northwestern home state of Chihuahua a series of cattle-raising and exporting latifundia. His son-in-law Enrique Creel, a son of the U.S. consul in Chihuahua, was to develop the manufacturing and banking aspects of the family fortune. Even if the old, formerly conservative landowners could never realistically dream of regaining political power, they could regain some of their previous influence by associating with influential liberals like the Terrazas-Creel family. As the number of rural mounted police was insufficient,[16] General Díaz must have come to the conclusion that he needed the haciendas with their private guards for maintaining order in the country.

Gone were the days when high society could snub a Spanish-Indian president. The liberal revolution opened the door through which many mestizos entered and rose to prominence. Thus, the 1883 marriage of Porfirio Díaz and Carmen Romero sealed the union of the liberal army, the church and the landed aristocracy. As a result, some scions of the old Escandón and Barrón families forgot their conservative and monarchist past and entered public service while others captured leading positions in banking. The marriage was significant for another reason. Díaz's father-in-law, Romero Rubio, had a considerable influence in liberal circles, to be sure not among liberal army officers, but among the civilians who had followed Juárez and Lerdo. By giving his daughter in marriage to Porfirio Díaz, by uniting his name to that of the military dictator, he made public his own and his group's reconciliation to army rule. The result was soon apparent: when Díaz reinstalled himself in the presidency in December 1884, he appointed his father-in-law as the powerful minister of interior (*gobernación*). Romero Rubio seemed to consider himself worthy of the highest office in the republic; he perhaps slightly looked down upon his mestizo son-in-law and accepted him only as a means to further his own presidential ambitions. As the constitution required that a former president could only be reelected after somone else had served a term in the office, he already imagined himself alternating the presidency with his son-in-law, only two years his junior. As long as the presidency remained in the family, he did not mind sharing it with the general. He did not lose his hope when the constitutional amendment of 1887 made immediate reelection of the president possible; after all, he would still have a chance in 1892.

Romero Rubio felt the need to build his own political machine, so as not to depend too much on his son-in-law. He began to gather a group of intellectuals and professional people, all very young, about twenty-five years his junior, in his office. They had studied under Barreda, the pedagogue who had brought positivist philosophy from France, and had been raised under Juárez and Lerdo in the belief that Mexico needed a civilian regime; although it now had a military president, he could be viewed as an instrument for consolidating peace in the country and, once this was accomplished, be expended with. But the constitutional amendment of 1890 opened their eyes to the possibility — very soon to be a fact — that the general was here to stay. Romero Rubio's ambition was not realized; he died in 1895. The young liberals either accepted high posts offered to them by the Díaz government or found consolation in the rapidly developing economy as leaders in banking and industrial corporations. Here they merged with the Escandóns and Barróns and with a group of French, British, and American businessmen like Thomas Braniff, a railroad constructor and then financier and hacendado. And so in time a new oligarchy of bankers, manufacturers, and hacendados arose out of the fusion of aristocrats, foreign merchants and liberal lawyers. The latter in particular came to accept the loss of freedom as a necessity during the transitional period between the priest-led Mexico prior to 1855 and the democracy which they were convinced would some day become a reality. This ideology was a convenient adaptation of Comte's stages of human evolution; the liberals themselves became known as *"científicos,"* the believers in science. Their ideologist, the mathematician Francisco Bulnes, justified the Díaz regime in 1899[17] with the theory that

wheat is superior in food value to maize and that consequently the maize-eating peoples (that is the immense majority of the Mexican nation) were inferior to the wheat consumers (that is the ruling oligarchy). Another leading intellectual of this group was the historian Justo Sierra, who had
supported Díaz as early as 1878 with his concept of "scientific politics" and a call for a strong government.[18]

The man who was to become the head of the *científicos*
was José Yves Limantour, son of a French financier who had
augmented his fortune by purchasing nationalized ecclesiastical properties. Born in 1854 — almost all leading *científicos*
were born in the decade of 1850–1860 — Limantour occupied government posts from an early age and edited a legal
journal. Opportunity knocked on his door in 1892 when Matías Romero, who had accepted the ministry of finance temporarily in a moment of economic crisis, brought the lawyer
of French descent into the ministry. Romero resigned at the
beginning of 1893, leaving the ministry in the hands of Limantour. Limantour was already rich, certainly the richest of
the *científicos*, and he now aspired to prestige and honor.
And so, after Romero Rubio's death, he inherited both leadership of the group and presidential ambitions. But he was to
rise no higher than finance minister. Díaz successfully played
him off against the popular General Reyes, boss of North-
eastern Mexico. When the vice-presidential position, nonexistent in the 1857 Constitution, was introduced in 1904 and
the presidential term was extended to six years, Díaz chose as
his running mate, instead of one of these rivals, the unpopular *científico* Corral.

From the beginning of the Díaz government, the United
States demonstrated an eagerness to set up business and invest in Mexico. To counteract possible American pressures,
Díaz reestablished diplomatic relations with France in 1880;
a year later, a new bank — the second one in the country —
was organized under French auspices in Mexico City and became the National Bank of Mexico. More difficult were the
negotiations with Great Britain, as a solution had to be found

for the renewal of payments on the old English debt. A compromise was in the interest of both countries, for on the one hand Díaz had faith in the stabilizing effect of his regime and was seeking to obtain a new foreign loan; on the other hand, the bondholders preferred to receive at least partial payment, rather than nothing, on their loan. Thus Great Britain and Mexico reestablished normal relations in the second part of 1884. Manuel Dublán, appointed toward the end of the year to head the finance ministry for Díaz's second term, reached a settlement with Great Britain in 1886. According to the bondholders, Mexico owed over £ 23 million including unpaid interest; they now accepted a conversion as a result of which the total debt was reduced to less than £ 15 million.[19] In the agreement the Mexican government reserved up to the end of 1890 the right to redeem the bonds at 40 percent of their face value. After the conversion Mexico negotiated a loan for £ 10.5 million in Western Europe, the proceeds of which went toward redeeming the outstanding bonds of the London debt. Consequently, Mexico's foreign debt in 1890 was reduced practically to the same level as it had been in the middle of the century.

With its credit reestablished, the Mexican government was now able to obtain funds for economic development. One project which was considered fundamental was the building of a railway line across the Isthmus of Tehuantepec. For obvious strategic reasons, Mexico decided that the line should be government-owned, in contrast to its general policy of placing railways in private hands, but it needed money for the construction. A loan of £ 2.7 million was granted in 1889, and the bonds given as payment for the construction were placed on the market by the contractors. In the next year, Mexico obtained a loan of £ 6 million – from European banks – for the redemption of the government subsidies with which the railroads had been partly financed. Thus Mexico's total foreign debt increased to £ 19.2 million. Then in 1891, the country was hit by a severe economic crisis produced in part by the depreciation of silver, the main item of

Mexican exports. At the same time the finance minister Dublán died and was succeeded two years later by Limantour. Thanks partly to political stabilization and hence lower expenditures by the army, Limantour managed to balance the budget and even obtained a surplus. Two more foreign loans followed, with the result that the total foreign public debt amounted in 1911 to approximately £ 30 million,[20] excluding the railway bonds. With European and United States banks, Limantour also negotiated two conversions, so favorable to Mexico that the real rate of interest on the loans decreased from 8 percent in 1888 to over 4 percent in 1910.[21]

The large foreign debt certainly did not seem excessive when compared with the expansion of the economy. In the thirty years from 1882 to 1911, the circulation of banknotes rose from 2 million to 116 million and demand deposits from 0 to 76 million pesos; total monetary circulation increased in the same period almost tenfold, from 36 million to 310 million pesos. The total assets of Mexican banks rose from 12 million to 1,116 million, which is, taking into account the gradual devalutaion of the silver peso by one half, a growth of fiftyfold in one generation.[22] Total credits granted by all banks increased from 3 million to 720 million.[23] By 1910 about two dozen banks with the right to issue bank notes existed in the country.[24] As yet there was no central bank; each institution had reserves in cash and metal bars. French influence in Mexican banking was dominant; French citizens controlled the National Bank of Mexico and also the Bank of London and Mexico, after the London Bank of Mexico and South America relinquished its control over its branch under pressure from the Mexican government and of a group of financiers represented by Braniff.[25] Mexican influence was perhaps much more extensive than ownership of stock alone would indicate for it can be assumed that at least some of the Frenchmen living in Mexico had the best interests of Mexico at heart.

The increase in banking enterprise was accompanied by more railroad construction and an increase in mining and industrial production. Díaz, who was of course primarily preoccupied with securing his grip on the country, encouraged the building of a railroad net and its natural complement, telegraph lines; together these provided the means by which troops could be moved rapidly from one part of the country to another and information could be transmitted from and to danger zones. The cutting of telegraph wires was punished at first by the death penalty meted out by the army, and as Díaz explained many years later in the previously mentioned interview: the railway "played a great part in the peace of Mexico." The centralization of power, already initiated by Juárez as an integral element of the liberal program to transform Mexico into a modern nation, was continued and completed by Díaz. In 1908 as he contemplated his long period of rule, he saw the establishment of order — called by him "peace" — as having been the necessary prerequisite of industrial and cultural growth; however, he probably gave little thought to these ramifications at the beginning.

In 1876, Porfirio Díaz had inherited 640 kilometers of railroads which consisted almost exclusively of the British-owned Mexican Railway.[26] Four years later, Mexico had 1,073 kilometers of railroad track, excluding urban and suburban lines. Following the precedent established by Juárez, Mexico began to subsidize foreign companies, now mainly American, on a larger scale. In 1881–1884, President González had granted concessions right and left with the result that at the end of his term Mexico had 5,731 kilometers of railways. However, this rapid expansion unbalaced the public treasury and the building proceeded at a slightly slower pace under Porfirio Díaz. By 1898, Mexico had 12,081 kilometers and the railroad network was basically the same as it is today. The breakthrough had taken place in 1884 when the Mexico City-El Paso, Texas, line of the Central Railway was completed; four years later, the Mexico City-Querétaro-Monterrey-Laredo, Texas line of the National Railroad was finished.[27] From then on, Mexicans could travel on land to the United States in relative comfort and Americans could also come to Mexico

City; as a result the United States began to exercise the influence so dreaded by Lerdo and all those who had not been able to forget the year 1848.

In 1910, Mexico could boast of 20,000 kilometers of railways. By that time, however, most of the network was in government hands. The idea that the nation should exercise influence on railroads was natural if it is remembered that the Mexican treasury had subsidized building them in a proportion which economic historians estimate at between one-third to two-thirds of their total cost. As early as 1868, Juárez had had the government buy stock of the Mexican Railway in order to secure representation on its board of directors.[28] Theodore Roosevelt's attack against railroad and industrial monopolies in the United States had made it easier for Limantour to wrest the control of most Mexican railways from foreign hands; Limantour had feared that powerful railroad, mining and oil interests, most of them American, might conspire against the interests of the Mexican economy and later perhaps against Mexican independence. Hence in 1904 the Mexican government, under Limantour's direction, purchased the control of National and Interoceanic Railways and, in 1908, acquired the Central Railways and merged all these lines into National Railways of Mexico. The new company had a total capital of 460 million pesos — $230 million — of which over one half belonged to the nation. Thus Mexico acquired control of 13,744 kilometers of railroads, over two thirds of the Mexican railroad system. While the first purchase was paid with the proceeds of a foreign loan, the years of 1907—1909 were years of financial crisis and, since Mexico had no money to buy the controlling interest of the Central Railroad, it guaranteed the obligations of the National Railways for over 100 million pesos. This was the basis of the so-called railroad debt which was to cause so many headaches to Mexican statesmen after the Civil War of 1910—1920.[29] The cost of "mexicanization" was high.

The impact of the railroads on the Mexican economy was revolutionary. In contrast to the industrial nations of the

North Atlantic — Britain, France, Belgium, Germany, and the United States — Mexico had, due to its geography, neither waterways — navigable rivers or canals — nor good highways. In fact, the roads were so bad that as late as 1877–1882 the tonnage hauled by mule train exceeded the quantity of freight shipped by wagon on almost all routes.[30] As is well known, transport by mules was costly and had been for centuries an effective obstacle to the development of the Mexican economy. But now the railroads provided cheap transport of heavy or bulky goods such as minerals. The railroad companies charged exporters of minerals lower rates and thus accelerated the growth of mining. The contribution of the railroads to Mexico's industrial and agricultural development was also far from negligible. The steel foundry in Monterrey flourished thanks to the transport of iron ore from faraway Durango and of coal, from a shorter distance, by railroad. And the spectacular rise of cotton farming in the northern Laguna district, of sisal (*henequén*) cultivation and processing in Yucatán, and of sugar manufacture in the state of Morelos were clearly made possible by railroads connecting these regions with the main lines or as in the case of Yucatán, with sea ports. Railways were also a factor in the flowering of the textile industry in central Mexico, for they made it economical to ship the excellent northern cotton over a distance of 1,000 kilometers to the factories of Mexico City.[31] All in all, the tonnage carried by Mexican railroads increased a hundredfold between 1873 (when the Veracruz-Mexico City railroad was completed) and 1910, and the number of tons of freight carried per kilometer increased two hundredfold. Mexico had indeed jumped from the era of mule trains to the railroad age.

In conjunction with the railways came the United States investments in mining. British ventures in the early post-independence days had in most cases failed. For example, the famous Real del Monte Company which functioned in partnership with the Count de Regla, suffered a net loss of 5 million pesos in a quarter of a century; in 1849, the concern was sold out to a group of Mexican financiers.[32] The new company seems to have fared much better but technology remained stagnant; Mexican capital was not sufficient to introduce significant changes. So the mines were sold again to foreign entrepreneurs and it fell to these to modernize them. While Porfirio Díaz was tightening his grip on the country in the 1880's, electricity produced mainly by water power was being introduced into mines. The cyanide process for extracting silver and gold revolutionized metallurgy, rendering obsolete the traditional "patio" process based on mercury.[33] Thus from 1877 to 1910, retrieval of silver deposits increased from 607 to 2,305 tons. Gold mining was even more spectacular; it jumped from 1 to nearly 40 tons. The Díaz regime witnessed the expansion of mining to hitherto almost unexploited metals: in the period from 1891 to 1910 the retrieval of lead increased from 38,000 to 120,000 tons and copper from 6,000 to 52,000 tons.[34] Investment was naturally considerable: in 1911, the value of American-owned mines was estimated at $223 million and smelters at $26 million; British mines were estimated to be worth $44 million. However, the value of the French and Mexican-owned mines was comparatively insignificant.[35] The American Smelting and Refining Company, controlled by the Guggenheim family, operated several mines and was the pioneer in introducing modern smelting processes into Mexico; with its five plants, this company was at the head of the smelting industry.

At the same time the oil industry developed with such a speed and became so profitable that several companies were soon fighting among themselves. This worked to Mexico's advantage. President Díaz requested that Doheny, the owner of the Huasteca Petroleum Company, never sell his holdings to Standard Oil without first notifying the Mexican government so that it could buy the property.[36] Díaz might have been a dictator, but he was also a good and effective patriot. He and Limantour granted the most valuable petroleum concessions to the British-owned *El Aguila* Company. Thus, the United States never held sway over Mexican oil industry as it did over mining. In 1911, one half of the foreign investment in Mexican oil was British, almost 40 percent American, and the rest French.[37]

The first decade of the twentieth century also witnessed the birth of Mexico's modern steel mill; it was built in Monterrey, an important railroad center, within convenient distance from coal and iron deposits. In 1911, it produced over 60,000 tons of iron and steel, an impresssive achievement.[38] The capital of the company was partly French, partly Mexican.[39]

The traditional cotton textile industry was relatively stagnant at the beginning of the Díaz regime. However, toward 1890 many Mexican manufacturers sold their factories to French merchants who modernized them and also built new ones run by hydroelectric power. For example, power facilities in the new, modern plant of Río Blanco in the vicinity of Orizaba, where rain and water in mountain streams are plentiful, were completed in 1897, four years after the first use of electric power in a cotton textile mill in the United States.[40] The French manufacturing concerns also owned large department stores in Mexico City, where their products were one of the chief items along with merchandise imported from France. The dynamic growth of the cotton textile industry can be illustrated by two sets of figures: the number of spindles increased from over 100,000 in 1845 to more than 700,000 in 1910; the number of lengths of cotton fabrics rose from around 1 million in the middle of the nineteenth century to 3 million in 1878, from which it then jumped to almost 19 million in 1906.

Total investment in mining, oil production, railways, manufacturing, public utilities, commerce, and banks around 1910 can be estimated at $2 billion; of this rough sum, foreign interests accounted for over two thirds;[41] Mexicans contributed less than one third of the total. Their investments were mainly in banks, manufacturing and commerce. This seems to contradict and, in fact, it does contradict the traditional impression that Mexicans were not interested in modern business. It is an open question where the Mexican capital for industrial development came from, whether from banking and commerce, or from agriculture and real estate, or elsewhere. The figure does not include investment in land; this sphere was dominated by Mexicans.

The value of total mineral and metallurgical production — overwhelmingly for export — increased tenfold during the Díaz regime, from 26 million pesos in 1877 to 270 million in 1910.[42] Manufacturing grew more slowly, from 90 million pesos in 1892 to 205 million in 1910. Total agricultural production increased even more slowly, at about a 50 percent gain in fifteen years from 1892 to 1907. However, a distinction must be made between industrial raw materials intended either for domestic or for export markets, for example cotton, and foodstuffs produced for internal consumption. The former increased much faster than the latter. While cotton farming in traditional areas like Veracruz remained stagnant, it developed from scratch in Northern Mexico, where the desert in the environs of Torreón, west of Monterrey, was transformed by irrigation; all in all, cotton harvests almost quadrupled from 1892 to 1910. Sisal (*henequén*) cultivation in the Yucatán peninsula was even more dynamic, for it increased tenfold under the Díaz regime and practically all of it was exported. Crops restricted to old farming areas and cultivated basically for domestic consumption, like sugar cane, were less spectacular; still, harvests more than doubled from 1892 to 1910 and the production of sugar trebled in the same period due to technological advances. Thus, tropical and semitropical agriculture paralleled the industrial growth. Foreign investments became conspicuous in cotton and coffee plantations, among others. Not all foreigners made a profit, however. Many abandoned Mexico after suffering considerable losses; the story of fantastic profits derived from Mexican soil and labor usually omits these casualties.[43] In cotton, Mexican hacendados managed to hold their own; the leading progressive cotton farmer of the North was Francisco Madero, who was later to become president of Mexico. Sisal and cane remained primarily in the hands of Mexican hacendados.

Cultivation of foodstuffs in the temperate zone was less successful. Of the two most important products, wheat production increased by about one third from 1892 to 1907 and maize by only one fifth, if allowance is made for the fact that 1892 harvests were the lowest in the whole period. This increase apparently sufficed to feed the population of Mexico, which rose during 1893 to 1907 from 12 million to more than 14 million;[44] this increase occurred mainly in the maize-consuming classes. In bad years, some maize — around 10 percent of the harvest — was imported but thanks to the railways, its price was kept within limits so the poor did not go hungry; this situation continued until 1910.[45] If it is considered that foreign immigration was relatively insignificant, then the increased harvests of wheat — which was not exported — indicate that the number of persons eating bread rather than maize was increasing; in other words, a middle class was growing under the Díaz regime. However, this class still remained small compared to tortilla-eating country and city poor.

Nevertheless, by 1900 it was obvious that the cultivation of maize was stagnating in the country of its origin; maize fetched higher prices than in the United States, despite the abyss between laborers' wages in the two countries. The scientist Bulnes blamed the high cost of Mexican maize on exhausted soil; its yield could of course be augmented by fertilizing and irrigation, but the hacendados preferred to devote their attention to other crops such as wheat, potatoes, red peppers, rice, and wine, the demand for all of which was increasing. Agriculture was becoming diversified. Bulnes had not discerned this new trend and so he blamed the stagnation on the habits and the behavior of hacendados, practically all of whom were Mexicans. Actually, some hacendados of the temperate zone might have been almost as modern in their outlook as their cotton-producing colleagues of the North, and their farms nearly as profitable.[46]

Overall economic progress of Mexico, though small by present-day standards, seemed spectacular to contemporary observers; it gave Mexican cities and Mexican industry a modern appearance and it began to transform the conservative countryside. During the first decade of the twentieth century, it looked as if this development would continue without setbacks or interruptions. However in 1906, threatening signs of overproduction appeared on the horizon, together with labor unrest in mining and industry; today it is impossible to say which of them came first. As is common in history, disasters seldom occur singly: economic decline goes together with social tension and the latter, with political disintegration, and all this is occasionally aggravated by natural catastrophes. In Mexico the disasters began on 31 May 1906 in Cananea, in the far northwestern state of Sonora, when copper miners called a strike for better wages against a United States firm, Green Consolidated Copper Company; their wages were three pesos a day, among the highest in the country, and now they demanded five.[47] In the ensuing riot several miners and American supervisors were killed. A few months later, stock sales collapsed, to be followed by a decline in general production of copper in Mexico[48] and the appearance of a rather new phenomenon in Mexico, unemployment, hardly known in a country where economic development had so far been continuous. Half a year later, the market for textiles began to be glutted,[49] while an almost three-hundredfold rise in cotton exports caused an increase in its price. The owners shut the factories while the workers demanded better wages and living conditions, especially in the Orizaba area where factories were run like barracks. Their delegates even conferred with President Díaz and agreed on a compromise. The plants were to be reopened on 7 January 1907, but during an incident at the Río Blanco factory, the largest of them, a clerk was killed and the company store was looted and then burned. The government's reaction was brutal: federal troops killed several hundred people and the next day executed several members of the rural mounted police who had refused to fire on the crowd. All this hit Mexico like a bombshell. The public suddenly realized that not everything was well with the regime. True, Díaz could still enforce law and order, but at what price and for how long?

In the United States the crisis became known as the Panic of 1907 and had no serious consequences but in Mexico it affected the whole economy. Cotton textile production declined for the first time after a generation of steady growth: it fell from 19 million lengths in 1906 to 14 million in 1909 and the number of cotton laborers decreased from 36,000 in 1907 to 32,000 two years later.[50] Business was beginning to pick up in 1910, but by this time it was too late to reverse the trend. Many decisive events had occurred in the meantime.

As has been said above, almost all the banks of the country were organized as commercial banks and bank loans were legally restricted to six months or less; hence they could not grant to the hacendados the long-term credit so much needed for the development of agriculture. However, there was a way around this requirement: a tacit agreement was made between the banker and borrower that the short-term loan would be extended indefinitely. This became a common practice, especially as the clients belonged more or less to the same social group as most bankers. The system was reminiscent of the ecclesiastical loans of the late colonial era. In 1907, of the total bank credits for 631 million pesos, over 90 percent were legally short-term, although many of them, perhaps most of them, were in fact long-term loans granted to landowners. It is not known to what degree the hacendados used the loans for agricultural improvements or to cover their personal expenses and maintain an aristocratic style of life; a few of them may have diverted the funds to the purchase of urban real estate or productive investments other than agriculture, especially manufacturing. The latter certainly showed considerable foresight, as will be seen later. The subterfuge by which long-term loans appeared to be short-term, of course presented constant danger to the liquidity of banks;

the Panic of 1907 brought them to the brink of bankruptcy.[51] They curtailed the credit when it was most needed and called in the swollen debts. Many farmers were ruined, or in imminent danger of being so; their spokesman Esquivel Obregón, himself a landowner, wrote several newspaper articles accusing the banks of bad faith; though he obviously displayed ignorance of international economy, in the already heated atmosphere, his argument was bound to stick. The public discovered an additional reason to hate the *científicos*. Even the largest landholders felt the pinch; for example, the Madero family in the North, with interests in agriculture, textile manufacture, wine distilleries, mining and refining, rolling mills and banking, and with a combined fortune of almost 50 million pesos or $25 million.[52] The crisis especially hit cotton exports from the future president's farms; as late as 1910, the Madero family's debts to various Mexican banks were said to total 8 million pesos.

In 1908, Limantour, the finance minister, found a temporary way out by getting the three largest banks in Mexico to agree to form the Bank for Irrigation Works and Agricultural Development. The new institution promptly obtained a foreign loan of $25 million, or 50 million pesos; its proceeds replenished the coffers of commercial banks, the debtors nominally repaying their short-term debts, and, in exchange, mortgaging their haciendas to the new government bank. Such borrowers were able to save their properties — for the time being at least — for now the banks' pressure on them was relieved. The board of directors of the bank was controlled by the well known *científicos*; hence it is not surprising that the bank actually helped less than one hundred large debtors.[53] This only added more fuel to the fire.

As long as there was prosperity, landowners and other members of the upper and middle classes did not openly oppose such manifestations of favoritism; they were taken for granted and were considered the price one had to pay for economic development. As long as dictatorship meant progress, it was tolerated as a lesser evil. Once prosperity turned into a depression, however, the usefulness of the regime began to be questioned. The so-called Liberal party, a little group of radical journalists centered around Ricardo Flores Magón, had been agitating against Díaz for years and recently, since the publication of its program on 1 July 1906 in the United States, had increased its influence among the youth. At the same time, the middle classes, impoverished by the crisis and incited by the followers of General Reyes, were pointing an accusing finger at the clique of the *cientificos*; now even the upper classes with close government connections began to fear that order and peace, so elaborately built and maintained by the dictator, might go with him. Stability depended on one single person. If this person died, would Mexico return to disorders again? It was necessary to select a successor, that is a Vice-President who would be just as able as Díaz but who would be a civilian, not an army man, for now the Mexican people were ready for democracy; a man who would guarantee the peace and order needed by large industrial, mining and mercantile concerns, as well as political freedom. Vice-President Corral was hardly the man for the task.

There was another important factor: a generation gap which cut across class lines. Practically all cabinet members and almost all state governors were over sixty-years-old; most of them had been in office more than a decade. Most *cientificos*, the technical advisers, were only in their fifties. The present regime offered little prospect of change, for in the event of the president's death, Vice-President Corral would carry on with all the rest of the aging *cientificos* considered already old by men in their twenties and thirties, who also had their ideals, their ambitions for power or wealth or social status.[54] It was fruitless to preach the virtue of peace to these young men: to them dictatorship appeared to be the worst evil; unlike their fathers, they were not raised during civil wars.

But President Díaz had not lost his political sense. Perhaps sincerely wishing to satisfy the growing general discontent and guide the nation through the transition period up to the moment of his end, perhaps only maneuvering with the expectation of crushing his enemies in due time, the general declared at the beginning of 1908 that he would retire in 1910, at the end of the present term, and that he welcomed the formation of an active opposition party. "The nation is ready for her ultimate life of freedom," he declared. The declaration created a sensation in Mexico. Here the dictator himself offered to terminate his dictatorship and replace it by liberty as originally promised by the 1857 Constitution; it seemed entirely in agreement with the dictum of Bulnes that "the successor of Porfirio Díaz should be the Law."

One man took the general at his word. Francisco Madero, a member of one of the richest families of Mexico, had studied business administration in Paris and agricultural economics in California. In the autumn of 1893 the twenty-year-old Madero returned and devoted the following fifteen years to cotton farming on his father's land, as well as on other properties he leased, through which he amassed personal capital in excess of $250,000.[55] Like many, if not most Mexicans of the time, he felt a sincere admiration for the president, but he had an equally sincere faith in democracy and in the necessity of introducing full freedom as promised by the Constitution of 1857. In contrast to so many other educated Mexicans who felt the need for a change, Madero was financially independent; he had time and money, so he sat down and wrote a book, *La sucesión presidencial en 1910, (The Presidential Succession in 1910).* The book, released at the beginning of 1909, acknowledged the historical merits of the Díaz regime and proposed a peaceful change by means of a compromise: the general would remain as president but the vice-presidency would be given to a new party, the National Democratic party, which the author was about to organize.[56]

The book was a tremendous success and its author became the overnight favorite of liberal and opposition groups. It became clear, however, that Díaz and Corral were determined to have another reelection; accordingly the government started to persecute the opposition. In due time the president and the vice-president were of course reelected and Madero, now presidential candidate of the opposition party, was jailed in San Luis Potosí. But Díaz's decision to back down on his word produced terrible consequences for his country. Madero broke jail, fled disguised as a railroad worker to Texas, and proclaimed a revolution in a manifesto dated 5 October 1910 from San Luis Potosí, the last day of his stay in that city. The manifesto declared null and void the elections for president and vice-president, magistrates of the Supreme Court, and deputies and senators; Madero announced that he was assuming the provisional presidency "with all necessary powers to fight the usurper government of General Díaz until the people should choose its government according to law."[57] The manifesto also urged that the principle of no-reelection should be included in the constitution. The same weapon Díaz had so effectively used first against Juárez and then against Lerdo was to turn against him. Madero ended with a call to his fellow citizens to take up arms and to overthrow the Díaz regime; the revolution was to start on Sunday 20 November.

The revolutionaries were prepared; they had managed to stockpile arms purchased in part on the credit of the Madero family. But as had happened before in Mexican history, it was impossible to defeat the government in the heavily garrisoned region of Central Mexico. The local leader of the revolutionary movement in Puebla, which was drawn largely from textile workers,[58] was Aquiles Serdán, the owner of a shoestore. When the police came to search his house two days before the revolution was scheduled to break out, Serdán, his brother, wife, sister, and mother as well as a few of his closest associates resisted with arms in their hands in the expectation that shooting would serve as the signal for their followers to attack the army barracks. Their hope did not materialize, however, and the defenders perished in an uneven struggle against government forces. Perhaps Serdán was predestined for a martyr's death, for he was the grandson of General Alatriste, a former liberal governor of Puebla State executed by the conservatives half a century earlier. Alerted by the events, the regime tightened its controls and nothing happened on 20 November. However, when the revolutionary army under Pascual Orozco captured the border town of Ciudad Juárez — where Juárez had spent some time during the French occupation of Mexico — on 9 May 1911, the regime hastened to negotiate a conditional surrender whereby Díaz and Corral would resign by the end of the month and an interim president would call for general elections. Madero entered Mexico City in triumph on 7 June.

5

The Civil War
1910–1920

> In the confusion into which life was now thrown ..., hu-
> man nature, always rebelling against the law and now its
> master, gladly showed itself ungoverned in passion ... The
> sufferings which revolution entailed ... were many and ter-
> rible, such as have occurred and always will occur, as long
> as the nature of mankind remains the same.
>
> Thucydides, "Corcyraean Revolution,
> *The History of the Peloponnesian War*

In the crowd that greeted Madero at the railroad station in
Mexico City was Emiliano Zapata, a peasant and livestock
trader from the sugar-cane-growing state of Morelos, who
had been in revolt against the local hacendados and the government since the previous year and who had, not long ago,
endorsed the Manifesto of San Luis Potosí.[1] The manifesto
had included a clause dealing with the usurpation of lands
owned by small, mostly Indian, proprietors by the ministry
of development or the tribunals; the manifesto declared that
if such despoilments were found unjust, the lands should be
returned to their former owners. A large landholder himself,
Madero perhaps had in mind mainly the Yaqui Indians of the
far Northwest, who had been dispossessed of their lands and
sold as slaves to tropical planters of Southeastern Mexico.
Such flagrant injustice had to be corrected.[2] The agrarian
clause of the San Luis Potosí Manifesto was subject to
broader interpretation, however. It could have implied a con-
demnation of any encroachment, invasion, or intrusion of village lands by haciendas; this is probably the meaning Zapata

gave it and this might explain why he declared his allegiance to it.

By 1910, the idea that the existing system of land tenure and agriculture was not satisfactory had been accepted by most responsible Mexicans. The ideological father of reformist ideas was none other than Bulnes, who as early as 1899 had attacked hacendados for not investing in irrigation works[3] and condemned mortgaged latifundia to extinction; according to Bulnes, middle-size irrigation farms were the solution for Mexico. As we already know, Bulnes took the inferior position of peasants and laborers for granted; he was interested in economic development which he saw being hampered by large estates and their owners.   Ten years later, the lawyer Andrés Molina Enríquez dealt with the same subject in his book *Los grandes problemas nacionales (The Great National Problems).* Time was running short, and signs of agrarian discontent could be discerned; adding the social argument to the economic one, Molina recommended a division of haciendas in cereal-producing, overpopulated Central Mexico where agricultural production was technologically backward and estates pervaded by "feudal" spirit. Molina Enríquez coined the phrase, "a hacienda is not a business enterprise, but a feudal domain." Information available today suggests, however, that at least some haciendas of Central Mexico were run for profit.

The conditions of so-called resident peons in the middle of the nineteenth century were described in Chapter 3. What were these conditions in the first decade of the twentieth century? Here we must distinguish between Southeastern Mexico and the rest of the country.

Debt-serfdom was an established fact throughout the Díaz regime in Yucatán.   This was no doubt due to a deeply rooted local tradition which was intensified by the isolation of the peninsula from the rest of Mexico; even though a fairly dense railroad network existed in Yucatán, it was not connected with the railways of Central Mexico, and the tropical rain forest, the lagoons, marshes, and rivers made traveling by land from the peninsula, from Mérida to, say, Veracruz, extremely difficult. In the first decade of the twentieth century, the rapid growth of sisal farming made local hacendados look for other sources of manpower; in their desperation for labor they resorted to the purchase of Yaqui Indians from Northwestern Mexico. Conditions akin to slavery existed also on some tropical plantations located in almost inaccessible valleys of the districts bordering on the Gulf of Mexico.

In Central and Northern Mexico, however, the rapid population growth during the Díaz regime, especially among peasants and laborers, made peonage superfluous. Mobility of laborers was a characteristic feature especially in the North with its mines and the opportunity to work across the Río Grande into the United States.[4] The construction of railroads and overall economic progress had loosened the rigid relationship between landowners and their peons in most of Central and Northern Mexico.

Resident peons must be distinguished from seasonal laborers and sharecroppers. Many estates were so enormous, especially in the North, that owners found it impossible to prevent squatters from settling on outlying sections of their property. This was of course illegal occupation of land but hacendados had to be particularly careful in expelling the squatters, for the colonial laws which made it possible for the settlers in certain cases to claim as their own the ground on which they lived and which they tilled had not been annulled in the independent Mexico.[5] Anyway, hacendados sometimes found it to their advantage to have some such settlements on their property, for their inhabitants could form a reserve of labor. It was only necessary to bring them under control, to legalize their status. Thus, the squatters often became tenants. Tenants normally worked part of the year for the hacienda as seasonal laborers or sharecroppers, or both. Seasonal laborers did not enjoy some of the advantages granted to permanent hacienda peons, and their freedom was bought at the price of greater poverty. They were rarely able to pay their rent in cash so they were forced to pay with their work; if

they resisted, their animals — they usually owned a few head
of cattle — were taken away. In extreme cases they could be
evicted although this does not seem to have been a frequent
procedure; it was to the hacendado's convenience to have
them at his disposal. Thus tenants were treated as potential
peons. The hacendado was a lord on his territory. In some
cases tenants became sharecroppers, perhaps not always to
their disadvantage. The owner was responsible for the maintenance of order on his estate and, therefore, it was in his interest that everybody had some means of livelihood. Social in-
equality was taken for granted by both hacendados on the
one hand and peons, tenants, and sharecroppers on the other.
What the tenants resented were the abuses against which it
was difficult, if not impossible, to find redress through normal channels, which were often obstructed given the close relationship between hacendados and state governors and district chiefs.

Finally, tenants dwelling and working on haciendas as seasonal laborers and sharecroppers must be distinguished from
peasants living in villages on their own land. Indian villages
were a typical feature of Central, Southern, and Southeastern
Mexico. As mentioned in the previous chapter, many villages
lost their lands, or part of them, as a consequence of liberal
reforms enacted in and after 1856. Many, if not most of
these lands ended up in the hands of hacendados. Thus it
happened that peasants who had been landowners in their
own right had to apply at neighboring haciendas for work.
They became seasonal laborers and the rest of the year farmed
their own meager patch of land. Sometimes they had to rent
parcels of land that once had been their own and work them
as sharecroppers or simple tenants. This of course must have
been particularly irksome to them. The increase in the population of the villages only worsened their plight. The peasants felt that the hacendados had stolen their land — even
though in fact their own ancestors might have sold it to the
hacendados — but because it had been sold at such a low price
considering its present value, the peasants felt that their fa-

thers had been cheated by the hacendados. They felt it was only just to demand that their ancestral lands be restored to them. However, land titles were often either misplaced or vaguely drawn and this explains the enormous amount of litigation between individual landowners[6] and between hacendados and villages throughout the colonial and independent period.[7] This is why Madero specified in his revolutionary manifesto that usurpations must be revised; there was no question of outright, immediate restitution.

The situation was particularly bad in the state of Morelos — the northern corner of the ever-rebellious and vengeful "hot country" — where recent increases in sugar-cane cultivation had induced local hacendados to seek more land. There were many haciendas and also many villages in Morelos; the state was over-populated. The problem came to a head near Cuautla where large haciendas nearly choked a small cluster of villages. The ancestors of the peasants had taken part as soldiers on the side of Morelos and Juárez, and their descendants were well armed. No wonder they resented being treated as inferiors; they saw the day coming when haciendas would absorb the ground on which they dwelt. This they were determined to prevent.

Anenecuilco, the village in which the agrarian revolt started, was a hamlet with less than four hundred inhabitants possessing in total only some 50 hectares of land. As early as the eighteenth century, the villagers had fought what they considered an encroachment of their lands by neighboring haciendas. Since most of them had lost the original deeds granting them an ample area of land, they asked the authorities in 1798 for slightly over 100 hectares, or 1 square kilometer, of land.[8] At that time, the village population totaled ninety-four persons, about thiry families which might have found this amount of land sufficient. But in the course of time, the haciendas managed to seize about one half of it and, at the same time, the village population increased about fourfold. As a result, most, perhaps almost all, adult males of Anenecuilco were compelled to work as parttime laborers on haciendas. But even in the poorest villages there were a few comparatively prosperous families or individuals. Anenecuilco was no exception to the rule. Here one of the wealthiest men was Emiliano Zapata, who had inherited a little land and livestock and who became a cattle-dealer and excellent horseman. This gave him prestige and authority and so he was elected the leader of the village.

The crisis in the relations between villages and estates came to a head after the crop failure of 1909 and the subsequent high price of maize. The desperate peasants of Anenecuilco asked the nearest planter, who happened to be the state governor Escandón, to let them plant maize on disputed land. He rented the land instead to farmers from another neighboring village. The rainy season of 1910 was already underway and it was urgent that the sowing of maize begin immediately. So Zapata had his villagers arm themselves and together they expelled the renters from the fields. This was the beginning of the Mexican agrarian revolution. (Actually several agrarian uprisings took place in Yucatán in the first decade of the twentieth century, followed in 1909 by a revolt of Mérida workers, but they did not influence the rest of the country.[9])

Conditions similar to those in Anenecuilco prevailed in other parts of Central Mexico. For example, residents of the Michoacán fishing village of Naranja had lost the means to pursue independent livelihoods by 1885, when their mayor sold the title to nearby marshes to two Spaniards who drained them and established a fertile hacienda.[10] The Spaniards did not recruit their labor force from among the impoverished villagers but brought from the Bajío resident peons who felt superior to the Tarascan-speaking peasants. By 1910, the village of Naranja consisted of landless peasants on the one hand and a small group of merchants, who were at the same time municipal officials, on the other. The affluent and powerful merchants sided with the hacendados.

The villages that had preserved their land were also stratified. In the state of Morelos itself, not all villagers had lost their communal lands. A few of them had preserved them thanks to their geographical isolation, among them Tepoztlán, hidden in a deep valley surrounded by cliffs. The fact that Tepoztlán had preserved almost all its common lands, which consisted mostly of forests, does not mean that all its inhabitants had access to land however. The village was controlled by a closed group of merchants, landowners, and livestock raisers who used the communal lands as pasture and prevented the land-hungry poor from cultivating it.[11] These wealthy *caciques* naturally sided with government authorities. Thus, the whole countryside was sharply split between the rich and the poor. It is not certain if Madero was fully aware of the situation and its implications in 1910. Madero himself was a good hacendado who not only raised the wages of his workers but also gave them hygienic living quarters and saw to it that they received free medical attention; having no children of their own he and his wife fed dozens of children in their own home and gave shelter and education to a number of orphans, as well as substantial contributions to charity.[12] But Madero must have known of injustices perpetrated by other hacendados, especially in the state of Morelos. Hence he was sympathetic to Zapata, in particular as the latter was in control of the important region south of the capital and was offering Madero political support. The two conferred the next day in the Madero family's Mexico City home, located in a fashionable section where streets were named after European capitals.[13]

For Madero it was important to bring this agrarian rebel to his side. His own movement had so far been restricted to urban centers. Even the Liberal party had not made much headway in the countryside despite its program to redistribute land and abolish debt servitude. The countryside lagged behind the cities in political awareness. Anyway, in 1908 the Liberal party had split: one wing had drifted into the anarchist camp; the other eventually joined Madero's nonreelectionist movement. Thus Madero reaped some benefits from the decade-long political activity of the Liberal party.

Now Madero wished to capitalize on the growing agrarian discontent. He sincerely wished to establish a democratic government with broad popular support — after all, peasants, tenants, and peons formed the majority of the population — and he understood the need of agrarian reform. But when Zapata demanded that lands be immediately returned to the villages ("*pueblos*"), Madero responded that this could only be done within the law and then went on to suggest that Zapata prepare to disband his army. This Zapata refused to do and so they parted.

Madero was not a free agent. In order to avoid further bloodshed, by the terms of the armistice, he had renounced the provisional revolutionary presidency assumed by him in October 1910; now he was merely a presidential candidate. León de la Barra, a lawyer who had served under Díaz, was acting as interim president and there was a new cabinet in which Madero's uncle Ernesto occupied the post recently held by Limantour. Also contrary to the San Luis Potosí Manifesto, the personnel of the Supreme Court as well as the Senate and the Chamber of Deputies remained unchanged. Except for a few changes at the top, the Díaz establishment was intact. This was especially true of the army.

The manifesto of San Luis Potosí had offered a permanent military career to those civilians who would enlist in the revolutionary, voluntary forces.[14] Again, the armistice between the Díaz and the Madero armies provided that hostilities should cease with the understanding that the revolutionary army units were to be discharged, thus leaving the task of preserving internal order primarily to the professional federal army. For Madero to have accepted a deal with the Díaz regime and not to have fulfilled his own program as outlined in his manifesto, was an error which was to cost him his life twenty months later.

On the day following his conference with Zapata, Madero had a meeting with General Bernardo Reyes. In Madero's scheme for the establishment of democracy it was essential to gain the support of Reyes for his candidacy; for what would happen if this most popular army man who had opposed the *científicos* decided to run for the presidency. Even if Madero won, the army would most probably revolt if Reyes did not give Madero his support. It was imperative for Madero to come to terms with him. It did not seem too difficult, for the two Northerners had many common friends and Reyes himself was sixty, past the age when a man usually became president for the first time. They agreed that Reyes would renounce his candidacy in exchange for being appointed minister of war and that he would urge his followers to vote for Madero.

But a split which soon appeared between Madero's supporters and the radical revolutionists emboldened the reactionary segments of Mexican society. Almost all the important newspapers, some of which had opposed Díaz in the last years of his rule, now joined hands in an anti-Madero campaign. Bulnes commented some time later that "After submitting for thirty-three years to the yoke of a government-censored press, the public wanted to reap the benefits of a free press, however unworthy of freedom it might be."[15] Reyes changed his mind and announced his candidacy at the beginning of August. Some of Madero's closest followers, whose zeal exceeded their judgment – especially his brother Gustavo – organized street manifestations against Reyes and forced him into exile. Yet orderly elections were held in October; Madero was elected president by an overwhelming majority. Not daring to attack the national idol, the opposition concentrated on an attempt to capture the vice-presidency. Of the total count of over 19,000, approximately 10,000 voted for Madero's candidate Pino Suárez, 5,500 for the conservative León de la Barra and close to 3,500 for Vázquez Gómez, spokesman for revolutionaries disillusioned with Madero.[16] Madero assumed office 6 November 1911, five months after his triumphal entry into the capital. When Madero, acclaimed by the multitude, came to the Chamber of Deputies to be sworn in as president of Mexico, the traditional military guard was absent. Madero had indicated that the guard was not necessary.[17] This slight to the military was not forgotten. The army in 1911 was different from the army which had served the nation during 1860–1870. The liberal, revolutionary army had been built during Juárez's presidency on the ruins of the old professional arny of Santa Anna's times. The new army often consisted of lawyers turned officers, but even this army was regarded with mistrust by civilian presidents like Juárez who discharged part of it after his final triumph. The situation in 1911 was different from that of 1860–1870. No civil war had taken place — yet. Madero ordered most of revolutionary troops to be disbanded; but he did not discharge the army taken over from the Díaz regime. This was a professional army with officers graduated from the military academy; they had a strong *esprit de corps* and they took it for granted that the country should always be ruled by one of them and wasted no love on Madero and the civilians surrounding him. Thus plans for the restoration of the old regime were conceived in the barracks. It was not easy to estimate the effectiveness of the army in the present circumstances; it remained to be seen how the new democracy and the people would react. Thus the first attempts at subversion failed. It must be mentioned that Porfirio Díaz had nothing to do with these plots. On leaving Mexico, however, he had left behind a troublesome nephew Félix Díaz, son of Díaz's brother who had been killed in the revolt against Juárez.

The opportunity for an army coup seemed favorable: Zapata had proclaimed a revolt against Madero only two and a half weeks after the latter's inauguration; in his Manifesto of Ayala, he recognized General Pascual Orozco as the chief leader of the revolution.[18] It was rumored that Pascual Orozco, who had contributed so much to Madero's military triumph, was not happy with the new government, for he had expected to become minister of war. So Reyes, again back home, revolted in December; the revolt was quickly quelled and Reyes himself was locked up in the military prison at Tlatelolco, once the home of a Franciscan college for Indian youths, built on the spot where Cuauhtémoc had made his last stand. Zapata's guerrillas were restricted to the state of Morelos. They did not represent danger to the central government in spite of the short distance between them and the capital; on the other hand, they could not be defeated and thus were a constant nuisance. The revolt led by Orozco early in 1912 in Chihuahua posed a more serious threat, since Orozco had supporters in other parts of the country. His revolutionary manifesto proclaimed a radical agrarian reform as well as other reforms taken from the 1906 Liberal party program.[19] General Victoriano Huerta, an old professional army commander, was dispatched by Madero to fight the uprising; Orozco was finally beaten in August but his guerrillas now began to plague the state. While this was going on, Félix Díaz revolted in October in Veracruz and was also imprisoned in Mexico City. Neither Reyes nor Díaz was executed; they continued plotting a revolution from their prison cells.

Madero, however, remained faithful to democratic procedures. Early in 1912 he said: "Those gentlemen who miss the methods of the dictatorship should be assured that I have avoided them not through lack of energy, but because I am determined to do everything possible to implant democracy in Mexico. And I will do it in spite of them." Even though "in critical moments those methods can be indispensable, it would be a disillusion for me to have recourse to them."[20] Toward the end of the year, he was less optimistic: "Because if a government such as mine which has honorably kept its promises," he said to the Congress in September, "which has done everything for the good of the republic that was within the reach of its understanding, which was installed by the almost unanimous vote of the Mexicans, something that had never happened before; if such a government cannot endure in Mexico, gentlemen, we should conclude that the Mexican people are not fit for democracy and that we need a new dictator who, sabre in hand, will silence all ambitions and will smother the efforts of those who do not understand that liberty can only flourish under the protection of the law."[21] Perhaps Madero recalled the words pronounced by General Díaz on leaving the country for exile in June 1911: "The new men will soon discover that the only way to rule the Mexican people is the way I ruled them." The simple truth was that having been freed from obedience, Mexicans wished to enjoy their freedom. But they went to the other extreme: now nobody wanted to obey anybody.

Madero did not remain inactive, though; he instructed his government to study the agrarian question.[22] But this study proceeded slowly; hence, Madero was losing popular support. More radical measures were urgently needed. Influenced by Molina Enríquez's book, the Madera party deputy Luis Cabrera proposed in December 1912 a bill which would give the president the power to expropriate lands in order to grant them to villages that had lost them or simply that needed them.[23] No action was taken on the bill, however.

The president also attempted in October to reform the army by introducing compulsory military service.[24] He rightly thought that the soldiers from all social classes who were serving a civic duty should not be treated as playthings in the hands of scheming officers, as soldiers recruited from the poorest segments of society had so far been. Of course, the army officers sensed an immediate danger in Madero's proposal.

The press campaign against Madero stepped up. His personal honesty was never questioned, nor could he be accused of boundless ambition or a desire to be reelected. He remained a modest and sincere man throughout his term in office. Madero's enemies did find a weak point however. He had always been an obedient son and a dutiful relative. It so happened that the Madero family was extremely large, even for Mexico. Trusting that his relatives would be honest, Madero brought three of them to the cabinet, in particular to the all-important ministry of finance, not to speak of minor appointments.[25] Madero's brother Gustavo, member of the Chamber of Deputies, undertook the task of organizing mass support for the president. He used strong-arm methods, understandable in the light of the vicious anti-Madero propaganda, and was soon hated by the reactionaries. It was whispered that now that presidential reelection was ruled out, Gustavo would succeed his brother in the office.[26] Porfirio Díaz had never given cabinet posts to his relatives, sons or sons-in-law;[27] it perhaps never occurred to him to think of his descendants or relatives as presidents of Mexico. Playing upon the fear and prejudices of the people, the reaction was able to say that the Madero family, no longer content with its opulence, now aspired to become a dynasty.

In this atmosphere of confusion, the extreme elements of the army decided to strike. The plan consisted of freeing Bernardo Reyes and Félix Díaz and marching to the national palace which would in the meantime be taken by cadets and from which Reyes would proclaim his provisional presidency.[28] The deadline was set for early Sunday morning, 9 February 1913. The first stage of the plan was accomplished without any difficulty; but when Reyes and his followers reached the main square, they were greeted with machine-gun fire. Contrary to their expectations, the loyalist troops in the national palace had disarmed the cadets. Riding on horseback Reyes was an easy target and was felled by the first blast, a picturesque figure to his last breath. The rebels, commanded by Mondragón and Díaz, withdrew to the army arsenal situated in a building originally destined for a government tobacco factory, about 2 kilometers from the main square across the city center. Madero, at his post in the national palace, appointed General Victoriano Huerta as the new commander of loyalist troops to replace the former commander who had been wounded. The period known as the Ten Tragic Days was about to begin. An old admirer of Reyes, Huerta should have been the last man to be trusted by Madero. Perhaps Madero now reflected how useful loyal revolutionary troops could have been. During the next ten days, an artillery duel took place between the rebels in the fortress and the loyalists led by Huerta in the national palace, while an unpleasant dusty wind swept through the city, spreading the stench of the bodies of innocent civilians killed in the streets; it was as if the army, after being relegated for almost two years to second place, wanted to show who was master. Actually Huerta was only defending the palace in order to become president himself; for this he of course needed Madero's resignation first. As a stalemate in the fighting was reached, the United States Ambassador Henry Lane Wilson became an intermediary between Huerta in the national palace and Félix Díaz in the fortress. In the final settlement, Huerta was to become provisional president with a cabinet composed of Díaz supporters; still president, Madero was placed under arrest by Huerta on 18 February. Having heard the news of his brother Gustavo's assassination in the citadel, Madero resigned on 19 February. Three days later, Madero and his vice-president, Pino Suárez, were shot to death "while trying to escape." Thus Madero's hope of establishing democracy in Mexico ended with his death.

Huerta's *coup d'état* and the murder of Madero and his closest associates aroused indignation all over the country. As on previous occasions, the army, lined solidly behind Huerta and Díaz, had full control of Central Mexico with the exception of the state of Morelos held by Zapata. Just as in 1911 the North had dealt the decisive blow to the Díaz dictatorship, it now fell again to the North to raise the first voice of protest. As soon as Huerta had declared himself president, he sent a message to all state governors demanding their allegiance. Most of them immediately recognized the new government; others remained silent. However, one courageous man did not wait to see what the others would do: on the same 18 February, Venustiano Carranza, governor of Coahuila, called an emergency session of the state Congress which denied recognition to Huerta, gave emergency powers to the governor, and invited other states to follow. Carranza was already a man of national prominence; a son of a hacendado who had been a colonel under Juárez, Carranza had been a public official under Porfirio Díaz and then an early supporter and a leader of the Madero movement.[29] His relationship with Madero was intimate; after all, the interests of the Madero family were centered in Coahuila — Madero's grandfather had been governor there — and Carranza's property, mainly a latifundium of around 80,000 hectares, was located in the same state.

The governors of two northwestern states, Chihuahua and Sonora, did not answer Huerta's request for allegiance. The Madero movement had been strong in both states: in the former, because of discontent with the ruling clique and rumblings of an agrarian revolt, recently exploited by Pascual Orozco; in the latter, because of agitation created by striking miners and the Yaqui Indian lands issue. The governors of both states had of course been followers of Madero. Their failure to answer was viewed by Huerta as a sign of disloyalty. In Chihuahua, the army was strong enough to arrest the governor; two weeks later, he was shot while "attempting to escape," an already familiar procedure. In Sonora, however, the army was unable to act similarly.[30]

The three northern states had the advantage of bordering on United States territory, where it was never too difficult to obtain military supplies. Hence, these states became the cradle of the revolt against Huerta. One month after Madero's assassination, Carranza resolved to formalize his revolutionary program: in what became known as the Manifesto of Guadalupe, the Coahuila rebels designated Carranza, who was not a military man, the first chief of the constitutionalist army and stipulated that he would hold general elections after the final defeat of the spurious Huerta regime. The foremost task was to reestablish the constitution of 1857 with amendments that would make presidential reelection and a repetition of Huerta's illegal acts impossible.[31] A different situation developed in Chihuahua. The assassination of Abraham González, who would probably have followed Carranza's leadership, left a vacuum which was at once filled by popular leaders like Francisco Villa, owner of a butcher shop and born into a peon's family.[32] It seems that Villa was devoted to González and Madero, who exercised a restraining influence on him; his heroes gone, Villa would listen neither to Carranza nor other revolutionary chiefs. He soon became internationally famous for his bravery and cruelty. He certainly

more than avenged the death of his idols. Again different
conditions prevailed in Sonora. After the inevitable initial
confusion, the governor pledged allegiance to Carranza and
appointed Alvaro Obregón as chief of military operations in
the state. The youngest of eighteen children of an impoverished landowner, Obregón did not have much opportunity
for education, but he was imaginative, ambitious and enterprising: he invented a machine for sowing chickpeas, and by
1910 owned a modern farm of around 200 hectares.[33] His
talent for soldiering was discovered during the Orozco rebellion of 1912. The primitive, warlike Yaqui Indians formed
the backbone of his army, at least at the beginning .

Several months after Madero's murder, most of the North
was already in the hands of the new revolutionary armies. It
looked like a repetition of Madero's revolt of 1910–1911.
Yet there was a profound difference between 1911 and 1913.
While two years earlier no deep gulf separated Madero and
the Díaz regime and eventually they signed an armistice, the
blood that had been shed as a result of Huerta's actions now
precluded any agreement between him and Carranza. The revolutionaries meant to have Huerta's body or perish in the attempt. The limited warfare of 1910–1911 broadened into a
full-fledged civil war in which the whole nation, millions of
people, were engaged. The state of Morelos continued under
the control of the imperturbable Zapata; if he shed no tears
for Madero, who was in his eyes a traitor, Zapata did keep up
his local war against Huerta. But now all over Central Mexico
guerrilla bands began to spring up and harass the federal army. Some of them chose to affiliate themselves to Carranza,
others to Villa, depending often on their proximity to this or
that Northern commander.

The landowning segment was prominent in Carranza's entourage; for example, his chief of staff was a former Madero
supporter from a leading landowning family of San Luis Potosí.[34] Officers in Obregón's army descended from more
popular strata; one of his closest associates was a Sonora
schoolteacher, Plutarco Elías Calles, later to become presi-

dent. Schoolmasters, the intellectual proletarians of the Díaz regime, were born revolutionists.[35] Generally speaking, the educated people occupied leading posts, for they were needed as physicians, advisers, or propaganda writers. One of them was Mariano Azuela, born in the state of Jalisco in a region famous for its rural middle class. He had been an active propagandist for Madero and after his downfall went into hiding and in 1914 joined a pro-Villa guerrilla band where he served as camp doctor.[36] He described his own position there in a novel, *Los de abajo*,[37] one of the best novels of the revolution. Azuela's work has a unique freshness; he wrote his short, colorful portraits, in which he never spared himself, immediately after his personal experience, in contrast to several other more sophisticated writers who reconstructed the events one or two decades later in more elaborate novels.[38]

Leaders and officers of guerrilla bands, some of whom were later incorporated into the revolutionary army but many of whom went under when they did not accept subordination to Carranza, were often independent farmers or peasants living on small or middle-sized isolated homesteads, or rancheros as they have always been called. They were not laborers — in fact, they might have had peons of their own — but they tended to be poor and they of course were uneducated. They joined the revolution most often to avenge a personal insult or an injustice, not to change society. The hero of *Los de abajo* is modeled after these men.[39]

The hungry ones fought for food, the landless for land, the wronged ones for redress of their grievance; neither Carranza nor Villa had trouble in recruiting men. Although common soldiers came from all the lower classes of society, most of them probably were agricultural laborers, for after all these formed the majority of Mexico's population. The ranks of the guerilla band in *Los de abajo* appear to consist of peons; for as one of them exclaimed, "who remembered the wretched hut where you live like a slave, always under the vigilance of the master or of the sullen, bad-tempered foreman, with the inescapable obligation to be up before sunrise, shovel and basket or plough handle and share in hand, to earn the daily bowl of maize-mush and plate of beans?"[40] Many if not most peons were peasants or tenants working as parttime laborers; they felt like peasants and aspired to own land, or to own more land. Even the fulltime peons wished to have land in order to cultivate it themselves in the traditional way and this eventually began to reflect on the revolutionary program.

Not many peons and peasants flocked to Huerta, irrevocably identified with the ancient regime, despite his initial efforts to appear as a champion of agrarian reform, which managed to confuse quite a few young, inexperienced radicals. He had appointed Toribio Esquivel Obregón as minister of finance, who, it will be remembered, criticised the banks for squeezing the debts out of hacendados in 1908; he took part in Madero's fight against the Díaz dictatorship but then, disillusioned, turned away. But now a new opportunity presented itself. Many large estates were not productive and were heavily mortgaged and Esquivel Obregón surmised that hacendados would be willing to sell them;[41] he suggested that the state should extend credit through the emission of guaranteed government bonds to the landless wishing to acquire land. Thus haciendas would eventually be subdivided. His assumption was that landowners wanted to part with their property in order to make more productive investments, in contrast to the common conception that estates were a status symbol and as such had to be kept in the family at any price. Before this theory could be tested, however, the new military dictatorship became involved in mounting financial difficulties so that projects of agrarian reform were dropped.

Huerta had to fight on the defensive against the steadily growing, if badly armed, troops of Carranza, Villa, and Zapata. So far he was able to continue in power thanks to his possession of the capital; the fact that he was recognized by European powers made it possible for him to obtain a new foreign loan.[42] He thus received means to pay for imported military equipment. His survival depended on these imports and these again depended on his possession of the Veracruz harbor and the communication lines from there to Mexico City.

It was with the avowed object of starving out Huerta that the United States President Woodrow Wilson ordered in April 1914 the landing of American military forces in Veracruz. Wilson, who had assumed office on 4 March 1913 and who refused to recognize the military regime in Mexico City, showed sympathy for the revolutionary movement and thus completely reversed the policy of his predecessor Taft and his ambassador in Mexico, Henry Lane Wilson. Had Félix Díaz struck one month later, perhaps the Madero government or, at least, Madero's life might have been saved by timely instructions cabled by President Wilson to his notoriously anti-Madero ambassador. At any rate, the death of Madero and the existence of a military dictatorship in Mexico was at the beginning of March a tragic *fait accompli*. But United States occupation of Veracruz provoked a reaction unforeseen by Wilson. He did not know that the memories of the 1846–1848 war were still alive though dormant in Mexico. There had really been no xenophobia under Porfirio Díaz and foreigners, especially Americans, were welcome. This feeling continued under Madero. But the disappearance of government authority as a result of the Reyes-Díaz uprising made it possible for an American ambassador to temporarily become the arbiter of Mexican politics and to tip the balance in favor of the reaction. If Huerta was known to owe his power, at least in part, to the ambassador's intervention, the American occupation of Veracruz, directed against him, now gave him an opportunity to appear before the Mexican public as a defender of national sovereignty against foreign intervention and, thereby, to gain some popularity in a country where foreign invasions had been a common experience in the nineteenth century. It could be pointed out that Veracruz was not far from the Tampico oil fields and hence that the American intervention in Mexican domestic affairs was a pretext to get a permanent foothold on the national territory; were not the constitutionalists getting their supplies from the United States?

Had not Madero himself invaded Mexico from the neighboring country? To Wilson's surprise, not only Huerta but also Carranza condemned the aggression.[43] Mexican sensibilities were such that had Carranza not done so, he would have been branded as an American agent and the cause of the revolution would forever have been linked with the powerful neighbor. Whatever President Wilson's true intentions, he did contribute to Huerta's downfall: the latter resigned in July 1914 and went into exile. In November the perplexed United States troops evacuated Veracruz after over half a year of occupation.[44]

As long as Huerta held Mexico City, the revolutionary factions were united in the decision to punish the usurpers; this was the *raison d'être* of the revolution. But it was also understood that this would only be the first step, after which extensive reforms would follow. Of the several issues that were on the revolutionists' minds, two — involving the Spaniards and the church — were echoes of past revolutionary struggles. Others such as economic imperialism and economic nationalism, were just beginning to take shape. So agrarian reform became the new, central issue. At the beginning it was justified as a punishment of the Díaz supporters. As early as 4 March 1913, two weeks after Madero's murder, a San Luis Potosí schoolteacher demanded the confiscation of all haciendas belonging not only to Huerta, Félix Díaz, and their associates, but also those belonging to supporters of Porfirio Díaz, and their division into lots of 10 hectares for each family. This political measure would obviously have deep social significance, as most hacendados in the republic had after all supported Díaz.[45] This schoolteacher, a former Madero enthusiast, did not mention the estates of the Madero family, but it must have been obvious that under the cloak of a simple political measure, a radical agrarian reform was being proposed. Several months later, one of Carranza's generals divided an estate belonging to Félix Díaz; a few similar subdivisions followed.[46] But Carranza would not be deflected from his main war aim, the defeat of Huerta. Since landowners were men with a tradition of leadership, Carranza did not want to estrange them from the movement.

Now that Huerta was gone, keen competition arose between the revolutionary factions for popular support. Which one of them represented the true revolution? The rivalry between Carranza and Villa became more intense. An attempt to patch up the differences made during a convention in the town of Aguascalientes failed in November 1914[47] and, as the United States had just evacuated Veracruz, a new civil war without foreign interference began between the revolutionary factions. Zapata joined Villa and together they expelled Carranza and Obrégon from Mexico City, where they had been since August. Zapata did not have to fear Villa, at least not for the moment, because the latter's base was in the North. So the two got together in Mexico City; a unique photograph was taken of them in December, with the uninhibited Villa occupying the presidential chair and the distrustful Zapata sitting on his left. Carranza withdrew to Veracruz and his cause seemed to be lost; most of the country was now in the hands of the Villa-Zapata coalition which represented the more popular elements of the country. In order to win peasants over to his side, Carranza proclaimed the need for the formation of small holdings, the dissolution of latifundia, and the restitution of lands unjustly taken from villages. A manifesto known as "Additions to the Plan of Guadalupe" was followed in January 1915 by a corresponding decree. Its author was Luis Cabrera, now Carranza's finance minister. Thus, Carranza scored a point in the ideological war.

Equally important was the promise in the manifesto to introduce legislation for the improvement of the conditions of wage-earners. The 1906–1907 strikes had revealed the power of the working class and Liberal party members and industrial workers had been active in the Madero revolution. Taking advantage of the freedom under Madero, a few former leaders of the Liberal party in Mexico City together with several European socialists founded a center called *Casa del Obrero Mundial* (House of the Worker of the World) in 1912 which spread anarcho-syndicalist ideas.[48] Carranza found it to his convenience to renew the relationship betwen labor and the revolution, interrupted under Madero and Huerta. His generals, Obregón as well as the latter's friend, Calles — two men from the progressive state of Sonora — had taken the initiative by introducing minimum wages in areas controlled by them in the first part of 1914; similar action was taken elsewhere by other progressive, young generals. Hence, when Carranza and Obregón entered the capital in the summer of 1914, they established friendly relations with labor leaders.[49] Finally, in February 1915, the Carranza government and the leaders of the *Casa* signed an agreement by which Carranza promised laws for the betterment of the working class in exchange for political support. Here was a weapon which was beyond the reach of Zapata and Villa. While Carranza was making an alliance with urban workers and simultaneously competing with Villa and Zapata for the peasants' support, General Obregón reorganized his forces and in April 1915 utterly routed Villa's army near Celaya, between Querétaro and Guanajuato, in the bloodiest battle of Mexican history. Barbed wire and trenches, then the latest European fashion, proved effective against Villa's hitherto invincible cavalry.[50] The battle proved to be decisive. Other battles followed; in one of them Obregón lost his right arm. Villa's power waned and by the first week of October he abandoned the entire North save for Chihuahua; Zapata's army left Mexico City in August 1915 and thereafter remained confined to Morelos and parts of neighboring states. Thus the constitutionalists effectively controlled the whole country except parts of the Northwest and the sugar-cane district south of Mexico City. Despite his antipathy for Carranza, Wilson could not help but recognize his government on 19 October, 1915. It looked as though Mexico could enjoy some peace after five years of civil strife. But this was not to be. Parts of the country continued to be devastated by guerrillas and neither Villa nor Zapata would give up their strongholds.

Nevertheless, Carranza was firmly established in power; the

reaction was completely beaten. Felix Díaz's attempt, in February 1916, to start a new revolution with slogans of agrarian reform, intended to bring confusion into revolutionary ranks, collapsed.[51] Perhaps in order to attract Villa, Díaz had somewhat copied Villa's agrarian decree of May 1915 in his own manifesto, but it could not be expected that the latter would second a movement sponsored by Madero's assassin, even if it were disguised as an agrarian reform. Meanwhile, Carranza strengthened his government in March 1916 by appointing Obregón, his best general, as minister of war. At the same time, he gave the ministry of foreign relations to his son-in-law Cándido Aguilar.[52] Carranza did not have to worry about the possibility of another United States invasion of Mexico since Wilson was becoming more and more entangled in World War I.

The time had arrived to hold elections for a national Congress that would formulate a new constitution embodying the aspirations of millions of peasants and laborers who had so generously sacrificed themselves during the revolution. What could the government now offer them? The mood of revolutionary intellectuals was analogous to that prevailing in 1856–1857, but now there was a different objective: then the liberals wished to destroy the power of the church; now the revolutionaries felt similarly about the haciendas. They felt that now that the ordeal was behind them, a new, better constitution would be the result. With these thoughts the deputies who had been elected in October 1916 assembled the following month in Querétaro, which was the place selected by Carranza to underline the similarity between the present situation and the triumph of Juárez over Maximilian half a century before.

Carranza submitted his own draft of the constitution which basically did not go beyond amending several political articles of the existing 1857 Constitution: he recommended no reelection for president or for state governors, elimination of the vice-presidency — the office being resented because of the way in which Díaz had used it for his political maneuvering — and so on; and he proposed a few additions to Article 27, which specified that no corporation could own real estate and which had been used to deprive villages of their common lands. It was obvious to everyone that the agrarian reforms proposed by the liberal program had failed and that, barring exceptions, Indian peasants had not become independent farmers. Carranza recognized the right of villages to own property but he reaffirmed the clause prohibiting the church from owning real estate; finally he suggested that banks should be allowed to accept mortgages, an important proposal in view of the banking situation discussed earlier.[53]

In December it became clear, however, that Congress or at least its most articulate members — among them the young officer from Michoacán Francisco Mújica — wished to include profound social and economic reforms in the constitution.[54] There was a generation gap between Carranza and the great majority of revolutionists, deputies, civilians, and army men under him. Carranza was born in 1859; the others, including Obregón were twenty or more years younger. Some Madero supporters now working for Carranza, for instance Luis Cabrera, were somewhat older but they were soon to be replaced by their younger colleagues. In group photographs in which he appears surrounded by his associates, Carranza with his grey beard looks like a patriarch. The day was not far away when he would be thought of as an obsolete figure. However, age was not the only divisive factor. Another element was social position: Carranza and his chief of staff who was thirty years his junior belonged to the upper class while most deputies were not only young, but from the middle class.

It was these new men from the middle class who succeeded in introducing agrarian reform into Article 27 of the constitution: the text of the amendment began by stating that property of land is vested originally in the nation which in turn may transfer it to private persons. This idea paraphrased the old Spanish principle according to which property is originally vested in the king who has the right to make grants of it to individuals; as early as 1912 Luis Cabrera had said that the only country from which Mexico could learn was New Spain. Hence according to Article 27, the nation could and would impose restrictions on private property in order to achieve an equitable distribution of wealth, to break up latifundia, foster small and middle-size farms, create new settlements by endowments of land, and develop agriculture. Villages lacking enough land to be relatively self-sufficient would receive it from adjoining large properties. Grants of land to villages made thus far, in accordance to Carranza's 1915 decree, were hereby confirmed. Here again the text of the article echoed the viceregal legislation concerning the breaking up of latifundia in favor of villages and new settlements. According to the new article, all land lost by villages since the 1856 disentailment law would be returned to them; restitutions carried out so far according to the 1915 decree were hereby confirmed. Thus the disentailment procedures carried out by Lerdo and Juárez were to be reversed. Furthermore, the president could annul grants made under Porfirio Díaz, as a result of which land and natural wealth had been monopolized by both individuals and companies.

Not satisfied with stating a general program for agrarian reform, the constitution specified that the federal and state congresses would issue laws concerning the division of large estates, whereby the owners should break up and sell in easy payments all land in excess of a specified amount. The large estate owners would receive bonds of a new public debt as a guarantee of the payment; the buyers would not be permitted to sell until they had completed their payments to the former owners. It remained to be seen if enough people found it profitable to purchase land; while hacendados could be forced to divide their properties by the threat of expropriation, no one could force people to make an unprofitable investment in poor land. Furthermore, not many persons could be expected to buy if there was hope of obtaining free land or if they feared losing the recently acquired land as a result of a future, more radical, reform. At any rate, it appears that the 1917 Constitution, far from introducing socialism, implemented the proposals of some 1856 liberals who had dreamt of a middle class of landowners as the solution to Mexico's perennial troubles. The same spirit inspired another section of the article which offered to safeguard the communal use of village lands pending the preparation of a law dealing with their division among the users.

In a deliberate departure from the 1856 internationalist spirit, section 1 of Article 27 specified that only Mexican citizens and Mexican companies could own land; the government could, however, concede this right to foreigners willing to renounce the protection of their governments. Another paragraph reserved the direct ownership of all subsoil wealth to the Mexican government which could grant concessions for its exploitation to individuals or companies. This departure from the mining laws of the Díaz era was again reminiscent of Spanish colonial legislation. Moreover, it was a manifestation of growing Mexican nationalism, for at present almost all mines and all oil fields were in the hands of foreigners; the provision was bound to breed trouble between Mexico and some other countries.

In a measure designed to modernize the country's economic structure as well as to hit the Díaz plutocracy, Article 28 reserved the issue of banknotes to a single, government-controlled bank. Again, this provision was not going to be popular among those foreigners who held the controlling interest in Mexican banking. Luis Cabrera, as finance minister, had just ordered — at the end of 1916 — a provisional attachment of the banks: the government forced them to deliver their reserves in precious metal, valued at over 50 million pesos, and, thus, brought the metallic peso back into circulation. After four years of monetary chaos, the peso was stabilized at its prerevolutionary exchange rate of 2 pesos to $1.00 United States. Since the government was unable to set up the national bank of issue, only coins circulated in the country; this lasted until the formation of the Bank of Mexico in 1925.[55]

Another attack against the former laissez-faire policy was presented in Article 123, devoted to the protection of wage-earners. Some of its sections codified protective measures already accepted in more advanced countries, measures such as establishment of the eight-hour day; other sections reflected local conditions. This is especially true of provisions regarding strikes, a weapon labor had been using so effectively in recent years. The impression is that while the constitution made lock-outs of workers by employers difficult, it made strikes fairly easy; it was felt that this was the only way to raise the traditional, low wages of Mexican workers. Having reduced the presidential term to its original four years, the constitution provided for presidential and congressional elections in the near future.

Carranza took the oath to obey the constitution on 31 January 1917. He might have had misgivings about its social and economic clauses but he did not worry about them, as they had to be implemented by special laws, a time-consuming procedure in itself. However, the nationalistic spirit of the document probably pleased him; even before his inauguration as president on 1 May, Carranza was embroiled in difficulties with Woodrow Wilson. Although he proclaimed Mexican neutrality after the United States declared war against Germany in April, Carranza let it be known that his sympathies were with Germany. In the end, in order to avoid trouble with its southern neighbor, the United States State Department approved the shipment of ammunition to the Mexican government. Mexico learned how to take advantage of the United States' involvement in World War I.[56]

Following the familiar pattern, Carranza was able to get his followers elected as governors of most states; a few of them were his relatives: for instance, his son-in-law General Cándido Aguilar left the cabinet to become governor of Veracruz, his home state. Relatives of his closest associates were also favored, such as the brother of his finance minister who was elected to the governorship of his home state, Puebla.[57] But Carranza was not always successful; for example, in Sonora, General Plutarco Elías Calles, known to owe allegiance to Obregón, was at the helm. The latter resigned as war minister on the very same day Carranza was sworn in as constitutional president; for "reasons of health," Obregón gave up his commission as general and returned to his farm in Sonora. Obregón, a widower with two children since 1907, had remarried a year before[58] and his resignation could be interpreted as a desire to turn his attention to his personal life and, in view of his physical disability, perhaps retire altogether from public life. But of course it was construed rather as an indication that he did not wish to be held responsible for Carranza's future policy and that he would aspire to the presidential candidacy in 1920. Iturbide, Guerrero, Santa Anna, and Díaz had all resigned and withdrawn to their haciendas before taking the leap to supreme power; now of course the term "hacienda" had fallen into disuse, but the mechanics of the situation were identical. It had become a tradition in Mexico that those who seek to become national leaders, *caudillos,* must feel strong enough to retire temporarily from a position of power. Had Obregón remained in Carranza's cabinet, he might have succeeded to the presidency without bloodshed. Unfortunately, tradition required that a national leader stage a military revolt, preferably from his home state.

Obregón had good reasons to believe that peasants and workers would support him. The majority of Congress was dissatisfied with the slow pace of the agrarian reform;[59] even the president's son-in-law was showing some impatience. Local agrarian commissions continued to grant land to villages, however, and up to 1920 villages had received 132,000 hectares. But an agrarian reform law promised by the constitution was not even submitted to Congress. Like Madero before him, Carranza seemed to lack a sense of urgency. Meanwhile, rising prices forced wage-earners to strike for higher wages; as employers were not in the habit of raising wages of their own accord, they simply had to be forced to do so. Many strikes were suppressed by the government, however. As a man estranged from the government, Obregón was in a position to capitalize on the agrarian and labor discontent. Although held to be a partisan of social reforms and the inspiration behind the radical articles of the constitution, he had not really made his views clear; he refused to be pinned down on a question of political theory. However, he was known as a hard-boiled realist with a keen sense of humor, uncommon in Mexican statesmen.

On 1 June 1919 Obregón announced his long-awaited candidacy. While acknowledging Carranza's merits, Obregón said that unscrupulous leaders had betrayed the revolution. He implicitly condemned the recent assassination of Emiliano Zapata; thereby making an obvious bid for agrarian and, in general, popular support. A new leadership was needed, said Obregón, which he would provide. And yet Obregón would not identify himself with any group or ideology; he stated that he was not offering any program, for programs "are little better than rhymed prose."[60] Two months later, however, he signed a secret pact with the Regional Confederation of Mexican Workers (CROM) — a federation of labor unions founded a year before — in which in exchange for the support of his candidacy he committed himself to foster the rights of wage-earners and to create a ministry of labor headed by a man recommended by labor; this meant that the CROM would recommend its leader Luis Morones, a former electrician. Consequently, far from remaining above programs and parties, Obregón accepted a very definite program benefiting a certain group and even a certain individual. By joining with labor, Obregón followed in the footsteps of Carranza, who had done so on a small scale in 1914.

At this stage, Carranza still could have decided to back Obregón and later events showed that it was folly not to have done so. Carranza could not have been reelected anyway, so why not leave the presidency to his former war minister? Instead, Carranza picked as his candidate the Mexican ambassador to the United States Bonillas; it was a poor choice for ambassadors to Washington could be suspected of having sold out to the United States. Obregón, on the other hand, was powerful and moreover he was known to favor radical reforms, while Bonillas, once president, would probably listen to Carranza's advice; the sacred principle of no reelection would thus be thwarted. These motives were attributed to the president by the opposition. But there was an idealistic streak in Carranza; after all, his revolt against Huerta could not have been motivated by thirst for power or money. He believed in a government of civilians, not of any army men. Carranza and Bonillas, two civilians, were a poor match for the host of generals. The situation differed from earlier conflicts between the army and the civilian government, however. The military revolt against Madero had been a reactionary movement. Although the Díaz uprising against Lerdo could not be viewed as reactionary, the Díaz regime turned out to be more conservative than civilian governments of Juárez and Lerdo. Now the army, or at least its most popular representative, was more progressive than civilians like Carranza, Cabrera, or Bonillas. With his victory over Huerta, Carranza undermined the very foundations of the system to which Madero and he were tied.

Obregón did not refer to Zapata's assassination in vain. The new leader of the Zapata movement Gildardo Magaña, an educated young man of a middle-class background, now oriented the movement toward supporting Obregón. Zapata would not have approved it, but he was dead. So at the end of March 1920 the two forces allied themselves against Carranza,[61] an event which was to save Obregón's life two weeks later. The candidate was campaigning all over the country and, in a careless move, obeyed an order to appear before a court in Mexico City. While he was there tension mounted between his home state, Sonora, and the federal government. Obregón, in immediate danger of being arrested, managed to escape disguised as a railroad worker, just as Madero had done ten years before. Obregón's pact with labor worked; no doubt, railroad workers contributed greatly to the revolutionary triumph. The train headed south to the state of Morelos where the agrarian rebels took care that the candidate got out of Carranza's reach. Obregón's faithful followers in Sonora proclaimed the rebellion on 23 April in the Agua Prieta

Manifesto which declared Carranza deposed and the state governor, Adolfo de la Huerta — no relative of Victoriano Huerta — provisional president. A civilian, he was perhaps chosen to counteract Carranza's antimilitary propaganda.

Carranza and his close associates boarded a train for Veracruz. It was too late. The whole country was in turmoil. In the state of Puebla, the train was attacked; Carranza had to leave it and retreated on horseback with an escort and a handful of friends into rugged, forested mountains. There, in the village of San Antonio Tlaxcalantongo, Carranza was murdered on the night of 20 May 1920. A few days later Congress elected Adolfo de la Huerta interim president of Mexico. As expected, presidential elections gave Obregón an overwhelming majority and he was sworn into office on the night of 30 November 1920. A new cycle in Mexico's history had begun.

6

Social Reforms
1920–1940

> The fusion of the high and the low . . . enabled the state to
> raise up her head after her manifold disasters.
>
> Thucydides, "Fall of the Four Hundred,"
> *The History of the Peloponnesian War*

The half year presided over by Adolfo de la Huerta proved to
be useful. Now that Carranza was gone, there was no reason
for Francisco Villa to go on fighting. Two months after Carranza's death, the government agreed to grant Villa a hacienda of 80,000 hectares, where he would establish his permanent residence with an escort of fifty men selected by him
and paid by the war ministry; the unique document of conditional surrender was signed on 28 July 1920.[1] The government had to purchase the property first, but it was well
worth its price of 800,000 pesos. Villa retired to private life
and probably realized his life-long dream. Where Carranza
had failed by the force of arms, Huerta succeeded by good
will; henceforth he could count on Villa's loyalty.

When Obregón took office on 1 December, nothing happened. Villa probably assumed that de la Huerta's presence in
the cabinet was a sufficient guarantee that the president
would abide by the agreement. The country which had lost
around one million citizens[2] wanted peace, and Obregón capitalized on this desire. Above all, peace was needed for the
reconstruction of the devastated country. Oil extraction along
the eastern seaboard was about the only prosperous activity. The president, an entrepreneur in his own right, wanted
to foster industry and agriculture and also to fulfill his com-

mitments to labor and peasants; but it soon became clear that it was difficult to simultaneously carry out both an economic and social program. Investors would hardly want to buy land which the government might take away, nor invest in industries that might go under as a result of the excessive demands of labor. The destruction of the old ruling classes had created a vacuum which was filled by the army and this, in turn, needed the support of labor and peasants. While the demands of industrial wage-earners were being satisfied fairly easily by the formation of unions and an increase of wages, the demands of peasants seemed to require a sweeping transfer of property, as promised by the 1917 Constitution. Obregón resisted these demands, however, and prevented their realization in northern Mexico; after all, he was now planning to enlarge his Sonora farm which eventually became a hacienda with 3,500 hectares cultivated by as many as 1,500 laborers.[3] Central and eastern Mexico, however, were another matter; here in two states, Morelos and Yucatán, Obregón carried out the revolution's promises. In Morelos the hacendados were now either in exile or ruined and sugar factories had been burned down, so the national economy would not suffer from agrarian reforms here; besides, Obregón would thus repay the Zapata soldiers who had saved his life and helped him to the presidency. This he did by breaking up haciendas and giving one fourth of the total area of the state to villages. Haciendas were left with a minor proportion of their land. For example, the rather small Atlacomulco estate owned by the conqueror's descendants now residing in Italy, lost 1,289 hectares to neighboring villages and 195 hectares to its own inhabitants; its original 2,206 hectares were reduced to 722.[4] In Yucatán, no agrarian movement akin to Zapata's had existed, for the Mayas had not forgotten their defeat in the war of Castes. Perhaps in part to weaken the local oligarchy that was ever striving for an autonomous if not independent government, the Mexican authorities encouraged Mayan peasants to demand land. President Obregón divided among them almost one fifth of the area of the state; thus Yucatán was bound more closely to Mexico. All in all, in the four years of his term Obregón distributed around 1 million hectares, eight times more than Carranza.

Nevertheless, Obregón had good reason to restrain agrarian reform. He did not have to fear the hacendados whose power had been broken; rather, he had to fear the possibility that the United States would put military pressure on Mexico. After World War I, when Europe was busy with its problems, the northern neighbor had emerged as a colossus; moreover, the newly elected President Harding had friends connected with large corporations, especially oil companies with interests in Mexico. Furthermore, Obregón was not recognized by the American government as legitimate ruler of Mexico. A campaign against "bolshevist" Mexico was unleashed in the United States' press. Oil companies were scared, or pretended to be, by the possibility that their properties would be confiscated and their concessions annulled as a result of the 1917 Constitution; American landowners, especially important in Chihuahua and Sonora, also felt strongly about the pending implementation of agrarian clauses in the constitution. The atmosphere was tense. Obregón must have recalled the dictum attributed to Porfirio Díaz: "Poor Mexico, so far from heaven and so near the United States."

Obregón accepted the realities confronting him; he limited agrarian reform basically to regions further south, in particular to Morelos and Yucatán where no American landowners existed. He could not of course revoke the 1917 Constitution but beyond his support for labor he took no steps that would infuriate the oil companies. His primary task, as he saw it, consisted in achieving the diplomatic recognition which would make it possible to obtain a foreign loan to finance a reconstruction.[5] But in order to attain the recognition, he had to make concessions; in particular, he had to come to terms with the Internation Committee of Bankers on Mexico, acting on behalf of the foreign bondholders of the Mexican public debt. Obregón decided to reach a settlement with them at any price: his finance minister, Adolfo de la Huerta, and Thomas W. Lamont of J. P. Morgan signed an agreement in June 1922 whereby Mexico accepted that its foreign debt be increased by almost 368 million pesos. The increase in debt consisted of railway bonds so far not guaranteed by the government; since the railroads had been operated by the government since Carranza, the bankers concluded that Mexico should guarantee all railroad obligations. The total debt was thus raised to over 1 billion pesos; adding to it the accrued interest, the total rose to almost 1.5 billion. During the so-called Bucareli conference which took place in Mexico City from May to August, Mexico "extra-officially" ceded subsoil to the exisiting oil companies. After this final concession the United States recognized Obregón at the end of August 1923.[6]

It was high time. Now that reelection was constitutionally ruled out, Mexican presidents had to cope with the problem, unknown to Porfirio Díaz, of picking their successor. Díaz could devote all his time to administration: he did not need to worry about succession; his reelection was taken for granted. But now, besides administrative work, presidents had to keep a watchful eye on politics: some of the more prominent cabinet members who thought themselves worthy of the highest office were preparing the ground for their candidacy, discreetly at the beginning and more openly as time went on, with the hope that the president would decide in their favor. As individual ambitions clashed and as this might hamper and eventually disrupt the smooth flow of administration, the president did everything in his power to postpone making his decision. The question on the president's mind was: would the losers or the loser abide by his decision or would they or he campaign in opposition to the hand-picked candidate? In the latter case, the men disappointed by the president's choice might unite and invite the country to revolt against the government. After all, Obregón himself had not recognized Carranza's choice and had, instead, initiated a successful revolt. This could easily repeat itself. Hence for Obregón it was essential to resume normal diplomatic relations with

Washington: then, should the dissatisfied elements rise against the government, he could count on obtaining military supplies from the United States. As long as he was not recognized, however, Washington could declare an embargo on all shipments of arms to Mexico and this could favor the rival faction, especially if it were backed by the oil companies. The memory of the civil war was fresh. Presidential elections were scheduled to take place on the first Sunday of July 1924 and approximately one year was considered necessary for the campaign. Furthermore, as Article 82 of the constitution stipulated that a future president must not be absent from the country during the last year before elections, the official candidate obviously had to know that he was the president's choice one year before; if not, he could spoil the president's plans and, of course, his own chances by being abroad. However, once a candidate knew he had been chosen, it was difficult to stop him from proclaiming his candidacy. Consequently, it can be assumed that Obregón communicated his decision to his candidate, Calles, about the middle of 1923 at the latest but that they kept it in secret until the resumption of relations with Washington were announced. This occurred on 31 August; Calles made public his candidacy on 5 September.[7]

Actually, Obregón had been considering two possible candidates: Adolfo de la Huerta, the minister of finance, and Calles, the minister of the interior. Both were from Sonora and both had been his friends and associates for years. Both held important posts in the government: de la Huerta, a civilian, was well suited for the ministry of public finance and General Calles, as minister of the interior, kept in close touch with state governors and army units. As de la Huerta had been placed in the presidency for half a year in 1920 — with the sole purpose of presiding over the election of Alvaro Obregón — he was thought by some to be the logical successor. He most probably thought so himself. Whatever might have been Huerta's qualities, Obregón decided that they were outbalanced by the bond between Huerta and Francisco Villa. Should de la Huerta become president, it was not difficult to envisage his government under Villa's influence. This of course might endanger Obregón's life itself. Whatever, if any, fears Obregón might have harbored, they were allayed by Villa's assassination in July 1923. De la Huerta's position was weakened and his suspicions were aroused. He resigned from the cabinet a few weeks after Calles announced his candidacy.[8]

Events moved swiftly toward their logical, and bitter, dénouement. De la Huerta proclaimed a military revolt two and a half months after his resignation. He counted on the support of large segments of the army, which had numbered over 100,000 when Obregón had assumed office at the end of 1920[9] and which Obregón had subsequently reduced by 40,000. Hence he had to face a similar situation to that faced by Juárez in and after 1867. In both cases, the state of the country's economy had necessitated a drastic reduction in military expenditures, the difference being that during 1867–1876 a military, national hero capitalized on the army's discontent against two civilian presidents, while now a civilian leader at the head of discontented segments of the army was a poor match for a national military hero in power. In the event that some or most of the army would revolt, Obregón could mobilize peasant and labor organizations and also purchase equipment in the United States. He did both, the uprising was crushed and Calles was dutifully elected by an overwhelming majority.

It is not impossible that Obregón had reasons known only to himself for picking Calles. In retrospect, it seems legitimate to speculate that Obregón had conceived early the idea of getting himself reelected, following the example set by Díaz who had in 1880 put into office his friend González; a person of his exceptional gifts would certainly think years ahead. Plutarco Elías Calles — known as Calles — came from an old Sonora family: his great-grandfather had been a governor and a hacendado; his father was a deputy and prefect. However, Calles was an illegitimate child; like other Sonora revolutionary leaders, he was a self-made man.

There was one cabinet member whom Obregón never considered as a possible successor: his minister of education, the writer and philosopher José Vasconcelos. And yet, as seen in retrospect and as revealed by the tone of his autobiography, *El desastre,* Vasconcelos was deeply hurt by Obregón's choice.[10] Vasconcelos's encouragement of elementary education as well as of arts and culture in general were, no doubt, the most positive achievement of Obregón's term; for while external pressures prevented the president from carrying out his social and economic program, they did not affect education and culture. Be that as it may, Vasconcelos was justly proud of his accomplishments in office and it is plausible to assume that he aspired to the highest reward. Vasconcelos, a pro-Madero journalist in 1910, had been minister of education in the short-lived pro-Villa government established in 1914 in Mexico City. His hostility to Carranza became an asset in 1920 when Huerta appointed him rector of the National University. This was a stepping stone to being appointed minister of public education under Obregón. The unique contribution of Vasconcelos as minister of public education was the establishment of rural elementary education. Elementary education, first developed on a modern basis by Juárez and expanded under Porfirio Díaz, had been mainly an urban phenomenon. Rural areas were covered by municipal schools, parish schools and by hacienda schools supported by landowners. The rural schools were of course insufficient and this accounts for the high degree of illiteracy in 1910: 70 percent of the total population over ten years of age was illiterate.[11] Furthermore, Article 3 of the 1917 Constitution had banned schools run by the clergy and it could be anticipated that hacendados would either be unable or unwilling to continue subsidizing schools, however small might be the cost. A new approach was needed. Finding inspiration in the Spanish missionary activity of the colonial period, Vasconcelos channeled the revolutionary enthusiasm of schoolmasters into founding schools in often remote districts where little Spanish was spoken.[12] At that time more than one million Mexicans did not speak Spanish.[13] As certified teachers were insufficient, volunteers were often used. Thus the Mexican rural school began; the schools not only taught children how to read and write — in Spanish of course, for the government continued the policy of integrating the Indians into the Spanish-speaking Mexican nation — but also instructed adults in arts, crafts, modern agriculture, and hygiene. The school often became the social center of the village and thus was reminiscent of the old Catholic missions. Hence, while Cabrera drew his inspiration for agrarian reform from New Spain, so too did Vasconcelos in his educational projects. Rural schools, nonexistent in 1921, amounted to 2,000 in 1925, at the outset of the Calles administration.

Vasconcelos was also a patron of the arts and under his auspices Mexican mural painting was born. Its creators, Diego Rivera and José Clemente Orozco, purported to spread revolutionary ideas; Rivera covered the walls of the ministry of education with his vivid paintings and Orozco painted murals at the National Preparatory School, once the college where Sebastián Lerdo had been rector. The most profound painter of Mexican muralism, Orozco had accompanied the pro-Carranza revolutionary workers to Veracruz in 1914.[14] The revolutionaries had settled in a derelict convent in Orizaba and in an abandoned church printed a journal for which Orozco supplied caricatures; he also made posters for the mostly illiterate masses. His 1922 murals were of course partly revolutionary propaganda. Although Vascancelos must have disliked the anti-Hispanic bias especially evident in Diego Rivera's work, the murals in general fitted into his scheme of popular education. Thus atheists like Orozco and Rivera and the philosophical idealist Vasconcelos temporarily found a common goal; soon, however, they would part company.

Whatever might have been his true feelings, Vasconcelos bowed to Obregón's presidential choice; but he remained indifferent during the Huerta uprising and not making any effort to conceal his antipathy to Calles, resigned from the cabinet as soon as the latter was elected in July 1924. Vasconcelos found consolation during the next years in philosophy; in one of his treatises he advocated a fusion of all races, out of which the superior Ibero-American "cosmic race" would e-merge.[15] (Ten years later, however, Vasconcelos prided himself on his pure Hispanic ancestry.)[16]

After Vasconcelos public instruction was supervised mainly by Moisés Sáenz, a disciple of John Dewey and a Protestant preacher — a unique case among Mexican functionaries and politicians — and by 1932 there were 6,800 rural schools.[17] Yet illiteracy was hard to beat. Despite the enormous effort, in 1930 60 percent of the population over ten-years-old was still unable to read or write, a decrease of only 10 percent from 1910; of course, the total population had also increased, from over 15 million in 1910 and 14.3 million in 1921 to 16.5 million in 1930.[18]

Now that order was reestablished in the country and the Mexican government was recognized by the United States, Calles was in a better position than Obregón to foster economic development. He invited Alberto Pani, finance minister since de la Huerta's resignation in 1923, to continue in the cabinet. Pani was a civil engineer already prominent in the last years of the Díaz regime; as university graduates, engineers, like lawyers and doctors, were part of the social elite, providing they were either successful or of upper class birth. Pani had joined the Madero movement and thereafter occupied important posts under all the revolutionary presidents, Madero, Carranza, Obregón, and now Calles, and thus earned the scorn of Vasconcelos. As a young impecunious humanist and pedagogue, Vasconcelos had perhaps hoped to be rewarded by Madero with the undersecretaryship of public education and had been hurt when Madero gave it to the affluent technician Pani. Pani's first task consisted in negotiating a new agreement with foreign bondholders. In June 1924 Obregón had suspended the payments agreed upon in 1922; he put the blame squarely on de la Huerta for having signed a contract onerous for Mexico. The truth was that now that the Mexican government was recognized by the United States Mexico did not need the good will of the bondholders any more.[19] Consequently, Pani obtained in 1925 from the bond-holders a reduction of the foreign debt. In addition, the bondholders gave up their claim to some of the best land-holdings of the country. The Bank for Irrigation Works was a government-controlled bank to which less than one hundred hacienda owners had mortgaged their property for 50 million pesos during the 1908–1910 period.[20] The Bank had bor-rowed this amount abroad and now foreign creditors could any moment put their hands on valuable real estate. In the arrangement negotiated by Pani, the Mexican government itself became responsible for the Bank's bonds and these ceased to be guaranteed by mortgages and properties of the Bank. Needless to say, the hacendados were not able to regain their mortgaged properties; some of these were used for agri-cultural colleges and other government projects, while others were turned over to private banks in 1927, especially the Na-tional Bank of Mexico, as part payment of gold and silver reserves borrowed by Carranza.[21] It was just as well. Even if a provident, but under the circumstances not very farsighted hacendado had redeemed his mortgage to the bank, he would not have enjoyed the property for a long time; it would have been divided up later as a result of the agrarian reform.

Pani had equal success in domestic economic and financial improvements. The upsurge in silver mining made it possible for the government to save over 50 million pesos in seignior-age. These were used in 1925 as the initial capital for the government-controlled Bank of Mexico, which was to have the monopoly for the issue of banknotes. After almost a de-cade of exclusively coin circulation, the banknote reform took a long time to take root. Pani was also instrumental in financing the construction of large irrigation works and mod-ern highways; the building continued under subsequent ad-ministrations until it reached the stage we know today.

Both manufacturing and agricultural production — the lat-ter less so — rose sharply in 1925[22] after the stagnation of Obregón's days and the last years of the Díaz régime. Mining, exclusive of oil, which had dropped by about 40 percent during the civil war, reached its prerevolutionary level under Obregón and continued its steep climb under Calles. The increase began before Pani's reforms and therefore cannot be attributed entirely to them. Capital for the expansion of mining came from abroad, with the exception of such Mexican enterprises as the Monterrey Steel Foundry. The capital for the expansion of manufacturing and farming probably came from some of the former landowning and banking families of the Díaz era.

Fortunately for their survival, many hacendados had commercial establishments and real estate in the cities, and with the enterprising spirit inherited from their forebears, they could now use their profits either to reactivate their impoverished estates or invest in new industries. Moreover, some of the wealthiest hacendados had been bankers under Díaz and continued in this profession. The most fortunate ones were owners of the relatively few haciendas on the outskirts of large cities, now growing fast as a result of the exodus of the unemployed poor from the countryside. Such land would later be developed for residential purposes, thereby increasing instead of diminishing the landowner's wealth.[23] Finally, some of the impoverished rural landowners found respectable positions in banks or secured enough credit to establish a business.

Idle capital and cheap labor were waiting for a stimulus. It came from Calles, who was determined to give guarantees to private enterprise. In the country, the irregular agrarian troops, organized to combat the 1923 antigovernment uprising, proved troublesome; Calles had them disarmed with the help of the army and police.[24] Agrarian reform was at the same time stepped up, and although Calles was by nature urban-minded, more land was granted to villages during his term: 3 million hectares compared to 1 million during Obregón's term. The agrarian reform proceeded without adversely affecting agricultural production. The iron hand of the new president let itself be felt even more in manufacturing, hitherto plagued by strife. Calles's minister of industry and labor was Luis Morones, a former worker in the Mexican Light and Power Company[25] and later head of a federation of labor, the CROM. Morones did not think himself sufficiently rewarded by Obregón, who had given him only a minor, though remunerative job, thereby violating the 1919 pact. Thus, strikes, which had been controlled by Carranza, multiplied under Obregón; in 1924, the last year of his administration, there were 136 strikes with 24,000 participants. In 1925, the first year of the Calles regime, the number of strikes dropped to 51 with 9,861 strikers and in 1928 they dwindled to next to nothing. Although CROM membership rose, this only resulted in the strengthening of the government's grip on labor. After all, Morones was minister not only of labor, but also of industry. The revolutionary energy of Mexican workers had in the meantime found a new outlet in terrorist activity against the church.

The church had on the whole opposed Madero and then supported Huerta. This policy proved fatal. A spiritualist himself Madero was tolerant of all creeds and he had let a new Catholic National party be organized, something that would have been impossible under Porfirio Díaz. Democracy under Madero was so complete that the party was able to have several state governors elected. In its own interest, the church should have supported Madero against army uprisings then plaguing Mexico. But it did not and, consequently, almost all the revolutionary leaders, both military and civilian, were even more anticlerical than their forerunners of 1857. Thus, Article 130 of the 1917 Constitution prohibited political parties with any reference to religion in their name. But the constitution did not prohibit the formation of Catholic labor unions. It had probably never occurred to the deputies that the church would succeed in organizing workers. Taking advantage of this loophole in the constitution, Catholic labor unions came into being and integrated a federation in 1922;[26] most of the members were in Jalisco and Michoacán. This was unwelcome competition to CROM, which had inherited fanatical anticlericalism from the Spanish anarchist founders of the House of the Worker of the World; CROM resorted to terrorist acts. Dynamiting of churches increased in 1925, at the outset of the Calles regime. While during 1858–1860 the issue was merely church property, now the survival of the church and religion itself was at stake. Catholic unions in the cities were easily suppressed, but now the struggle spread to the countryside: peasants in the Bajío — the states of Jalisco, Michoacán, and Guanajuato — many of whom owned land and consequently were not interested in agrarian slogans — now revolted against the government with the cry "long live Christ the king." In one Michoacán village peasants had just purchased parcels from an hacendado; the same land was being claimed by landless tenants and peons from elsewhere and there was danger that the peasants' purchase would be annulled by the government. The peasants saw agrarian reform as an enemy and so they revolted under the leadership of their parish priest. Many other villages did the same. The guerrilla war in which schools were burned and ninety priests were shot or murdered marred the rest of the Calles administration.[27]

Time was drawing near when the president would have to make known his decision as to his successor. All of Calles's cabinet members, except the War Minister Amaro and Labor Minister Morones, had a university degree or at least had been to schools of higher learning. Calles, a schoolteacher, felt somewhat inferior in their company; Obregón would not have cared, for his intellectual gifts made up for his lack of formal education. But Calles was not of the same stature. Of the two self-educated cabinet members, Calles preferred the company of Morones to that of the taciturn Amaro. The minister of labor believed for a time that he would be the candidate but, in the middle of the presidential term, it became clear that Obregón aspired to be reelected and toward the end of 1926 Congress amended the constitution to permit one, just one, nonconsecutive presidential reelection;[28] the amendment was published in January 1927. The method Obregón chose was exactly the same as that used by Porfirio

Díaz; once reelected, would Obregón then make Congress amend the constitution again with the object of permitting a second, and later an indefinite reelection? Or would he be satisfied with the first amendment which would make it possible for Calles to get reelected in his turn? No doubt, these questions were on everybody's mind. A year later, in January 1928, a new amendment extended the term of the next president to six years; Díaz had done the same in 1904.

It will never be known if Obregón offered the presidential candidacy to Calles in 1923 on the condition that it would be returned to him in 1928. At the beginning of his term Calles had built a political machine of his own — the labor organizations controlled by Morones; he also managed to show that he was different and in many ways a better administrator than Obregón. However, toward the end of 1926, Calles and Obregón must have agreed on Obregón's candidacy. Morones was probably the only cabinet member disappointed by Obregón's candidacy and he did not conceal his hostility.

Attempts of ambitious and able individuals to perpetuate themselves in power always presented a problem in Mexico where the educated middle classes were republican and liberal in spirit while the Indian and peasant population, accustomed for centuries to obey the landowning oligarchy, was more inclined to submit to army rule personified by a monarchy or an autocracy. The contrast between the urban middle class and the rural population was one of the underlying causes of wars and revolutions in Mexican history. Iturbide, Santa Anna and Porfirio Díaz, each in his turn attempted and the latter succeeded in perpetuating himself in power. Juárez was an exception, for he managed to continue indefinitely in office thanks only to republican and liberal support; moreover, he was the most fortunate of them because he was severed from the Presidency only by his death. But if Santa Anna improved on Iturbide and Díaz on Santa Anna, Obregón did not improve on Díaz; he resorted to the same, now obsolete and crude, method of reelection. Obregón could justify his reelection on the ground that there were no other generals capable of ruling the country. Calles himself, by his ill-advised attack on the church, had divided the peasantry. Hence Obregón seemed the suitable candidate. A few generals, however, did not share his opinion and hurriedly revolted in the first days of October 1927. The revolt was nipped in the bud, but it still remained to be seen how the country at large would react to the reelection. It seemed prudent to improve the then-tense relations with the United States; the main obstacle was American oil companies, as ever in favor of a military intervention in Mexico. In the United States, however, after the revelations of the Teapot Dome scandal, American public opinion would no longer support military intervention in Mexico. Oil production in Mexico decreased by one half from 1921 to 1926; existing oil wells were being exhausted and the companies would not drill new ones in an atmosphere of uncertainty.[29] The effect on Mexican government revenues was disastrous; immediate remedial measures were needed. Mexico and the United States met half-way; the tension decreased when Dwight Morrow, a partner in the J.P. Morgan Company, was appointed ambassador to Mexico in September 1927 and initiated what later became known as the Good Neighbor Policy. Obregón was reelected on 1 July 1928, but seventeen days later was slain by a Catholic terrorist.

He became the fifth leading revolutionary leader to be assassinated, sharing the fate of Madero, Zapata, Carranza, and Villa. While all the top revolutionaries were felled by an assassin, destiny was kinder to the conservatives and reactionaries: Porfirio Díaz died in 1915 and Limantour twenty years later, both in Paris. While Madero was put to death for having dared to disturb the peace of the Díaz regime, General Huerta died in exile in 1916 and the perpetual plotter, Félix Díaz, many years later, in 1945, almost eighty years old. Only Reyes met a violent end, but in a battle, not before a firing squad or by assassination. The fate of the leaders of the 1910–1920 revolution is reminiscent of the principal fighters for Mexican independence one century before, Hidalgo, Allende, Morelos, and Guerrero, the first three executed by the order of viceregal authorities and the fourth as a victim of the domestic reaction. Again, the leaders of the Pro-Spanish party and army fared much better; those remaining in Mexico saved themselves by promoting or joining the movement for independence. Nemesis reached one of them, Iturbide, some time later, but others like Generals Bustamante and Santa Anna lived to a ripe old age. The liberal revolution of 1867 had had a similar beginning but in the end Juárez made Maximilian Habsburg and a few Mexican generals pay for the blood of Ocampo with their lives.

When Obregón was struck down by an assassin's bullets, panic seized all those present at the banquet organized in the peaceful suburb of San Angel to celebrate his victorious re-election. As the news spread through the city, many politicians reacted with despair. True, Calles was still president — his term was to expire on 30 November — but, as the assassin himself declared shortly afterwards, Obregón was the foundation of the building on which Calles was standing.[30] Calles had not been present at the banquet for the sake of appearances, for the candidate was supposed to have been elected without the government's support; separation of administration and politics was upheld also in order to sustain the fiction that candidacy had emerged spontaneously from below and that the ensuing campaign had been carried on by popular elements. The despair of the politicians gave way to the suspicion that Morones bore responsibility for the assassination[31] and this implied the responsibility of Calles himself as the protector of Morones. Although it was soon established that only a small group of Catholic terrorists was involved, many people continued to believe that a larger plot was behind it. Carranza was held politically responsible for Zapata's death, Obregón, in his turn, for Carranza's end, and Villa's slaying could be attributed either to Obregón or to Calles, or to both of them. It did not seem to make sense that the church would strike at Obregón, who had made known, though naturally not in public, his intention to terminate the religious war. From the principle *cui prodest* it was inferred that Obregón's death would benefit only Calles, for he could now seek reelection himself.

Calles did not lose his head. Before the end of July, he appeased Obregón's supporters by making Portes Gil minister of the interior and by firing Morones. Fortunately for himself in the short run, and even more fortunately for Mexico in the long run, he developed in the following month a new method of governing the country. Now that the last great national *caudillo* was gone, he announced to Congress on 1 September that the country should be ruled by laws and institutions. This of course sounded a bit like the dictum that "the successor of Díaz should be the law," but Calles explained that by the institutions he meant political parties. Perhaps out of decency and modesty, perhaps out of fear, he refused to step into Obregón's shoes and solemnly declared that he would never again aspire to the presidency, although, should need arise, he might assume military responsibilities. He concluded by guaranteeing to the nation the conduct of the army.[32] With Obregón gone, obviously only Calles could assure a peaceful transmission of the presidency but he would thus retain a considerable measure of power, especially if a civilian president was chosen.

This happened when Congress elected the minister of the interior, a former schoolteacher and lawyer Emilio Portes Gil, as interim president beginning 1 December, for a period long enough for a national political party to organize, select a presidential candidate, and campaign on his behalf. On 30 November, Calles handed the office over to his successor and on the next day, while Portes Gil was starting his work with a cabinet basically similar to the previous one, the former president announced the formation of the National Revolutionary party which would unify the efforts of numerous parties already existing under the labels "agrarian," "socialist," and the like, as well as organizations of peasants who had received land from the government.[33] This was the instrument designed by Calles to reserve for himself the controlling interest in the government, for while he would keep an eye on the army through War Minister Amaro, he would manipulate politics through the new party he had formed.

Aaron Sáenz, a man of thirty-seven and a younger brother of the well known educator appeared to be second in command in Calles's new party. Sáenz had worked under Obregón since 1913 and under Calles as minister of foreign affairs; later he had served as governor of his home state Nuevo León and, more recently, as Obregón's campaign manager. During the fateful banquet, Sáenz had sat on Obregón's left. Discreet, as became a Protestant in a country where everyone was either a Catholic or a freethinker, Sáenz was one of the few politicians who managed to preserve the friendship of both Obregón and Calles. This was the man chosen by Calles for the presidency. At the party convention, celebrated in the first months of 1929 at Querétaro, however, Sáenz was outmaneuvered by Portes Gil and others.[34] In the first place, the federation of labor unions (CROM), formerly the bulwark of Calles, now tarnished as a result of Obregón's death, did not join the party.[35] Hence peasant, not labor organizations dominated the convention. A decade later, Portes Gil wrote that Sáenz was not a man who would appeal to peasants and common people in general but rather to industrialists, which would be natural for a person born in the manufacturing heart of Mexico.[36] So, Ortiz Rubio, a compromise candidate, was chosen. However, though Sáenz was deprived of the presidency, he went on to become the leading manufacturer of sugar and alcohol in Mexico. New cane fields and factories were developed in northern Mexico, and it can be assumed that Sáenz not only represented his own interests there but also those of Obregón and Calles.[37] Tied to Calles by family bonds,[38] Sáenz's relations with succeeding presidents remained good.

In March 1929, some generals revolted against such a prolongation of the Calles regime. Calles assumed the ministry of war and with the help of agrarian militias, defeated the insurrection; he resigned again at the end of May and left on a tour of Europe. Calles considered the domestic front safely under control. He was not mistaken. In the first place, the provisional president Portes Gil reached a settlement with the church. Both sides having made concessions, Catholic worship, suspended three years before by the clergy in protest against persecution, was resumed in the middle of 1929.[39] No friend of the church, Portes Gil succeeded where Calles, using strong-arm methods, had failed in pacifying the country. Obregón's assassination had convinced the government that it could not rule Mexico indefinitely in opposition to the church.

Meanwhile, the presidential elections were scheduled to take place in November; the official candidate Ortiz Rubio was opposed by José Vasconcelos. Vasconcelos, the former minister of education had abstained from politics during Calles' administration and had not opposed Obregón's reelection. Now that Obregón was gone, he was free to express his hatred of Calles and, thus, at the earliest opportunity he became the presidential candidate of the opposition. His favorite target during the campaign was American Ambassador Morrow and he accused the Mexican national leaders of having sold out to the United States. The campaign, in fact, was reminiscent of the conservative criticism raised almost exactly a century earlier against the liberals and the first American minister in Mexico, Poinsett. Vasconcelos's main support resided not among organized workers and peasants but only among intellectuals, his disciples and former students, all of them believers in the superiority of Hispano-American "idealism" over the United States "materialism." Hence, Vasconcelos was bound to lose. After the elections, he went to the United States where he wrote among other things, an anti-American and anti-Protestant history of Mexico.[40]

Calles returned after the elections, in December 1929, and almost immediately expressed concern about the rapid pace of agrarian reform. In one year Portes Gil had distributed more than 1 million hectares, while Calles had dispersed 3 million in four years. However, before these two men could clash, Portes Gil turned over the office at the beginning of

February 1930 to the president-elect Ortiz Rubio, whom Calles soon brought under his control. It was under Ortiz Rubio that the position of Calles was institutionalized. He became known as the ex officio chief, *"jefe nato,"* of the party, and as the "supreme chief of the revolution," a title used especially by the daily paper *El Nacional* published by the party.[41] In practice it meant that commissions called on Calles first and on the president afterwards, which was of course not conducive to the prestige of the highest office. Calles also sat in on cabinet meetings and came to consider this as his right.[42] For a man with ill health like Calles, who spent a great deal of time in country homes, in spas and visits to foreign sanatoria, this position was a perfect solution.

Thus when Calles declared, in June 1930, that agrarian reform was a failure and suggested that it should be terminated as soon as possible in order to end the uncertainty in the countryside,[43] redistribution of land in the following years dropped sharply.[44] The federal labor law issued in 1931 to satisfy the promises of the 1917 Constitution, specified among many other things, the rights of permanent agricultural workers;[45] the implication was that the traditional hacienda with its resident peons was here to stay.

Hence everybody was surprised when Calles suggested in an interview granted in the latter part of May 1933 that agrarian reform should be resumed. (By this time, Ortiz Rubio was no longer president; by his continuous reshuffling of cabinets, Calles made life for him so difficult that he resigned and in September 1932 Congress elected Abelardo Rodríguez, a close friend and business associate of Calles, to serve for the rest of the term, until November 1934.) Calles began the interview by repeating his already familiar assertion that the division of land so far was a failure from an economic point of view because of the small size of *ejido* parcels, but that it had of course been necessary to destroy the power of the landlords.[46] As the hacendados, however, could not reestablish the peonage nor revive the old farming methods, Calles proposed that the distribution of land to villages should be resumed until its full completion within the next presidential period; he prophesized that, if not in its entirety, at least four fifths of the peonage would disappear. Simultaneously, the government should force the estate owners to subdivide the remains of their properties and sell them in fractions so as to enable *ejido* members not satisfied with their meager parcels to purchase them and become modern farmers. Thus there would arise a healthy mixed economy conducive to progress. It was time, Calles concluded, to formulate a detailed program of action for the next six years. As supreme chief of the revolution, Calles was, even if in a minor degree, heir to Obregón's prestige, just as the latter had in a way inherited the prestige of previous national leaders or heroes. Since declarations of the *caudillos* to the press were considered *ex cathedra*, the suggestions of the former president were accepted without question.

Since 1930, when Calles had put a brake on granting land to villages, a crisis had shaken the world economy to its very foundations. It produced a disaster in Mexico which depended so much on exports and the world market. While the production of crops for the domestic market, especially maize, remained fairly stable, depending only on a good or bad harvest, the export crops like cotton and sisal declined on the average by over one half — if value rather than volume is considered.[47] A similar decline occurred for mining and metallurgy. The decline of silver mining and of oil extraction had even started before 1930, due to the worldwide demonetization of the metal, the gradual exhaustion of existing wells, and the unwillingness of the companies to drill new ones. The result was wide-spread unemployment in the countryside, much higher than official statistics allowed, for by custom, the unemployed would go to live with their relatives: "where one person eats, another one can eat too."[48] During 1930–1932, the area devoted to the cultivation of export crops was probably reduced by one half and the number of farm hands diminished in a similar proportion. This must have led to the conclusion that the unemployed laborers should be allowed to practice subsistence agriculture – that is, cultivation of maize – on the now unused land. Hacendados would thus be relieved of their traditional duty to feed their peons.

The depression strengthened nationalistic and socialistic trends everywhere; in the United States, Roosevelt inaugurated his New Deal in March 1933 and in April sent Josephus Daniels, a personal friend, as ambassador to Mexico. Whatever agreement as to the termination of social reforms Calles might have closed with Ambassador Morrow in exchange for concessions by the committee of foreign creditors, it now seemed invalidated. Here then was a unique opportunity to complete agrarian reform and to nationalize subsoil wealth, both promised by the 1917 Constitution but postponed for years.

The effects of the depression as well as the permissive attitude of Washington account for an upsurge of the agrarian movement in the spring of 1933. Since Calles was known to have put a brake on the reform in the past, the agrarian movement was a vague, indirect rebellion against his leadership. The question was: who will be president next? It was felt in political circles that the country needed a strong president, a man of courage and character who would be able to complete the six-year term and lead Mexico out of the impasse it had found itself in after Obregòn's death. Whoever the next president was, however, he should never, under any circumstances, be able to reelect himself. Thus, in April 1933 Congress annulled Obregón's amendment and reinforced in most emphatic terms the constitutional ban on reelection. The fact that Calles could never, not even in an extreme case, become president again, was bound to depress his authority. Now, on 1 May, Portes Gil and other politicians acting on behalf of agrarian leagues of several states issued a manifesto urging resumption of agrarian reform and the nomination of General Lázaro Cárdenas, the minister of war, as presidential candidate of the official party. After serving as governor of Michoacán, his native state, Cárdenas had occupied several cabinet posts; he was hard-working, efficient, unassuming, and

loyal to Calles. Cárdenas had the support of Calles' friends
such as Aarón Sáenz and two of Calles' sons, one of whom
was governor of Sonora.[49] They did not speak for their father,
however; it seems that he would have preferred a different
candidate. But he could not halt the tide of the public opinion and, when Cárdenas resigned two weeks later and agreed
to become candidate, Calles reversed his stand on the agrarian
reform. Did he change his views under the pressure of events
or did he simply attempt to ride on the crest of the wave? His
sincerity was subjected to a test half a year later, when the
National Revolutionary party met in Querétaro — always the
fateful Querétaro — to discuss the draft of the Six-Year Plan,
which had been prepared by the government in the meantime.

Agrarian reform in actual practice had been restricted to
land grants to villages; no hacienda land had so far been given
to permanent peons residing on haciendas. The reason was
obvious: if the peons were granted land, the haciendas would
lose not only their centrally located lands but also their labor
force. It would be the end of the hacienda itself. It so happened that not only Obregón but also Calles and most of his
leading generals had acquired landed estates; admittedly they
were small compared with those of the Díaz oligarchy, but
a farm with an intensive agriculture and animal husbandry
could be just as profitable as one of the old estates. Hence
the draft of the Six Year Plan made no mention of resident
peons. When a San Luis Potosí schoolmaster and agrarian
leader proposed at the Querétaro convention that resident
peons should be given the right to obtain land, the representative of the Calles interests, the editor of *El Nacional*, accepted the proposal in principle but stated that the problem required further study; the question was *where* peons should
or could obtain land. A disturbance arose at the meeting and
the convention finally approved the right, under certain conditions, of permanent peons to receive land.[50] From then on,
the hacienda was marked for extinction.

In labor matters, the plan was more radical.[51] The party
and the government should side with workers in "the class

struggle inherent in the system of production" and should strengthen trade unions. The plan did not specify what the class struggle should lead to, however. Given the worldwide trend toward self-sufficiency, the plan recommended that Mexico should stimulate the creation of new industries; products of the rich subsoil should also be industrialized as far as possible. The plan did not make it clear who should be in charge of this process, the state or the private enterprise; it did state, however, that formation of cooperatives should be fostered. In spite of having adopted for the program a term current in Soviet Russia, it would seem that some of its makers had in mind a gradual transformation of Mexican society into cooperative socialism. Cárdenas, whom the convention designated on 6 December as the party's presidential candidate, clarified this point in one of his campaign speeches: the instruments of production would be given "to the organized proletarian masses;" the Mexican revolution would progress toward socialism but not toward state communism "because it does not harmonize with the nature of our people . . . nor do we desire to substitute for the individual employer the state as employer."[52]

The convention resolved that the Six Year Plan should go into effect at once. Even before the end of 1933, Congress amended Article 27 of the constitution and three months later approved the Agrarian Code, a detailed law implementing the constitution.[53] Its important feature was the limit set on the division of land. In the first place, buildings of any kind and irrigation works were excluded from land grants. Also exempted from land grants were holdings of irrigated lands whose area did not exceed 150, or in certain cases 100, hectares and holdings of seasonal, unirrigated lands of up to 300 or 200 hectares respectively; plantations of certain tropical crops were freed up to 300 hectares; lands planted with alfalfa and industrially important crops like sisal might be entirely exempted under certain conditions, as also might lands devoted to sugar cane on properties with mills that belonged to the owner of the land, up to the amount required to furnish cane for the average production. The maximum limits on private property seemed reasonable enough, for it still made profitable farming possible. Landowners had the right to choose the land which would be free from nationalization. Such units not subject to expropriation were called small properties. The law also stipulated that cultivatable land granted to villages and other population centers should at once be divided into individual holdings. The size of the parcels was not specified; it obviously depended on the area of expropriated land and on the number of applicants. The grantees would be owners of their individual lots subject to the following limitations: they might never sell, mortgage, or lease their lots. Henceforward, peasants would be protected but at the same time forced to farm their land with their own hands; penalties were established for violators. Hence it was not true ownership but rather usufruct; property was vested in the village. Individual cultivation was normal on maize lands which predominated in Mexico; certain crops, however, required the combined efforts of peasants or laborers for cultivation. In the latter case, the law stated that such lands should be held and cultivated on a communal basis and that special government banks would organize production and marketing. Woodland and pastures granted to villages would remain common property. All land granted under the agrarian reform was termed *ejido* (the law gave a new meaning to this old word); besides *ejidos*, villages could still own communal property from previous years and individual peasants could retain private property inherited from their forebears as well as *ejido* lots. The result was bound to be complicated. The important difference was that *ejido* lands and their new owners would be under government control. Finally, the law made it easier for peasants to obtain land; as a result, land grants in 1934 rose to 680,000 hectares, several times as much as in the previous year.

Labor agitation also increased, however: the number of strikes jumped from thirteen with 1,000 participants in 1933 to 202 with almost 15,000 participants the following year. The tide was turning left.

By this time, the Mexican economy had partially recovered from the slump. The currency had been devalued from its rate of 2 pesos to $1.00 to 3.60 pesos to $1.00. As a result, the export balance that had slipped to only 120 million pesos in 1933, went up in one year to 310 million.[54] The Bank of Mexico finally succeeded in persuading the public to accept its notes and their circulation increased from 1.5 million in January 1932 to 100 million in the middle of 1934. The upturn in economic activity was on the way while Cárdenas was campaigning in the countryside, visiting villages, and talking to peasants. As the electoral victory of the official candidate was taken for granted he was touring the country largely for post-electoral purposes: he wished to get acquainted with the needs of the common people and to establish personal contact with them. In this, Cárdenas was so successful that he set the precedent for his successors.

It was not difficult for Cárdenas to understand the peasants. Having been born in the Michoacán village of Jiquilpan in 1895, he used to help his grandfather, once a soldier in the republican army under Juárez, to cultivate 2 hectares of rented land.[55] His father was a textile craftsman and later a small merchant. Opportunities in the village were limited, so the boy began to work in the local government office at the age of fourteen and then in a printshop. From here he joined the revolution in 1913. Several years later, he met another countryman from Michoacán, General Francisco Mújica. Mújica's father had been a schoolteacher and he himself had been to a seminary which he left to become a clerk and a radical journalist. In 1910, he joined Madero in Texas and three years later signed Carranza's Guadalupe Manifesto. He was a member of the constitutional Congress and probably one of the main authors of the radical sections of the new constitution. Eleven years older than Cárdenas, Mújica seemed predestined to exercise a strong influence on Cárdenas, whose formal education had been limited to an elementary school. They spent the years 1926–1927 together in Veracruz. The legend, denied by Mújica and never admitted by Cárdenas, goes that there, on warm tropical nights, Mújica expounded the doctrines of socialism to his young friend.[56] Thereafter, Mújica fell into disfavor with following presidents. Cárdenas rescued him from obscurity when he brought him to his cabinet on 1 December 1934 as minister of industry and commerce.

Mújica was perhaps the only true Cárdenas supporter in the cabinet which was composed largely of men associated with Calles; the minister of communications was Rodolfo Elías Calles, and of agriculture, Garrido Canabal, boss of the banana-producing state of Tabasco and a fanatical anti-Catholic hacendado.[57] Portes Gil, the minister of foreign affairs, could perhaps be classified as independent. Even supposing that the new president attempted to shake off Calles' yoke, he could still be held in check by the cabinet. Relaxed, Calles departed to Los Angeles for medical treatment.

From the first day, Cárdenas refused to live in the Chapultepec castle built on a hill overlooking the capital; it had been a symbol of authority since the time of Porfirio Díaz.[58] The president began to carry out the Six-Year Plan. Land grants in 1935 almost quadrupled those of 1934.[59] Labor agitation bore fruit: strikes rose to 642 with 145,000 participants in 1935; it was significant that, contrary to the previous year, the findings of labor courts in most cases were favorable to workers. As prices were rising, strikes for better wages and more benefits were not surprising.

After almost half a year's absence, Calles returned to Mexico and in June made a declaration to the press against the continuous labor agitation; he did not blame "a sincere friend of the workers like General Cárdenas,"[60] but the labor leader Lombardo Toledano, a son of an upperclass but impoverished family, and a former secretary to Morones. (At the beginning of 1936, Lombardo was to found with the president's support the Mexican Workers' Confederation, [CTM].) Everybody expected the president either to heed

Calles or resign. Strangely, however, the party paper *El Nacional* did not publish the declaration,[61] the first sign that the machine did not obey the supreme chief any more. Placing his electoral pledges above his loyalty to Calles, Cárdenas reorganized his cabinet, substituting his supporters for Calles' friends. Disconcerted, the ageing Calles left Mexico. When he again returned half a year later, Cárdenas had in the meantime reorganized all government branches, including the army. Finally the president had Calles and a few of his closest supporters expelled from the country in April 1936. For the first time in Mexican history, a *caudillo* was eliminated without bloodshed. But then Calles, in contrast to the charismatic Obregón, was perhaps not a true *caudillo*. The bloodless coup was surprisingly easy; it showed how weak Calles had actually been.

Having eliminated the Calles machine, Cárdenas broadened his popular support by accelerating social reform. On 1 May he invited the generals and politicians exiled by Obregón and Calles to return.[62] Most of them were classed as conservatives. Cárdenas went as far as to open doors for Porfirio Díaz Junior, who returned after an absence of a quarter of a century, as well as to José Vasconcelos, who was allowed to ridicule the socialist Mexico of the future as an instrument of Wall Street bankers.[63] As a politician Vasconcelos was harmless and therefore was left unmolested. After all, his extreme nationalism could be useful. Eventually, Vasconcelos found peace in the bosom of the Roman Catholic church; his virulent anti-Americanism lives on in the antiimperialism of the present Mexican left wing.

The president was preparing a large-scale redistribution of land; an opposition, perhaps even an armed one, of landlords was to be expected. What was needed was the neutrality of the church, which was difficult but not impossible to obtain now that the dictatorship of Obregón and Calles had ended. The new 1935 cabinet had made it clear that the harshest anticlerical regulations would be abolished: the new minister of agriculture was General Cedillo, a former peasant revolutionary and known to be rather friendly to the clergy; the man whom Cedillo had replaced, Garrido Canabal, was offered a diplomatic position abroad and his hold on the state of Tabasco broke down under government pressure and a revolt of local Catholics.[64] Garrido Canabal's decree ordering priests to marry as well as other anticlerical regulations were declared anticonstitutional. As the church was not a large landowner any more, there was a reasonable hope that large-scale agrarian reform might succeed.

Distribution of land was immediately stepped up. The Agrarian Code of 1934 had put definite limits on the breaking up of estates; the Federal Labor Law of 1931 had made no provision for a nationalization of private enterprise. Cárdenas needed a legal base for his policy of socializing the means of production, both rural and urban. Hence in September 1936 he sent Congress the draft of a law giving him wide power to expropriate all sorts of private properties or enterprises. The law went into effect a few weeks later. The president had told the manufacturers as early as February that if they were tired of the ceaseless demands of their workers, they could hand over their factories to them. This actually happened in some small mines and manufacturing plants rendered unprofitable by ever increasing minimum wages, among other things. Minimum wages also applied in agriculture; strikes became as frequent in farming as in other industries. The strikes of farm hands were led mostly by agitators of urban labor unions; the day seemed at hand when the Confederation of Mexican Labor, directed by the Marxist Lombardo, would control not only city labor but also hacienda peons.[65] The CTM might become the most powerful force in the country. This was against the president's conception of cooperative socialism. It also ran counter to his conviction that peasants were in no way inferior to city workers and intellectuals.[66] Thus, when peons of the rich cotton haciendas of La Laguna district struck for higher wages and benefits at harvest time in 1936, Cárdenas ordered the immediate splitting-up of all haciendas. Most of the land went to peons;

given the fact that cotton grew there with irrigation only, it would be cultivated collectively, with government credit and under government supervision. Hacendados kept the rest. Cárdenas commented in his diary that it was impossible in this case to bring landless peasants from other regions into La Laguna to apply for the remaining land,[67] though this was a familiar practice. As resident peons were in many cases unwilling to apply for land and the government was bent on destroying the hacienda, the local peons often had to be forced into action by importing landless peasants.

Hacendados, for their part, practiced the real and fictitious sale of their lands to their peons, renters, or sharecroppers. Cárdenas himself approved one such sale of an estate in small fractions to bona fide buyers.[68] But in most cases such sales were rejected, for it was felt that haciendas were merely attempting to evade the law and to perpetuate their hold on land and people. Hacendados who had no other property were often utterly ruined, for even if the Agrarian Code was obeyed, which was not always the case, their lives might have been in danger if they stayed behind. Azuela, always sympathizing with outcasts, described a former hacendado turned proletarian in his 1929 novel *Avanzada*. He also described, with less sympathy, another ex-hacendado who had been clever enough to find a leading post in a socialized sugar factory.[69] When the code was obeyed, landlords kept the best land, even though this might have been only a very small part of their original property.[70] Needless to say, division of estates disrupted production; it especially damaged cattle-raising for hacendados had no land on which to feed their cattle.

Division of land, which in 1936 amounted to 3.6 million hectares, rose the following year to over 5 million. Peasant cooperatives under government control — so-called "collective *ejidos*" — were established in Yucatán in August 1937; this, together with the construction of the Yucatán-Veracruz railroad, bound the peninsula closer to Mexico.[71] In October 1937 the fertile, irrigated lands in Sonora, belonging in part to United States citizens and in part to politicians of the Obregón-Calles group, were divided. In the nonagricultural sphere, National Railways were nationalized in June; this was the logical culmination of the policy begun thirty years before by Limantour. Cárdenas gave the railroads to a workers cooperative in 1938. The Bank of Mexico kept pumping money into circulation[72] and financing government projects like the new dam for the La Laguna cotton district and the purchase of farm equipment for collective ejidos. Meanwhile, reorganization and modernization of the sugar industry was under way. The main source of sugar in prerevolutionary Mexico, the mills of Morelos, had been devastated during the civil war of 1910–1920. When Cárdenas assumed office, most hacienda lands there already belonged to peasants. A few of the old private mills were working again, but they were insufficient; besides, they were small by modern standards, for each estate in the overpopulated state of Morelos had insisted on having its own mill. Using government funds, Cárdenas built one large factory for the whole region and at the beginning of 1938 turned it over to a cooperative of mill operatives and peasants.[73] A year later, the president expropriated a modern sugar factory, established in 1930 with a loan from the Bank of Mexico and owned by Aaron Sáenz; a similar cooperative was organized there.[74] However, the president's program, as expounded in his diary,[75] of gradually transforming private sugar mills into cooperatives of workers and peasants was cut short by other events.

The one industry which had not recovered from the depression, or recovered only insignificantly, was the oil industry. It goes without saying that labor agitation in oil fields increased under Cárdenas and that workers were supported by the government. By tradition, the companies considered themselves as a state within a state; they made loans to the Mexican government[76] and dealt with it on equal terms. An impasse was reached when the Federal Labor Court awarded oil workers a 27 percent wage raise plus social benefits but the companies refused to comply, arguing that the total increase would in reality amount to about 100 percent, which they declared to be extravagant and impossible to meet. It was obvious that they would never be able to reestablish their influence and that they would continue to keep oil extraction at a minimum. This clashed with the interests of the Mexican government. So Cárdenas nationalized their holdings on 18 March 1938 and turned their administration over to oil workers.[77]

Previous acts of socialization especially those in the agrarian field, had mostly affected Mexican citizens. Much as hacendados might have hated Cárdenas, they had no recourse to a foreign power. The expropriation of oil companies, however, evoked an immediate reaction from two powerful countries; Great Britain, whose subjects owned the best oil fields, denied Mexico the right to nationalize the property of her subjects and severed diplomatic relations; the United States merely demanded fair and prompt payment while a part of their press renewed attacks on "communist" Mexico. Mexico's economy suffered as a boycott by the oil companies forced it to sell oil to Germany and Italy. Many Mexicans imagined that another foreign military invasion was coming. Up to this time, Cárdenas had been under attack in his country for having sold out either to Wall Street or to Russia. In a surge of national passion, he was now upheld by everyone, including the archbishop of Mexico. Vying with middle class housewives, peasant women offered their gold jewelry to the national treasury. Never had there been anything quite like this.

General Cedillo used this opportunity to settle his accounts with Cárdenas. Unhappy with the "socialization" of *ejidos*, he had resigned a year before from the ministry of agriculture and retired to San Luis Potosí, where he had a private army and even airplanes.[78] In May 1938, two months after the oil expropriation, he revolted, accusing Cárdenas of leading Mexico to communism, and since the boundaries of San Luis Potosí were near the Tampico oil fields, Cedillo was thought to be linked with the foreign oil companies. The revolt, limited from the beginning to San Luis Potosí, collapsed in a few weeks, and its leader lost his life.

Yet it was a warning that other, more serious uprisings,

perhaps led by dispossessed landlords and dissatisfied manufacturers, and financed by the oil companies, might follow.
Consequently, Cárdenas decided to sacrifice social reform to
the quest for national unity. The number of strikes was reduced by half[79] and redistribution of land was slowed down
from 5 million hectares distributed in 1937, around 3 million
in 1938, 1.75 million in 1939, and, finally, to 1.7 million
hectares in 1940. The total redistribution of land in the six
years of the Cárdenas presidency amounted to 17.9 million
hectares. In May 1938, at the very moment of Cedillo's revolt, the government opened the Office of Small Property,
designed to protect landowners from peasant demands and to
issue certificates of exemption from expropriation to them.[80]

The reason for the change in policy was probably due, in
part, to the inefficiency of production cooperatives; the short
experience showed they were not viable. Perhaps this explains
why Cárdenas did not pick the socialist Mújica as his successor in 1939 but chose instead the secretary of war, General
Manuel Avila Camacho, known as a moderate and a Catholic.
Given the international situation, it probably seemed prudent
to Cárdenas to let the conservatives take over for a while, in
order to preserve what had so far been achieved: namely, the
division of almost one half of the arable land and the nationalization of a sizable part of public services and natural resources.

The Cárdenas regime ended in a confusion. On the election
day in July 1940 many workers dissatisfied with high prices,
unemployment, and Marxist control of labor unions voted
for the candidate of the reaction, General Almazán.[81] Some
socialist intellectuals disenchanted with the nomination of
Avila Camacho did the same, out of spite or desperation.
Nevertheless, the official candidate received the typically
overwhelming majority of votes and assumed office on 1
December 1940.

To everyone's surprise, Cárdenas did not attempt to imitate Calles by becoming another supreme chief of the revolution but left the business of government to his successor,

thereby setting a precedent for the present presidential system. Cárdenas's expropriation of the foreign-owned oil industry made him popular with all classes and earned him the stature of a national hero, and yet, in actuality, it was his agrarian reform program that had the deepest impact upon Mexico's traditional social structure and that more than any other measure brought to consummation, after almost two decades of setbacks, the social goals of the revolution and of the 1917 Constitution.

Statistical Tables

Sources: Nacional Financiera, S.A., *Statistics on the Mexican economy*, (Mexico City: Nacional Financiers, S.A., 1966). Its figures are corrected and completed with the data from the 1970 Census, the latest presidential message to Congress and other government sources.

Table 1. *Population growth*

Year		Thousands of inhabitants
1793	(Census)	5,200
1810	(Est.)	6,122
1838	(Est.)	7,004
1856	(Est.)	8,283
1877	(Est.)	9,384
1895	(Census)	12,632
1900	(Census)	13,607
1910	(Census)	15,160
1921	(Census)	14,335
1930	(Census)	16,553
1940	(Census)	19,654
1950	(Census)	25,791
1960	(Census)	34,923
1970	(Census)	48,225
1976	(Est.)	62,000

Table 2. *Land grants by presidential terms*

Presidents	Term	Thousands of hectares
Carranza	1915–1920	132
De la Huerta	May–Nov. 1920	34
Obregón	1920–1924	971
Elías Calles	1924–1928	3,088
Portes Gil	1928–1930	1,173
Ortiz Rubio	1930–1932	1,469
Rodríguez	1932–1934	799
Cárdenas	1934–1940	17,890
Avila Camacho	1940–1946	5,519
Alemán	1946–1952	3,845
Ruiz Cortínes	1952–1958	3,199
López Mateos	1958–1964	16,004
Díaz Ordaz	1964–1970	16,000[a]
Echeverría	1971–1975	10,000[b]

[a] Corrected figure.
[b] President's message, Sept. 1, 1975.

Table 3. *Beneficiaries of the Social Security Institute*

Year	Total beneficiaries (in thousands)
1944	356
1955	1,576
1965	6,745
1975	15,471[a]

[a]To this figure should be added 3,173,000 beneficiaries of the government employees Social Security Fund.

Statistical tables

Table 4. *Elementary education* (values in thousands)

Year	Schools	Schoolteachers	Pupils
1857	2	—	185
1874	8	—	350
1910	12	20	848
1930	11	28	1,300
1940	23	40	2,114
1950	14	66	3,032
1960	32	113	5,462
1965	38	152	7,263
1970	44	198	9,700
1975	—	282	12,700

Table 5. *Rates of exchange for pesos to U.S. dollars*

Year	Pesos for $1	Year	Pesos for $1
1877	1.04	1931	2.65
1894	1.98	1933	3.50
1900	2.06	1939	5.19
1910	2.01	1945	4.85
1917	1.91	1950	8.65
1925	2.03	1955	12.50

Table 6. *Monetary circulation*

Year	Millions of pesos
1911	310
1931	316
1940	1,060
1950	5,989
1960	16,889
1970	49,012
1974	97,474

Table 7. *Total bank credits*

Year	Millions of pesos
1911	720
1942	2,024
1950	8,972
1960	39,780
1970	194,522
1974	378,746[a]

[a]Of this amount, $237,753 was granted by government-controlled institutions.

Table 8. *Freight transported by railroads*

Year	Millions of ton-kilometers of freight	Year	Millions of ton-kilometers of freight
1921	2,262	1960	14,004
1930	4,041	1970	22,863
1940	5,810	1974	30,819
1950	8,391		

Table 9. *Growth of the highway system*

Year	Kilometers	Year	Kilometers
1925	695	1960	45,089
1930	1,426	1970	71,500
1940	9,929	1975	185,000
1950	21,422		

Table 10. *Production of pig iron and steel ingots*
(thousands of tons)

Year	Iron	Steel
1906	31	33
1910	55	68
1921	34	43
1930	62	103
1940	70	149
1950	286	390
1960	521	1,492
1973	3,113	4,760
1974	—	5,100

Table 11. *Electric power*

Year	Capacity of power plants (thousands of kilowatts)	Power generated (millions of kilowatt hours)
1900	20	56
1910	110	308
1920	120	336
1930	510	1,464
1940	681	2,529
1950	1,235	4,423
1960	3,021	10,636
1970	7,495	28,592
1974	9,990	40,766

Table 12. *Production of selected metals* (metric tons)

Year	Gold	Silver	Copper	Lead	Zinc
1901	14	1,795	33,943	94,194	900
1910	37	2,305	52,000	120,000	1,833
1920	22	2,069	49,192	82,518	15,651
1930	20	3,272	73,412	232,931	124,084
1940	27	2,570	37,602	196,253	114,955
1950	12	1,528	61,698	238,078	223,510
1960	9	1,385	60,330	190,670	262,425
1970	6	1,332	61,012	176,597	266,400
1974	4	1,200	82,700	218,000	262,700

Table 13. *Production of crude oil*

Year	Thousands of barrels
1901	10
1911	12,553
1921	193,398
1931	33,039
1941	43,386
1951	78,780
1961	116,825
1971	177,251
1975 (est.)	300,000

Table 14. *Production of selected crops* (thousands of metric tons)

Year	Maize	Wheat	Beans	Rice	Coffee	Cotton
1907	1,088	312	63	33	50	34
1920	2,349	280	116	31	36	32
1930	1,377	370	83	75	49	38
1940	1,640	464	97	108	52	65
1950	3,122	587	250	187	66	260
1960	5,386	1,190	528	328	124	470
1969[a]	8,997	2,047	811	367	440	398
1974	7,784	2,764	896	489	208	476

[a] 1970 Census.

Table 15. *Production of sugar cane and sugar* (thousands of tons)

Year	Cane	Sugar
1900	1,267	75
1910	2,503	148
1920	2,873[a]	118
1930	3,293	216
1940	4,973	2,944
1950	9,419	590
1960	19,542	1,498
1970	32,550	2,208
1974	29,500	2,522

[a] 1925

Chronology

1519 Cortés lands on Mexican coast and begins his conquest of the country

1521 Spaniards seize Tenochtitlan, the capital of the Aztec empire

1521–1821 Spanish rule; the viceroyalty of New Spain set up in 1535

1805 Discontent of Mexican landowners as a result of confiscatory policy of the government

1808 Revolt in Spain against French domination

Attempts of Mexico to achieve independence by peaceful means thwarted by Spanish residents

1810 Hidalgo's uprising against Spanish rule

1811 Hidalgo defeated and executed; Morelos carries on insurrection

1813 Morelos convokes first Mexican congress which declares independence from Spain

1815 Morelos defeated, captured, and executed

1820 Liberal revolution in Spain

1821 Iturbide achieves Mexican independence with support of the church

1822 Iturbide becomes emperor

1823 Army revolt forces Iturbide's abdication

1824 Federal constitution adopted; Guadalupe Victoria elected president

1829 Presidency of Guerrero; attempts to introduce liberal and social reforms

1830–2 Conservative regime of Bustamante and Alamán

1833 General Santa Anna president and liberal leader Gómez Farías vice-president

1834 Santa Anna suppresses liberal reforms of Gómez Farías

1836 Texas declares independence; Santa Anna defeated and imprisoned in Texas

1841 Santa Anna becomes president again

1844 Santa Anna ousted by army revolt

1845 Texas annexed by the United States

1846–8 War between Mexico and United States. Santa Anna returns and becomes president again, defeated on battlefield, leaves the country, peace treaty

1848 Moderate liberal government established in Mexico

1853 Successful conservative army revolt brings Santa Anna back from exile

1853–5 Last presidency of Santa Anna

1855 Revolution ousts Santa Anna; radical liberal government set up under Alvarez

1856 Lerdo Law

1857 Liberal constitution

1858–60 So-called Three Years' War between liberals under president Juárez and conservatives ends with liberal victory

1861 French invasion begins with support of Mexican conservatives

1863 French army occupies Mexico City and president Juárez withdraws to Northern Mexico

1864 Mexican empire set up with Maximilian of Austria as emperor

1866 Napoleon III decides to withdraw army from Mexico

1867 Mexican empire crumbles; Maximilian is defeated and executed and Juárez elected president

1871 Juárez reelected

1872 Juárez dies and is succeeded by Sebastián Lerdo

1876 Porfirio Días revolts against Lerdo and becomes president

1877–80 First presidency of Díaz

1880–4 Presidency of Manuel Gonzáles, a friend of Díaz

1884–1910 Second to seventh presidency of Díaz

1910 Madero starts revolution against Díaz

1911 Díaz resigns; Madero elected president

1913 Madero resigns under army pressure and is assassinated; General Huerta becomes president; revolts all over Mexico against Huerta

1914 Huerta resigns and leaves the country, which is split between several revolutionary factions

1915 Carranza prevails over his rivals, Villa and Zapata, and is recognized by United States

1917 New constitution approved by congress; Carranza elected president

1920 Obrégon overthrows Carranza

1920–4   Presidency of Obrégon
1924–8   Presidency of Calles
1928   Obrégon reelected but shortly afterwards assassinated
1929–1935   Calles, Supreme Chief of the Revolution
1934–1940   Presidency of Cárdenas
1935–7   Sweeping agrarian reform
1938   Expropriation of foreign oil companies
1939   Presidential campaign: Cárdenas selects Avila Camacho as successor
1940   Avila Camacho assumes office

Notes

CHAPTER 1. BIRTH OF MEXICAN INDEPENDENCE 1805–1821

1 M.P. Costeloe, *Church Wealth in Mexico* (Cambridge, England: Cambridge University Press, 1967) pp. 110–115; R. Flores Caballero, *Counterrevolution: The Role of the Spaniards in the Independence of Mexico 1804–38* (Lincoln, Nebraska: University of Nebraska Press, 1974) pp. 14–46; B.R. Hamnett, "The Appropriation of Mexican Church Wealth by the Spanish Bourbon Government: The Consolidación de Vales Reales 1805–1809," *Journal of Latin American Studies*, I/Part 2 (1969) pp. 85–113; and Asunción Lavrin, "The Execution of the Law of Consolidación in New Spain," *Hispanic–American Historical Review*, 53/Number 1 (1973) pp. 28–49.

2 N.M. Farriss, *Crown and Clergy in Colonial Mexico 1750–1821, The Crisis of Ecclesiastical Privilege,* Historical Studies XXI (London: London University Press, 1968) pp. 243–244.

3 R.A. Humphreys, "Isolation from Spain," reprinted in *The Origins of the Latin American Revolution 1808–1826,* edited by R.A. Humphreys and John Lynch (New York: Knopf, 1965).

4 H.M. Hamill, Jr., *The Hidalgo Revolt* (Gainesville, Florida: University of Florida Press, 1966) p. 54; and J. Rodríguez Frausto, *Hidalgo no era Guanajuatense* (Mexico City: Historia, León, 1953) pp. 111–115.

5 Lucas Alamán, *Historia de México* (Mexico City: Editorial Jus, 1942) pp. 330–332.

6 David A. Brading, *Miners and Merchants in Bourbon Mexico 1763–1810* (Cambridge, England: Cambridge University Press, 1971).

7 Hamill, *Hidalgo Revolt,* p. 113.

8 Jan Bazant, *Historia de la deuda exterior de México* (Mexico City: El Colegio de México, 1968) p. 10.

9 For Puebla, see: R. Liehr, *Stadtrat und Städtische Oberschicht von Puebla am Ende der Kolonialzeit* (Wiesbaden: Franz Steiner, 1974) pp. 178—188.

10 Hamill, *Hidalgo Revolt*, p. 156.

11 *Ibid.*, p. 154.

12 *Ibid.*, p. 179; Alamán, *Historia de México*, I, p. 45.

13 Hamill, *Hidalgo Revolt*, p. 136.

14 J. H. Parry, *The Audiencia of New Galicia in the 16th Century: A Study in Colonial Government* (Cambridge, England: Cambridge University Press, 1948) pp. 55—83.

15 R. M. Sererra, *Guadalajara ganadera, Estudio regional novohispano, 1760—1805*, Sevilla, Escuela de Estudios Hispano-Americanos, 1977.

16 Alamán, *Historia de México*, I, p. 419.

17 J. Bazant, *Cinco haciendas mexicanas: tres siglos de vida rural en San Luis Potosí* (Mexico City: El Colegio de México, 1975) p. 101

18 Wilbert H. Timmons, *Morelos: Priest, Soldier, Statesman of Mexico* (El Paso, Texas: Texas Western College Press, 1963) pp. 2—29.

19 Farriss, *Crown and Clergy*, pp. 194—199, pp. 254—265 (Appendix).

20 Alamán, *Historia de México*, III, pp. 528—529.

21 N.L. Benson, ed., *Mexico and the Spanish Cortes, 1810—1822: Eight Essays* (Austin, Texas: Institute of Latin American Studies, University of Texas, 1966) p. 8.

22 Farriss, *Crown and Clergy*, pp. 248—249.

23 *Ibid.*, p. 251.

24 *Ibid.*, pp. 248—249.

25 W.S. Robertson, *Iturbide of Mexico* (Durham, North Carolina: Duke University Press, 1952) p. 97.

26 This so-called Plan of Iguala is reproduced in: Alamán, *Historia de México*, V, pp. 888—894.

27 Robertson, *Iturbide*, pp. 67—69.

28 *Ibid.*, p. 76.

29 The full text is reproduced in: Alamán, *Historia de México*, V, pp. 907—910.

30 *Ibid.*, pp. 261—263.

CHAPTER 2. THE TROUBLED YEARS 1821—1855

1 Lucas Alamán, *Historia de México*, V (Mexico City: Editorial Jus, 1942) pp. 315—319.

2 *Ibid.*, pp. 439—440, 909

3 W.S. Robertson, *Iturbide of Mexico* (Durham, North Carolina: Duke University Press, 1952) pp. 157–159.

4 N.L. Benson, *La diputación provincial y el federalismo mexicano* (Mexico City: El Colegio de México, 1955) p. 85.

5 Robertson, *Iturbide*, p. 165.

6 *Ibid.*, pp. 174–175.

7 *Ibid.*, p. 180.

8 Jan Bazant, *Alienation of Church Wealth in Mexico: Social and Economic Aspects of the Liberal Revolution 1856–1875* (Cambridge, England: Cambridge University Press, 1971) pp. 15–16.

9 Jan Bazant, *Historia de la deuda exterior de México* (Mexico City: El Colegio de México, 1968) pp. 14–15.

10 Robertson, *Iturbide*, p. 159.

11 Published in London in 1825.

12 J. Poinsett, *Notes on Mexico* (London: John Miller) pp. 89–92.

13 *Ibid.*, p. 279.

14 Robertson, *Iturbide*, pp. 222–238.

15 By means of the Casa Mata Manifesto; N.L. Benson, *La Diputación*, pp. 90–91.

16 Robertson, *Iturbide*, pp. 252–253.

17 Alamán, *Historia*, I, pp. 404–408.

18 E. Turlington, *Mexico and Her Foreign Creditors* (New York: Columbia University Press, 1930); Bazant, *Deuda*.

19 J. Sierra, *Evolución política del pueblo mexicano*, Second Edition (Mexico City: Fondo de Cultura Económica, 1950) pp. 138–139; published in English as *The Political Evolution of Mexican People* (Austin, Texas: University of Texas Press, 1970).

20 R.W. Randall, *Real del Monte, a British Mining Venture in Mexico* (Austin, Texas: University of Texas Press, 1972) p.73.

21 H.G. Ward, *Mexico in 1827* (London: H. Colburn, 1828) pp. 64–69.

22 Ward, *Ibid.*, I, pp. 452.

23 The best description of this period is in: M.P. Costeloe, *La primera república federal de México* (1824–1835) (Mexico City: Fondo de Cultura Económica, 1975).

24 C.A. Hale, *Mexican Liberalism in the Age of Mora 1821–1853* (New Haven, Conn.: Yale University Press, 1968) p. 23.

25 Bazant, *Alienation*, pp. 19–22.

26 Mexican Department of the Treasury, *Memoria de Hacienda de 1870* (Mexico City: Mexican Department of the Treasury, 1870) p. 97; Dublán and Lozano, *Colección de Leyes,* II (Mexico City: Editorial Oficial) pp. 110–111.

27 Robert A. Potash, *El Banco de Avío de México* (Mexico City: Fondo de Cultural Económica, 1959).

28 In Yucatán, an entirely unsubsidized cotton industry was established by a local entrepreneur. Howard F. Cline, "The Aurora Yucateca and the Spirit of Enterprise in Yucatan, 1821–1847," *Hispanic American Historical Review*, XXVII (1947) pp. 30–60; reprinted in: Lewis Hanke, ed., *History of Latin American Civilization, Sources and Interpretation: The Modern Age*, II (London: Methuen, 1969) pp. 132–140.

29 Mora, *Obras Sueltas*, Second Edition (Mexico City: Porrúa, 1963) pp. 169; Hale, *Mexican Liberalism*, pp. 24, 72, 296.

30 It was alleged that the refusal of the church to grant him a canonship had driven him to liberalism.

31 W.H. Callcott, *Santa Anna, The Story of an Enigma who once was Mexico* (Hamden, Connecticut: Archon Books, 1964) p. 4; O.L. Jones Jr., *Santa Anna* (New York: Twayne Publishers, 1968) pp. 21–22.

32 Callcott, *Ibid.*, pp. 33–38; Jones, *Ibid.*, p. 31.

33 Jones, *Ibid.*, pp. 89–95.

34 Bazant, *Alienation*, p. 25.

35 Hale, *Mexican Liberalism*, p. 139.

36 Callcott, *Santa Anna*, pp. 100–102.

37 J. Bravo Ugarte, *Historia de México*, III, Part 2 (Mexico City: Editorial Jus, 1959) pp. 12, 282–284.

38 Callcott, *Santa Anna*, pp. 108–109 [quoting Clarence R. Wharton, *El Presidente, A sketch of the Life of General Santa Anna* (Austin, Texas: Gammel's Book Store, 1924) p. 64].

39 Ann Fears Crawford, ed., *The Eagle. The Autobiography of Santa Anna* (Austin, Texas: The Pemberton Press, 1967) pp. 15, 48.

40 Hale, *Mexican Liberalism*, pp. 290–291.

41 Zavala, *Viaje a los Estados Unidos del Norteamérica* (Paris: Imprimerie de Decourchart, 1834) pp. 32, 67, 141, and 367.

42 Hale, *Mexican Liberalism*, p. 203.

43 Alamán, *Historia*; Mora, *México y sus revoluciones*, 3 vols. (Paris: Liberia de Rosa, 1836); and Zavala, *Ensayo histórico de las revoluciones de México*, 2 vols. (Paris: Dupont et G. Laguióniz, 1831).

44 For the bias in Alamán's *Historia*, see: N.L. Benson, ed., *Mexico and the Spanish Cortes* (Austin, Texas: Institute of Latin American Studies, University of Texas, 1966) p. 209.

45 Bravo Ugarte, *Historia de México*, III, Part 2, p. 154.

46 Robertson, *Iturbide*, p. 219.

47 *Ibid.*, p. 119.

48 As reported by a U.S. Consul. Callcott, *Santa Anna*, p. 126

49 Justo Sierra, *Evolución política del pueblo mexicano* (Mexico City: Fondo de Cultura Económica, 1950) p. 157 [translated and quoted in: Ramon Eduardo Ruiz, ed., *The Mexican War: Was it Manifest Destiny?* (New York: Holt, Rinehart & Winston, 1964) pp. 110–116].

50 The extent of the independence is described in: John L. Stephens, *Incidents of Travel in Central America, Chiapas and Yucatán*, 2 vols. (New Brunswick: Rutgers University Press, 1949) and *Incidents of Travel in Yucatán* (Norman, Oklahoma: University of Oklahoma Press, 1962).

51 The social atmosphere of those years was described by the Scottish wife of the first Spanish minister to Mexico in: *Life in Mexico. The Letters of Fanny Calderón de la Barca* (Garden City, New York: Doubleday, 1970).

52 Reproduced in: C. Alan Hutchinson, "Valentín Gómez Farías and the Movement for the Return of General Santa Anna to Mexico in 1846," *Essays in Mexican History*, edited by Thomas E. Cotner (Austin, Texas: Institute of Latin American Studies, University of Texas, 1958) pp. 169–191.

53 Jones, *Santa Anna*, p. 108.

54 Bazant, *Alienation*, pp. 30–31.

55 Hutchinson, "Valentín Gómez Farías," pp. 169–191.

56 Justo Sierra, *Evolución politica*, p. 184 [translated by R.E. Ruiz, *The Mexican War*].

57 M. González Navarro, *Raza y Tierra* (Mexico City: El Colegio de México, 1970) pp. 43–89, 169.

58 See also: N. Reed, *The Caste War of Yucatán* (Stanford, California: Stanford University Press, 1964) pp. 30–34, 48, 56, 88, 102–104.

59 One such uprising is described in: Bazant, *Cinco haciendas mexicana* (Mexico City: El Colegio de México, 1975) pp. 69–70.

60 Hale, *Mexican Liberalism*, pp. 239–240.

61 Callcott, *Santa Anna*, pp. 291–294; Jones, *Santa Anna*, pp. 125–129.

62 Santa Anna's later attempts to regain importance failed; a forgotten man, he was permitted to return in 1874 and died in Mexico City two years later.

CHAPTER 3. THE LIBERAL REVOLUTION 1855–1876

1 C.A. Hale, *Mexican Liberalism in the Age of Mora 1821–1853* (New Haven, Connecticut: Yale University Press, 1968) pp. 13–15.

2 José C. Valadés, *Melchor Ocampo Reformador de México*, Second Edition (Mexico City: Cámara de diputados, 1972) p. 27.

3 Ocampo, *Obras completas*, II (Mexico City: F. Vázquez, 1901) p. 291.
4 *Ibid.*, I, p. 229.
5 *Ibid.*, I, pp. 12—15, 110—118, and 229.
6 *Ibid.*, II, p. 271.
7 Lucas Alamán, *Obras*, XII (Mexico City: Editorial Jus, 1947) p. 471.
8 Ocampo, *Obras*, II, p. 263.
9 *Ibid.*, I and III; Valadés, *Ocampo*, p. 201.
10 Ocampo, *Obras*, I.
11 The 1857 law lowering parochial fees remained on paper.
12 Malcolm D. McLean, *Vida y obra de Guillermo Prieto* (Mexico City: Fondo de Cultura Económica, 1960).
13 Secretaría de Hacienda y Crédito Publico, *Miguel Lerdo de Tejada 1812—1861* (Mexico City: Secretaría de Hacienda y Crédito Público, 1961).
14 Frank Averill Knapp, Jr., *The Life of Sebastian Lerdo de Tejada 1823—1889* (Austin, Texas: University of Texas Press, 1951) pp. 1—3.
15 Secretaría de Hacienda, *Miguel Lerdo*, p. 12.
16 Knapp, *Sebastian Lerdo*, p. 48.
17 Secretaría de Hacienda, *Miguel Lerdo*, pp. 15-24.
18 J. Sierra, *Evolución política del pueblo mexicano*, Second Edition (Mexico City: Fondo de Cultura Económica, 1950) p. 201.
19 Bazant, *Alienation of Church Wealth* (Cambridge, England: Cambridge University Press, 1971) and Walter Scholes, *Mexican Politics during the Juárez regime 1855—1872*, Second Edition (Columbia, Missouri: University of Missouri Press, 1969), pp. 7—8.
20 Bazant, *Alienation*, p. 114.
21 Bravo Ugarte, *Historia de México*, III (Mexico City, Editorial Jus, 1944) p. 232.
22 Bazant, *Cinco haciendas mexicanas* (Mexico City: El Colegio de México, 1975) pp. 97—100.
23 F. Chevalier, "Survivances seigneuriales et présages de la révolution agraire dans le nord du Méxique," *Revue Historique*, CCXXII (July—September 1959) p. 11.
24 T.G. Powell, "Los liberales, el campesinado indígena y los problemas agrarios durante la Reforma," *Historia Mexicana*, XXI (April—June 1972), p. 656; and Donald J. Fraser, "La política de desamortización en las comunidades indígenas, 1856—1872," *Historia Mexicana*, XXI/4 (April—June 1972), p. 631.
25 Bazant, "The Division of some Mexican Haciendas during the Liberal Revolution, 1856—1862," *Journal of Latin American Studies*, III/1 (May 1971), pp. 25—37.

26 He died in 1863 on the battlefield, after Juárez had accepted his offer to fight against the French invasion.

27 Bazant, "Division of Haciendas," p. 136.

28 Sierra, *Juárez, su obra y su tiempo*, Second Edition (Mexico City: Universidad Nacional Antónoma de México, 1948) pp. 155—163.

29 Bazant, "Division of Haciendas," pp. 167—173.

30 *Ibid.*, pp. 176—254.

31 *Ibid.*, pp. 36—37.

32 Scholes, *Mexican Politics*, pp. 68—72.

33 Bazant, *Historia de la deuda exterior de México* (Mexico City: El Colegio de México, 1968) pp. 75—77, 88.

34 Bazant, *Alienation*, pp. 229—237.

35 *Ibid.*, p. 235.

36 *Ibid.*, pp. 256—274.

37 Bazant, *Deuda*, pp. 91—96.

38 J. A. Dabbs, *The French Army in Mexico 1861—1867, A Study in Military Government* (The Hague: Mouton, 1963) pp. 252—254.

39 Dabbs, "The Indian Policy of the Second Empire," *Essays in Mexican History*, edited by T. E. Cotner (Austin, Texas: Institute of Latin American Studies, 1958) pp. 114—119.

40 *Ibid.*, p. 19.

41 F. Chevalier, "Conservateurs et libéraux au Méxique," *La intervención francesa y el imperio de Maximiliano* (Mexico City: Instituto Francés de América Latina, 1965) p. 15.

42 Ugarte, *Historia de México*, III, p. 345.

43 Scholes, *Mexican Politics*, pp. 109—110.

44 *Memoria de Hacienda*, Mexico, 1870, pp. 919—26.

45 Scholes, *Mexican Politics*, pp. 113—116, and 134.

46 Ivie E. Cadenhead, Jr., *Benito Juárez* (New York: Twayne Publishers, 1973) p. 117.

47 Ugarte, *Historia de México*, III, p. 345.

48 Scholes, *Mexican Politics*, p. 138.

49 *Ibid.*, pp. 150, 160, 163—166.

50 Ugarte, *Historia de México*, III, p. 359.

51 T. G. Powell, "Los problemas agrarios durante la Reforma," *Historia Mexicana*, XXI, No. 4 (April—June 1972), p. 671.

52 He died there in 1889.

CHAPTER 4. THE ERA OF PORFIRIO DÍAZ 1876—1910

1 J. F. Iturribarría, *Porfirio Díaz ante la historia* (Mexico City: Union Gráfica, 1967) pp. 1—16.

2 R. de Zayas Enriquez, *Porfirio Díaz, la evolución de su vida* (Chicago: D. Appleton, 1908) photograph facing p. 178.

3 Carleton Beals, *Porfirio Díaz, Dictator of Mexico* (Westport, Greenwood Press: 1971) picture facing p. 178.
4. *Ibid.,* p. 174.
5 Frank Averill Knapp, Jr., *The Life of Sebastian Lerdo de Tejada 1823–1889* (Austin, Texas: University of Texas Press, 1951) p. 157.
6 Iturribarría, *Porfirio Díaz,* pp. 17–50.
7 Harry Bernstein, *Matías Romero 1837–1898* (Mexico City: Fondo de Cultura Económica, 1873).
8 Knapp, *Sebastian Lerdo,* p. 136.
9 Interview with James Creelman reproduced in: Lewis Hanke, ed., *History of Latin American Civilization: Sources and Interpretations:* II (London: Methuen, 1969) pp. 256–266.
10 E. Gruening, *Mexico and its Heritage* (New York: D. Appleton–Century, 1940) p. 57.
11 Iturribarría, "La política de conciliación del general Díaz y el arzobispo Gillow," *Historia Mexicana,* XIV/1 (1964) pp. 81–101.
12 Luis González, "La era de Juárez," *La economía mexicana en la epoca de Juárez* (Mexico City: Secretaría de Industria, 1972) pp. 13–56.
13 F. Bulnes, *The Whole Truth about Mexico* (New York: M. Bulnes Book Company, 1916) pp. 89–90.
14 Ugarte, *Historia de México* III, p. 393.
15 *Ibid.,* p. 394.
16 P. J. Vanderwood, "Los rurales: producto de una necesidad social," *Historia Mexicana,* XXII/1 (1972) pp. 34–51.
17 In his book: *El porvenir de las naciones Hispano–Americanas ante las conquistas recientes de Europa y los Estados Unidos* (Mexico City: Imprenta de M. Nava, 1899).
18 Charles A. Hale, Scientific Politics and the Continuity of Liberalism in Mexico, 1867–1910, in J. Z. Vásquez, ed., *Dos revoluciones: Mexico y los Estados Unidos,* Mexico, Jus, 1976, pp. 139–152.
19 E. Turlington, *Mexico and Her Foreign Creditors* (New York: Columbia University Press, 1930) pp. 209–219; Bazant, *Historia de la deuda exterior de México* (Mexico City: El Colegío de México, 1968) p. 123.
20 Turlington, *Mexico,* p. 246.
21 Turlington, *Ibid.,* p. 345.
22 Mexico went off the silver standard in 1905; the new gold peso was valued at one half the United States dollar.
23 F. Rosenzweig, "Moneda y Bancos," *Historia Moderna de México, El Porfiriato, La Vida Economica,* edited by D. Cosío Villegas (Mexico City: Editorial Hermes, 1965) pp. 789–886.

24 Mortgage and other banks were comparatively unimportant.

25 D. Joslin, *A Century of Banking in Latin America* (London: Oxford University Press, 1963) pp. 209–211; L. N. D'Olwer, "Las inversiones extranjeras," *Historia Moderna de México, El Porfiriato, La vida económica,* edited by D. Cosío Villegas, Part 2 pp. 1053–1063.

26 F.R. Calderón, "Los ferrocarriles," *Historia Moderna de México, El Porfiriato,* Part 1 edited by D. Cosío Villegas, pp. 516, 539–540, 566, 625.

27 *The Mexican Year Book 1908* (London: Mexican Yearbook Publishing Company, 1908) pp. 333, 347.

28 *Memoria de Hacienda 1870* (Mexico City: Secretaría de Hacienda, 1870) p. 744; R. Vernon, *The Dilemma of Mexico's Development* (Cambridge, Massachusetts: Harvard University Press, 1963) pp. 35–40.

29 Bazant, *Deuda,* pp. 157–164.

30 J. H. Coatsworth, "The Impact of Railroads on the Economic Development of Mexico, 1877–1910," Ph.D. dissertation, University of Wisconsin, 1972, pp. 107–115, 130,154, 207–208.

31 D. Keremitsis, *La Industria Textil Mexicana en el Siglo XIX* (Mexico City: Sep–Setenta, 1973) pp. 160, 190.

32 R. W. Randall, *Real del Monte, a British Mining Venture in Mexico* (Austin, Texas: University of Texas Press, 1972) pp. 73, 210–212.

33 M. D. Bernstein, *The Mexican Mining Industry 1890–1950* (New York: New York State University, 1964) pp. 42–44, 51, 75.

34 El Colegio de México, *Estadísticas económicas del Porfiriato, Fuerza de Trabajo y Actividad Económica por Sectores* (Mexico City: El Colegio de México) pp. 136–140.

35 Bernstein, *Mexican Mining,* p. 75; D'Olwer, "Las inversiones," p. 1154 provides similar figures.

36 M. Rippy, "The Mexican Oil Industry," *Essays in Mexican History,* edited by T. E. Cotner (Austin, Texas: University of Texas Press, 1958) pp. 248–267.

37 D'Olwer, "Las inversiones," p. 1154; Desmond Young, *Member for Mexico, A Biography of Weetman Pearson, First Viscount Cowdray* (London: Cassell, 1966) pp. 58–191.

38 Vernon, *Dilemma,* p. 47.

39 D'Olwer, "Las inversiones," p. 1119; F. Rosenzweig, "La industria," *Historia Moderna de México, El Porfiriato,* edited by D. Cosío Villegas, Part 1 p. 459.

40 Keremitsis, *Industria,* p. 102.

41 D'Olwer, "Las inversiones," pp. 1150–1155; Vernon, *Dilemma,* pp. 42–43.

42 In pesos of 1900; these and all following figures are taken from: *Estadísticas económicas del Porfiriato, Fuerza de Trabajo y Actividad Económica por Sectores* (Mexico City: El Colegio de México, undated). For agricultural production there is a continuous series of figures from 1892 to 1907. The information for 1877 does not seem very reliable, however.

43 One such experience is described in: H. H. Harper, *A Journey in South—eastern Mexico* (Boston: De Vinne Press, 1910).

44 *Secretaría de Economía, Estadísticas sociales del Porfiriato 1877—1910* (Mexico City: Secretaría de Económia, 1956) p. 8.

45 El Colegio de México, *Estadísticas Económicas del Porfiriato, Comercio Exterior* (Mexico City: El Colegio de México, 1960).

46 Bazant, *Cinco haciendas mexicanas* (Mexico City: El Colegio de México, 1975) includes descriptions of both types of hacendados.

47 Bernstein, *Mexican Mining*, pp. 58—86.

48 El Colegio de México, *Estadísticas económicas, Fuerza de Trabajo*, pp. 47, 140.

49 Keremitsis, *Industria*, p. 219.

50 Secretaría de Economía, *Estadísticas sociales*, p. 106.

51 V. N. Bett, *Central Banking in Mexico: Monetary Policies and Financial Crises 1864—1940* (Ann Arbor, Michigan: University of Michigan Press, 1957) p. 11; Vernon, *Dilemma*, p. 55; J. D. Cockcroft, *Intellectual Precursors of the Mexican Revolution 1900—1913* (Austin, Texas: University of Texas Press, 1968) pp. 3—40, 62, 63; Rosenzweig, "La Industria," p. 323.

52 S. R. Ross, *Francisco I. Madero, Apostle of Mexican Democracy* (New York: Columbia University Press, 1955) pp. 3—4, 11—12.

53 J. E. Sterret and J. S. Davis, *The Fiscal and Economic Condition of Mexico* (New York: International Committee of Bankers on Mexico, 1928) p. 30.

54 Bulnes, *The Whole Truth about Mexico*, pp. 116—117; Cockcroft, *Intellectual Precursors*, pp. 44—46.

55 Ross, *Francisco I. Madero*, p. 12.

56 Conclusions of the book are reproduced in: M. Léon Portilla, ed., *Historia Documental de México*, II (Mexico City: Universidad Nacional Antónoma de México, 1964) pp. 423—425; Ross, *Francisco I. Madero*, pp. 4—12, 57—64.

57 The Plan of San Luis Potosí is summarized in: J. W. Wilkie and A. L. Michaels, ed., *Revolution in Mexico: Years of Upheaval, 1910—1940* (New York: Knopf, 1969) p. 37.

58 Ross, *Francisco I. Madero*, p. 121.

CHAPTER 5. THE CIVIL WAR 1910—1920

1 J. Womack, Jr., *Zapata and the Mexican Revolution* (Middlesex, England: Penguin Books, 1972) p. 137.

2 This and similar cases were enumerated in: J. K. Turner, *Barbarous Mexico* (Chicago: Charles H. Kerr and Company, 1911).

3 Bazant, *Cinco haciendas mexicanas* (Mexico City: El Colegio de México, 1975) describes a hacendado who did invest in irrigation works and who ran his farms as a business enterprise.

4 F. Katz, "Labor conditions on Haciendas in Porfirian Mexico: Some Trends and Tendencies," *HAHR*, 54/1 (February, 1974) pp. 45—46.

5 They were only annulled by Santa Anna in 1853, to be restored by Congress in 1856.

6 Such cases were described before 1910 by novelists such as Mariano Azuela and poets such as Manuel José Othón.

7 In 1898 Senator José López Portillo described a fight between two neighboring hacendados for a barren hill in his novel *La parcela*.

8 J. Sotelo Inclán, *Raíz y razón de Zapata* (Mexico City: Editorial Etnos, 1943) pp. 84, 101—105, 192.

9 M. Gonzalez Navarro, *Raza y tierra* (Mexico City: El Colegio de México, 1970) p. 226.

10 P. Friedrich, *Agrarian Revolt in a Mexican Village* (Englewood Cliffs, New Jersey: Prentice-Hall, 1970) pp. 26ss., 112—113.

11 O. Lewis, *Life in a Mexican Village: Tepoztlán Restudied* (Urbana, Illinois: University of Illinois Press, 1951) pp. 51, 93, 230.

12 Ross, *Francisco I. Madero, Apostle of Mexican Democracy* (New York: Columbia University Press, 1955) pp. 12—13.

13 Womack, *Zapata*, p. 137.

14 E. Lieuwen, *Mexican Militarism, The Political Rise and Fall of the Revolutionary Army 1910—1940* (Albuquerque, New Mexico: University of New Mexico Press, 1968) pp. 8—12; Ross, *Francisco I. Madero*, pp. 170—216.

15 Bulnes, *The Whole Truth About Mexico* (New York: M. Bulnes Book Company, 1916) p. 174.

16 J. Bravo Ugarte, *Historia de México*, p. 434.

17 Ross, *Francisco I. Madero*, p. 219.

18 M. C. Meyer, *Pascual Orozco and the Mexican Revolution 1910—1915* (Lincoln, Nebraska: University of Nebraska Press, 1967) pp. 15—17.

19 *Ibid.*, pp. 64, 83—88.

20 Ross, *Francisco I. Madero*, p. 225.

21 Reprinted in: F. Bulnes, *The Whole Truth about Mexico*, pp. 30, 166.

22 Ross, *Francisco I. Madero*, pp. 241–245.

23 His speech, in which he acknowledged the merits of Molina's book as well as the bill, is reprinted in: Luis Cabrera, *El pensamiento de Luis Cabrera* (Mexico City: Talleres Gráficos de la Nación, 1960) pp. 179–210.

24 Ross, *Francisco I. Madero*, p. 249.

25 *Ibid.*, p. 223.

26 Bulnes, *The Whole Truth*, p. 175.

27 Many relatives of Díaz held other posts; Cabrera thus justified Madero's nepotism in: Cabrera, *El pensamiento*, pp. 161–178.

28 M. C. Meyer, *Huerta, A Political Portrait* (Lincoln, Nebraska: University of Nebraska Press, 1972) pp. 2, 14, 45–63.

29 S. G. Inman, *Intervention in Mexico* (New York: George H. Doran, 1919). p. 82; Charles C. Cumberland, *Mexican Revolution, The Constitutionalist Years* (Austin, Texas: University of Texas Press, 1972) p. 383.

30 Cumberland, *Ibid.*, pp. 15–16, 23–28.

31 The Plan of Guadalupe is reprinted in: M. González Ramírez, ed., *Planes políticos y otros documentos* (Mexico City: Fondo de Cultura Económica, 1954) pp. 137–140.

32 E. Beltrán, "Fantasía y realidad de Pancho Villa," *Historia Mexicana*, XVI/1 (1966) p. 72.

33 H. Aguilar Camín, *La frontera nómada. Sonora y la revolución Mexicana.* Mexico, 1977, Siglo XXI, pp. 222–4.

34 Cockcroft, *Intellectual Precursors*, p. 38; Lieuwen, *Mexican Militarism*, p. 21.

35 Bulnes, *The Whole Truth*, p. 140.

36 J. Rutherford, *Mexican Society during the Revolution, A Literary Approach* (Oxford: Clarendon Press, 1971) pp. 89, 96–99.

37 Published in English as: M. Azuela, *The Underdogs* (New York: New American Library, 1962).

38 Rutherford, *Mexican Society*, p. 71.

39 *Ibid.*, p. 198.

40 *Ibid.*, p. 199.

41 Meyer, *Huerta*, pp. 165–166.

42 Bazant, *Historia de la deuda exterior de México* (Mexico City: El Colegio de México, 1968) pp. 175–180.

43 Cumberland, *Mexican Revolution*, pp. 290–292. Carranza's minister of foreign affairs was the young lawyer Isidro Fabela, his representatives in the United States were two Urquidi brothers of an old Chihuahua landowning family.

44 R. E. Quirk, *An Affair of Honor, Woodrow Wilson and the Occupation of Veracruz* (Lexington, Kentucky: University of Kentucky Press, 1962) pp. 2–3, 70, 164–165.

45 Cockcroft, "El maestro de primaria en la Revolución," *Historia Mexicana*, XVI/4 (April–June 1967) pp. 565–587.

46 Cumberland, *Mexican Revolution*, pp. 231–240.

47 R. E. Quirk, *The Mexican Revolution, 1914–1915: the Convention of Aguascalientes* (Bloomington, Indiana: University of Indiana Press, 1960).

48 Cumberland, *Mexican Revolution*, pp. 252–262; J. Meyer, "Los obreros en la Revolución Mexicana: Los Batallones Rojos," *Historia Mexicana*, XXI/1 (1971) pp. 1–37.

49 Romantics of the *Casa* like former Liberal party leader Díaz Soto and Jahn, a survivor of the Paris commune, preferred to join Zapata. See: Womack, *Zapata*, p. 271.

50 Lieuwen, *Mexican Militarism*, p. 34.

51 Cumberland, *Mexican Revolution*, pp. 234–238.

52 *Ibid.*, p. 324.

53 *Ibid.*, pp. 340–351.

54 E. V. Niemeyer Jr., *Revolution at Queretaro* (Austin, Texas: University of Texas Press, 1974) pp. 210–224.

55 E. Turlington, *Mexico and Her Foreign Creditors* (New York: Columbia University Press, 1930) p. 268; Kemmerer, *Inflation and Revolution* (London: Oxford University Press, 1940) pp. 7–8.

56 Cumberland, *Mexican Revolution*, pp. 396–397; F. Katz, *Deutschland, Díaz und die mexikanische Revolution* (Berlin: Deutscher Verlag der Wissenschaften, 1964) p. 473.

57 Cumberland, *Mexican Revolution*, pp. 363–370.

58 Lieuwen, *Mexican Militarism*, p. 58; Cumberland, *Mexican Revolution*, p. 323.

59 Cumberland, *Mexican Revolution*, pp. 374, 382–385, 388.

60 R. Atkin, *Revolution, Mexico 1910–1920* (London: Macmillan, 1969) pp. 310–317. The manifesto is reproduced in: Cumberland, ed., *The Meaning of the Mexican Revolution* (Lexington, Massachusetts: Heath, 1967) pp. 9–14.

61 Womack, *Zapata*, pp. 487–490.

CHAPTER 6. SOCIAL REFORMS 1920–1940

1 M. González Ramírez, ed., *Planes políticos y otros documentos* (Mexico City: Fondo de Cultura Económica, 1954) pp. 262–263; E. Lieuwen, *Mexican Militarism. The Political Rise and Fall of the Revolutionary Army 1910–1940* (Albuquerque, New Mexico: University of New Mexico, 1968) p. 12.

2 M. González Navarro, *Población y sociedad en Mexico 1900–1970*, I (Mexico City: Universidad Nacional Antónoma de

Mexico, 1974) pp. 34—36.

3 N. Bassols Batalla, *El pensamiento de Alvaro Obregón* (Mexico City: Nuestro Tiempo, 1967) p. 13.

4 Gruening, *Mexico and its Heritage* (New York: D. Appleton-Century, 1940) p. 135 gives correct figures; Womack, *Zapata and the Mexican Revolution* (Middlesex, England: Penguin Books, 1972) pp. 508—512 (Epilogue); H. W. Tobler, "Alvaro Obregón und die Anfaenge der mexikanischen Agrarreform, Agrarpolitik und Agrarkonflikt 1921—1924," *Jahrbuch für Geschichte von Staat, Wirtschaft und Gesellschaft Lateinamerikas,* VIII (1971) p. 361.

5 Bazant, *Historia de la deuda exterior de México* (Mexico City: El Colegio de México, 1968) pp. 184—194.

6 John F. Dulles, *Yesterday in Mexico: A Chronicle of the Revolution, 1919—1936* (Austin, Texas: University of Texas Press, 1967) p. 171.

7 *Ibid.,* p. 184.

8 *Ibid.,* p. 191.

9 Lieuwen, *Mexican Militarism,* pp. 67—68.

10 A translated abridged edition of the four volumes of his autobiography was published as: J. Vasconcelos, *A Mexican Ulysses* (Bloomington, Indiana: University of Indiana Press, 1963).

11 E. N. Simpson, *The Ejido, Mexico's Way Out* (Chapel Hill, North Carolina: University of North Carolina Press, 1937) p. 659; D. L. Raby, "Los principios de la educación rural en Mexico," *Historia Mexicana,* XXII/4 (April—June 1973) p. 553.

12 Vasconcelos, *Obras Completas,* I (Mexico City: Libreros Mexicanos, 1958) p. 1328; D. L. Raby, "Los maestros rurales y los conflictos sociales en México," *Historia Mexicana,* XVIII/2 (October—December 1968) p. 190.

13 Ramon F. Ruiz, *Mexico. The Challenge of Poverty and Illiteracy* (San Marino, California: The Huntington Library, 1963) p. 40.

14 J. C. Orozco, *An Autobiography* (Austin, Texas: University of Texas Press, 1962) p. 51.

15 J. H. Haddox, *Vasconcelos of Mexico, Philosopher and Prophet* (Austin, Texas: University of Texas Press, 1967) pp. 53—63.

16 Vasconcelos, *Obras,* I, p. 301. Written when racism was in vogue.

17 Simpson, *The Ejido,* p. 282; J. A. Britton, "Moisés Sáens, Nacionalista mexicano," *Historia Mexicana,* XXII/1 (July—September 1972) p. 77.

18 Simpson, *The Ejido,* pp. 587, 659; Secretaría de Economía, *Anuario Estadístico* (Mexico City: Secretaría de Economía, 1939) p. 42.

19 Bazant, *Deuda,* pp. 194—198.

20 See Chapter 4.

21 Dulles, *Yesterday*, pp. 99, 287.

22 Vernon, *The Dilemma of Mexico's Development* (Cambridge, Massachusetts: Harvard University Press, 1963) p. 83.

23 In his novel *La región más transparente*, Carlos Fuentes described a hacendado who sold his estate to Americans at the beginning of the revolution and bought large tracts of cheap land near Mexico City. The novel was published in English as *Where the Air is Clear* (New York: Ivan Obolensky, 1960).

24 Lieuwen, *Mexican Militarism*, p. 85.

25 Dulles, *Yesterday*, pp. 273, 276, 293.

26 Gruening, *Mexico*, p. 341.

27 J. A. Meyer, "La Cristiada," *Extremos de Mexico* (Mexico City: El Colegio de México, 1971) pp. 225–240.

28 Dulles, *Yesterday*, p. 333.

29 E. Turlington, *Mexico and Her Foreign Creditors* (New York: Columbia University Press, 1930) p. 312; Bazant, *Deuda*, p. 198

30 Dulles, *Yesterday*, p. 371.

31 *Ibid.*, p. 381.

32 *Ibid.*, p. 386; M. León Portilla, ed., *Historia documental de México*, II (Mexico City: Universidad Nacional Antónoma de México, 1964) p. 492.

33 Dulles, *Yesterday*, p. 410; R. K. Furtak, *Revolutionspartei und politische Stabilitaet in Mexico* (Hamburg: Übersee-Verlag, 1969) pp. 15–22.

34 Dulles, *Yesterday*, pp. 429–434.

35 R. E. Scott, *Mexican Government in Transition*, Revised Edition (Urbana, Illinois: University of Illinois Press, 1971) pp. 122–123.

36 Portes Gil, *Quince años de polítical mexicana*, Third Edition (Mexico City: Botas, 1954) pp. 155–157.

37 Dulles, *Yesterday*, p. 582.

38 His sister was married to Plutarco Elías Calles Junior. See: Dulles, *Yesterday*, p. 34.

39 *Ibid.*, p. 463.

40 Published as: *Breve historia de Mexico* (Mexico City: Botas, 1936).

41 Dulles, *Yesterday*, p. 521.

42 Furtak, *Revolutionspartei*, p. 20.

43 Simpson, *The Ejido*, p. 113.

44 Secretaría de Economia, *Anuario Estadístico*, p. 191.

45 Simpson, *The Ejido*, pp. 120, 123.

46 *Ibid.*, pp. 440–442; Dulles, *Yesterday*, p. 551.

47 The figures are in: C. W. Reynolds, *The Mexican Economy, Twentieth Century Structure and Growth* (New Haven, Connec-

ticut: Yale University Press, 1970) pp. 392–400; Simpson, *The Ejido*, p. 682; and *Anuario Estadístico*, p. 1939.

48 Interview with Silva Herzog in: Wilkie, *Mexico visto en el Siglo XX* (Mexico City: Instituto Mexicano de Investigaciones Económicas, 1969) pp. 677–678.

49 Dulles, *Yesterday*, pp. 567–577; L. Cárdenas, *Obras, I Apuntes 1913–1940*, I (Mexico City: Universidad Nacional Antonóma de México, 1972) pp. 218–223.

50 M. Osorio M., *El Partido de la Revolución Mexicana* (Mexico City: Impresora del Centro, 1970) pp. 384–397; Simpson, *The Ejido*, p. 454.

51 The plan was published in English in: G. Bosques, *The National Revolutionary Party of Mexico and the Six-Year Plan* (Mexico City: National Revolutionary Party, 1937) pp. 129–212; a reference to Calles as *Jefe nato* was omitted in the translation.

52 Bosques, *Revolutionary Party*, p. 132.

53 The law was reprinted in entirety in: Simpson, *The Ejido*, pp. 759–808.

54 V. M. Bett, *Central Banking in Mexico* (Ann Arbor, Michigan: University of Michigan, 1957) pp. 66–68, 86–88, 114.

55 Cárdenas, *Apuntes*, I, pp. 5–41.

56 A. de María y Campos, *Mújica, Crónica Biográfica* (Mexico City: Ediciones Populares, 1939) pp. 208–211; Cárdenas, *Apuntes*, II (Mexico City: Universidad Nacional Antónoma de México, 1973) p. 558.

57 The persecution of the clergy under his rule was described in: Graham Greene, *The Lawless Roads* (Harmondsworth, England: Penguin Books, 1971); and Graham Greene, *The Power and the Glory* (Harmondsworth, England: Penguin Books, 1972).

58 Cárdenas, *Apuntes II*, I, p. 306.

59 There is a frequent discrepancy in official statistics; the figures here are taken from: N. L. Whetton, *Rural Mexico* (Chicago: University of Chicago Press, 1947) Table 19.

60 Dulles, *Yesterday*, p. 637.

61 Dulles, *Yesterday*, pp. 641–645.

62 Lieuwen, *Mexican Militarism*, p. 118.

63 Vasconcelos, *Qué es la revolución* (Mexico City: Botas, 1937).

64 Dulles, *Yesterday*, pp. 650–658 ("The Expedition to Tabasco").

65 R. E. Scott, *Mexican Government*, pp. 128–129.

66 When, in 1938, the official party was renamed the Party of Mexican Revolution; peasants, workers, and "working" intellectuals became its equal members. See: Furtak, *Revolutionspartei*, pp. 22–24.

67 Cárdenas, *Apuntes*, I, p. 631.
68 *Ibid.*, p. 357.
69 The novel was published in 1940.
70 For example, the Jajalpa hacienda between Mexico City and Toluca was reduced from 1,000 to around 150 hectares of land. See: R. S. Platt, *Latin American Countrysides and United Regions* (New York: McGraw-Hill, 1942) pp. 46–49; and, for the state of San Luis Potosí, see: Bazant, *Cinco haciendas mexicanas* (Mexico City: El Colegio de México, 1975) pp. 181–188.
71 The construction was completed in 1950.
72 The number of notes tripled from 1934 to 1936. See: Bett, *Central Banking*, p. 114.
73 Cárdenas, *Apuntes*, I, p. 385.
74 *Ibid.*, p. 411; some years later Aaron Saenz built another sugar mill of his own not far away.
75 *Ibid.*, p. 362.
76 Dulles, *Yesterday*, p. 632.
77 For a summary of the oil question, see: H. Cline, *The United States and Mexico*, Revised Edition (New York: Atheneum, 1971) pp. 229–260.
78 Lieuwen, *Mexican Militarism*, p. 116.
79 J. W. Wilkie, *The Mexican Revolution: Federal Expenditure and Social Change Since 1910*, Second Edition (Berkeley, California: University of California Press, 1970) p. 184.
80 A. L. Michaels, "The Crisis of Cardenismo," *JLAS*, 2/1 (May, 1970), pp. 51–79.
81 As Azuela aptly described in his novel *Nueva Burguesía*, published in 1941.

Index